MW00737080

Janet's Plan-its™ 2012
CELESTIAL PLANNER
Easy-to-Use Astrology Calendar

by Janet Booth

ISBN 978-0-9846499-0-7

Cover background image courtesy of NASA.
Cover talismans by Israel Regardie ©1972.
Design and layout by Bryan R. Bonina, Always Amazing Results, LLC
Ilene J. Wolf, Editor
Portrait by Ray Pioggia
Special thanks to Numerologist Sally Faubion for her insights on the year 2012.
Ephemeris pages reproduced by permission of the publisher:
Starcrafts LLC, 334-A Calef Hwy., Epping, NH 03042
"Global Pledge of Allegiance" by Edna Reitz, ©1988

While every effort to ensure the accuracy of information in this calendar has been made,
we cannot be held liable for errors, omissions or inconsistencies.

Published by:
Astrology Booth, LLC
P.O. Box 271133
West Hartford, CT 06127
AstrologyBooth.com

Printed in the USA

Janet's Plan-its 2012 Celestial Planner
CONTENTS

ABOUT THE COVER

This year's design was conceived by Janet Booth and Bryan R. Bonina. The front features the incredible five-pointed star shape formed by earth-Sun-Venus interactions. If you measure each time Venus passes between the earth and Sun and mark the spot in the zodiac, after eight years you're back nearly at the starting point. There will have been five passes, each two-fifths of the zodiac apart, forming a pentagram. The points of the pentagram slowly migrate to lower degrees, looking like a "spirograph," circling the entire zodiac over thousands of years. (See animation at lunarplanner.com/HCpages/Venus.html.) The unusual symbols in the corners are talismans depicting the "seal of the planet" for the rulers of the four season-starting signs. Counter-clockwise from lower left, they are: Mars (spring), Moon (summer), Venus (autumn) and Saturn (winter). An image of the constellation Draco is included on the back in honor of the Chinese Year of the Dragon.

**Visit JanetsPlan-its.com to learn about astrology
or for a personal consultation.**

Janet's Plan-its™ 2012
Celestial Planner

For more about major influences in 2012, read the Star Pages (p. 72).

Introduction

In ancient times, everyone knew the constellations, planets and moon's phases. These were the basis of stories, myths and songs, a teaching device before books or computers. At night, there wasn't much to do except enjoy the sky and learn from it. Nowadays, few people look up, night or day. But the stars and planets are still there, telling their stories to those who understand them and like a giant cosmic clock, showing us the time.

Astrology helps explain life in general and individuals' lives in particular. My goal is to put the power of astrology in the hands of everyone, rather than only those who study it in depth. Use this tool to whatever level of detail you wish in order to take advantage of the best moments the planets offer and dodge their difficult times. It's easy — just tap the knowledge of your celestial guide.

Overview of 2012

2012 is a Leap Year, a presidential election year for the U.S., and the most media-hyped year since 2000. Some people consider it significant that at the winter solstice, the earth is aligned with the center of our Milky Way galaxy, though this has been the case each winter solstice for many years, peaking in 1998. Various cultures from the Hopi to the Egyptians to the Mayans have mentioned this era. Because one of many cycles of the Mayan calendar (albeit a long one) ends at the winter solstice, Dec. 21, rumors of end times abound, as they did at the turn of the century and millennium. Of course, just like at a new year, another cycle begins. It's true we seem to have a major disaster somewhere almost monthly, but is "end times mentality" where you want to focus your energies? One thing we know for certain: this is a time of tremendous change and the ability to adapt to it will be an asset!

Uranus is on the ascent as we move into the Age of Aquarius, the sign it rules. Great Ages of over 2,100 years represent dominant themes in cultural and historical developments and take decades to change. Though there is no agreed-upon moment when the New Age begins, we're definitely at the doorway. In 2011, Uranus entered Aries, starting a new 84-year cycle through the signs. It ended a seven-year interchange with Neptune, where they were each in the sign the other rules, passing the baton from the ruler of the Age of Pisces to the ruler of the Age of Aquarius. From 2012 until 2026, as Neptune swims through the sign of the fishes, our collective consciousness is still strongly Piscean (trusting something greater than ourselves to take care of us rather than being empowered as individuals, the Aquarian goal). But Uranus is gaining the upper hand.

Uranus is famous for change as is Pluto, the primary planet of transformation, clearing the deck and starting over. Uranus and Pluto are at a key (and long!) turning point in their cycle of about 138 years, which began in the turbulent mid-60s. From 2010 until 2018, they are within the potent 5°-range of being "square" (90° apart). This positioning pushes for change, and they are in it precisely a record seven times between 2012 and 2015. Since energy and vibration are attributed to Uranus, a major shift in vibrational energy (as anticipated by some for this period) is consistent with this square.

At points in recent years, the planets seemed to gang up on us. There is some tough interplay this year, but not to the extent or with the degree of force we have just survived. A key difference in the planetary clashes of 2012 versus those from 2008 to 2011 is that now the slow-moving planets (Saturn, Uranus and Pluto) have moved beyond the early degrees of the season-changing signs they occupied then. (These power points of the zodiac indicate widespread impact.) There is reason to hope that 2012 may not be so bad.

This is supposed to be a lucky year according to Chinese astrology. The Year of the Dragon is associated with strength, health, power, good fortune, wisdom, happiness and success. It's considered auspicious, good for business and money-making, but also a time when everything is larger than life and things may seem better than they are. Exuberance can lead to over-spending. This year everyone can exhibit Dragon traits: flamboyance, ambition, courage, and a quick temper balanced by a soft spot. This Dragon is of the Water element, calming the Dragon's fire and aiding reconciliation after divisions.

Numerology tells us 2012 is a 5 year (20 + 12 = 32, 3+2 = 5), with the 32/5 being one of the better shift numbers, a lighter energy than some 5 years, which are always about major change. According to numerologist, Sally Faubion, it's a time to "look at things with a higher consciousness, to begin to see with different eyes. Realize we're all in this together and we have to come together to save Mother Earth."

A most hopeful sign is the "transit of Venus" on June 5. Similar to an eclipse, Venus is seen crossing the face of the Sun. This very rare phenomenon symbolizes love and harmony (ruled by Venus) going straight to our hearts (ruled by the Sun).

May you be filled with Venus's love, graced by the Dragon's luck, and sail through the choppy waves of 2012's changes!

Yours in the stars, Janet Booth

You can follow me on FaceBook and sign up on my website for my free eNewsletters. JanetsPlan-its.com

USING THIS PLANNER

Interpretations in this planner are based on solid astrological theories, but how a day affects your chart and your life can be different than its general nature suggests. For your most important activities (business start-ups, major purchases, marriage, surgery, etc.), it's always recommended you consult with your astrologer.

We can't be certain how much of life results from fate and how much from free will. Let's assume it's a combination and that our choices matter. Astrology helps us make better-informed selections. It offers an educated guess about the future based on similar conditions in the past. This is a bit tricky since there is never an exact repeat of the planetary patterns and each astrological indication can express in a multitude of ways. All planets and signs have positive and negative potentials. Rather than letting the planets have their way with you, put their energies to work and keep them busy in a manner of your preference. Get in the driver's seat and steer!

Janet's Plan-its™ Celestial Planner lists the generic nature of astrological occurrences and possibilities the planets present. As the planets and signs are mentioned, use the Keywords (p. 98) or the expanded list on JanetsPlan-its.com to arrive at your own speculations. Some days, the influences apply to your life noticeably. Other times, you may see the described situations happening around you but not to you.

To see your individual impact, consult your natal chart, determined by your exact date, time and place of birth. It's more accurate than any astrology calendar can be, though Janet's Plan-its™ is the next best thing. You could order a report that shows the links to your chart from the moving planets ("transits") and interprets them for you. To look for connections to your chart on your own, see the next section of this planner, Making It Personal. You might also want to learn to work with the ephemeris (see p. 62 – you'll find instructions there).

When a day doesn't sound so nice, you aren't doomed to have a bad experience. The message is a warning to watch out for difficult behavior in others and to monitor your own. It's just information to help you on your journey through life. An analogy is driving. You're going to get to your destination sooner or later, one way or another, but the trip is smoother if the traffic lights are green and you'll get there quicker than if the lights are red. When the planets play nicely together, it's like you're encountering green lights. Challenging planetary energy is like having to stop at red lights or even take a detour.

This planner applies to everyone, regardless of zodiac sign.

Don't be caught unaware – read ahead at least a couple weeks in advance.

MOON CYCLES

The Moon orbits the earth (and thus circles the zodiac from our viewpoint) in about 27 days. A New Moon happens as it passes the Sun, beginning a new cycle that takes on the flavor of the factors present at that moment, extending their sway over the next four weeks. Since the Sun is also in motion, it takes the Moon 29-30 days to pass the Sun again. Their cycle crests at the halfway point, which is the Full Moon. It marks a peak of awareness and often the culmination of a process or trend. Like a New Moon, the effects of a Full Moon are impacted by conditions occurring then. The Full Moon's influence starts two or three days before and extends two or three days beyond the exact date of the Full Moon (or much longer in the case of an eclipse). The Highlights for the weeks of New and Full Moons outline how to optimize their influences. See the Star Pages for discussions of eclipses, which are a stronger version of New and Full Moons. If there are no prominent patterns involving multiple planets at a New or Full Moon, a single planet connected to the Sun and Moon can wield significant power. Energy shifts at Quarter Moons, which are times for turning a corner. Both types require decisions. At a First Quarter Moon, rely on instincts. At the Third Quarter, let experience and information guide you.

The Moon changes the sign through which it travels every two to three days, giving a general indication of moods, behavior and circumstances (p. 75). The planner's daily pages tell you the Moon's position each day and exactly when it changes signs.

The amount of the Sun's light that the Moon reflects back to earth increases from New Moon to Full Moon, then decreases until the next New Moon. Every day, Janet's Plan-its™ shows you what the Moon looks like in its current phase. If you want growth in an activity, begin it during the waxing phase between a New Moon and a Full Moon (see illustration). Continue ongoing activities any time. A natural use of the Moon's cycle is to complete projects after a Full Moon and before the next New Moon (waning phase). If there's something you want to decrease, begin it during the waning phase. For example, hair shouldn't grow as quickly after a haircut then, and surgery to remove a tumor or reduce tissue is better during the waning phase.

The eight lunar phases relate to stages of your life and can be used for timing rituals, as detailed by guest writer, Maria Kay Simms, a Wicca High Priestess and professional astrologer (p. 90). Groups of four related moon phases across 2-1/4 year periods describe developments in the stories of our lives, according to astrologer Dietrech Pessin. She named them "moon families." Check her table of lunar phases for 2012 (p. 69). Degrees where New and Full Moons occur repeat from sign to sign for five to six months in "Moon Grooves" (p. 60).

Adjust for Your Time Zone: Eastern (E) and Pacific (P) zones are listed, adjusted for Daylight Saving Time. For Atlantic, add one hour to Eastern. For Central, subtract one hour from Eastern. For Mountain, add one hour to Pacific.

Moon Void of Course: (see Keywords on p. 98) Every two or three days, there is a period lasting from minutes to hours (sometimes an entire day!) when the Moon's motivating energy ebbs. It's fine to continue ongoing endeavors or complete projects but avoid beginning new initiatives after the time listed for the Moon becoming Void until after the Moon enters the next sign.

Day Ratings: Each day is rated as to the difficulty or ease that the planets present us. A **1** is most challenging; a **5** is the easiest. There aren't many **5**s. It's much easier for a day to be challenging than stress-free! The rating number appears next to the designation for the day of the week: **SA** = Saturday, **SU** = Sunday, etc. A **C** denotes a calm day with little or no astrological activity. Powerful days (marked **P**) are potent but not necessarily easy, just a stronger version of that day's rating.

Star Pages: A ★ on a daily line guides you to the **Star Pages** (p. 72) for interpretations and details about timing.

Weekly Highlights: These are a must read each week! In fact, read ahead. If a challenging period is coming up in a few weeks, you may want to handle important matters before then. More information is in the Star Pages.

Details: Below the weekly Highlights is a list in brackets of the details of the week's planetary activities. Some are explained in the Highlights or the Star Pages. You can piece together their meanings from the Keywords at the back of the planner.

2012 On a Page: See important information (p. 60) about periods when the planets appear to move backward, called Retrograde. There is also a handy list of the year's New and Full Moon dates and the zodiac degrees where they occur. When degrees are close to positions of planets in your birth chart (+ or − 2°), the cycle will affect you strongly.

Retrogrades: Try not to start anything new during Mercury Retrograde (days marked **MR**). If you must take action, be careful with all information exchanges, allow extra time to arrive for appointments and read contracts carefully before signing. When Venus is Retrograde (days marked **VR**), challenges arise in relationships or finances. We may have to repeat lessons or re-do activities in these areas. Recommendations for other planets' Retrograde periods are included in the Star Pages.

Ephemeris: This table (p. 63) shows the planets' zodiac positions and other astrological data useful for seeing when planets connect to your chart. It might look intimidating, but the instructions (p. 62) will guide you.

If you have your birth chart: To use it with Janet's Plan-its, read Making It Personal (p. 4). Also look for your chart's degrees in the 2012 All Star List (p. 70), which sorts the year's astrological happenings in zodiac order.

Planning with the Planets: When scheduling your important activities, look for days rated **4** or **5**, or at least try to avoid days rated **1** or **2**. It's also a good idea to steer clear of days when a planet changes direction, listed in 2012 On a Page. See **Best and Worst Days** for various activities (p. 95). Check the daily messages for days or portions of days that sound good for your plans. Avoid the Moon Void of Course (see above). For a complete picture of a given day, read earlier to find what's in effect then. You may need to back up several months or see As We Begin 2012 (p. 72) to take long-term factors into account).

Your Birthday Influences: Conditions at your birthday impact you from three months before your birthday until nine months after, when your next birthday's factors kick in. Read the Highlights and Star Pages for the week of your birthday. Check the closest prior New Moon. Look at the daily message for your birthday and a day before and after. A **4** or **5** rating indicates an upbeat year; a **1** or **2** shows a year of challenges. A **P** promises intensity that could go either way (see above). See if your birthday appears on the year's Best and Worst Days list.

To Your Health: Guest writer, Medical Astrologer Diane Cramer, contributes an examination (p. 93) of astrological associations with anatomy and affiliated conditions, along with ideas regarding good health for each sign.

Activities Associated With the Planets:

- **Moon:** spend time with family, do something for your home or décor, enjoy cooking or eating
- **Mercury:** make a decision, initiate an important communication, teach, learn
- **Venus:** handle relationship or monetary matters, be with loved ones, treat yourself to something special, make a purchase
- **Sun:** shine, enjoy the spotlight, lead, create, entertain, play, bring out your "inner child," be with children
- **Mars:** do something physical, be assertive, compete, watch out for anger or pushiness
- **Ceres:** nurture yourself or others, garden, commune with nature, enjoy the fruits of your labors
- **Jupiter:** travel, share your ideas, contact those at a distance, handle legal matters
- **Saturn:** get organized, write goals, act with authority, attend to your career
- **Uranus:** bring out your uniqueness, do something different or inventive, help people
- **Neptune:** rest, pray, meditate, spend time in the water (including hot tubs, pools), volunteer
- **Pluto:** release something, clean out closets, review investments, enjoy sensuality
- **Eris:** stand up for yourself, confront the competition, make waves, deal with discord or disorder

★ ★ ★ ★ ★
Janet's "cheat sheet" has symbols and keywords for planets and signs. Download it free at JanetsPlan-its.com.
★ ★ ★

If you're working with your chart:
- **Ascendant:** (1st House cusp) blow your own horn, seek attention, get a new outfit or hairdo
- **Midheaven:** ("MC") (10th House cusp) meet with your boss, go on an interview, enhance your reputation

MAKING IT PERSONAL

The planets appear to spin around us, their positions ever-changing, a bit like intricate clockworks. The difference is they never repeat the same configuration.

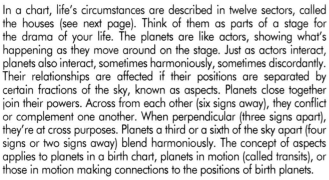

A planner like this tells you the energies at a given time in a generic way that anyone can utilize. What makes astrology personal comes from "stopping the clock" at the moment of your birth, from the viewpoint of your birthplace. **This determines your unique birth chart.***

In a chart, life's circumstances are described in twelve sectors, called the houses (see next page). Think of them as parts of a stage for the drama of your life. The planets are like actors, showing what's happening as they move around on the stage. Just as actors interact, planets also interact, sometimes harmoniously, sometimes discordantly. Their relationships are affected if their positions are separated by certain fractions of the sky, known as aspects. Planets close together join their powers. Across from each other (six signs away), they conflict or complement one another. When perpendicular (three signs apart), they're at cross purposes. Planets a third or a sixth of the sky apart (four signs or two signs away) blend harmoniously. The concept of aspects applies to planets in a birth chart, planets in motion (called transits), or those in motion making connections to the positions of birth planets.

Aspects are a little tricky to figure out. The easiest method is to count the number of signs between planets. (The signs are always in the same order, counterclockwise, Aries, Taurus, Gemini, etc., through Pisces.) The effect of an aspect is strongest if the degrees of the signs of both planets are within 2° of each other. For example, a planet at 14° Aries is opposite another at 16° Libra, but is not considered opposite a planet at 28° Libra. The leeway allowed from the exact fraction is called the orb. Astrologers debate how big of an orb has an effect. A pretty safe allowance is 5°. If you'd rather not try to figure out aspects, order a transit list and let a computer do it for you.

Everyone has the same houses in the same order. However, your birth time and place determine your personal alignment of signs relative to houses. The sign positions of the planets are based on their movement through the zodiac (transits). Their house positions in your chart are specific to your birth time and place, too.

Some keywords for the planets, signs and aspects are at the back of the planner. You can read more about them in the Study Booth at my website, and I offer conference call classes on various topics, as well.

Your chart's houses won't align perfectly with signs. Signs are exactly 30° while house size varies. If you don't have a transit report with exact dates, estimate when a planet enters or leaves your houses, judging by the time the planet spends in the sign and how far into the sign your house begins. The Star Pages tell when planets enter signs and how long they'll be there. (For the Moon, see the daily boxes on the weekly pages.) Find the house(s) where you have that sign, showing the department(s) of your life affected during the planet's visit. For instance, if your 1st House begins in the middle of Scorpio, then the Sun enters your 1st House halfway through its time in Scorpio, staying there about a month. If you want to be more precise, check the Ephemeris just before the Star Pages. (You'll find instructions there.)

Check the degrees and signs of New and Full Moons on 2012 On a Page. Locate their positions in your chart. A New Moon emphasizes a house (or a planet to which it makes an aspect) for the next four weeks. Do something new in the applicable part of your life. A Full Moon influence lasts a few days before and after the Full Moon. Eclipses are extra powerful New and Full Moons, with effects lasting several months. Take major action in the area of your life indicated by the house where the Eclipse occurs or by any aspect it makes. Also see if any of your planets are at "Moon Groove" degrees and will receive repeated attention.

To find your best time for an activity, locate that activity in the Houses table. See what sign you have at the beginning of that house (looking counterclockwise). Note when quick planets (Moon, Sun, Mercury, Venus or Mars) are in that sign and in that house. Check for aspects between slower planets in the Star Pages (p. 72) and on the All Star List (p. 70). Your planets and your life will be strongly affected if their degrees are within 2° of planets you have in the same sign or in a sign 2, 3, 4 or 6 signs away. Other good options are when New or Full Moons are in the applicable houses. There should be a New Moon once a year in each house and the same is true for Full Moons. The weekly Highlights and daily messages contain clues for dealing with people or what behavior to maximize or avoid.

EXAMPLE: Say you want to change your residence. Note any planets in your 4th House. Whether or not you have planets in this house, look at the sign beginning the house and find its ruling planet in the Keywords (p. 98). Scan the 2012 All Star List to see if any positive aspects (conjunction, semisextile, sextile, trine, quintile or biquintile) are at degrees of signs that aspect your 4th House planets or ruler. If so, such an influence improves your chances for several days around the time of such an aspect. Also read the weekly Highlights and the details below them for positive aspects involving your 4th House planets or ruler or the generic 4th House planet, the Moon.

An ideal time to start your search would be:

- in the two weeks following a New Moon (waxing phase); even better, if the Moon is going through the sign(s) in your 4th House
- on a day when a ruler or occupant of your 4th is in a positive aspect
- when the day rating is a **3** or better
- at a time when the Moon is NOT void (see Using This Planner, p.2)
- when neither Mercury nor Venus is Retrograde, unless you were born with that planet Retrograde, (℞ appears by its glyph)

First, search the year's Best and Worst Days (p. 95) for a Best real estate day or a Best day for a planet that occupies or rules your 4th House. (These are good days to use as long as they qualify in the other ways noted above, even if the Moon is not traveling through your 4th House). If the Best days are not in the waxing phase or are otherwise disqualified, next seek a qualifying day with a waxing Moon in your 4th House. The Moon moves through your 4th House two to three days each month but is not always in the waxing part of the cycle. For instance, if your 4th House begins with Sagittarius (ruled by Jupiter) and continues into the next sign, Capricorn, the Moon is in those signs and in the waxing phase from May until November. You want one of those days with a good aspect to Jupiter. Look after Venus is Direct in late June. The All Star List shows Ceres conjunct Jupiter July 10. The Ephemeris (p. 63) confirms they are close before the 7/3 Full Moon and Venus is nearby, too! The Moon is in Sagittarius July 1-2 but the day ratings are low. It's still in your 4th House in Capricorn on 7/3, and you can take your first step just ahead of the Full Moon that day, which is rated 3. The Highlights later that week mention a wonderful pattern involving the Moon. Use that time frame to take a subsequent step in your process. The first act might be contacting realtors or rental agents. The second step could be viewing a property.

---

*A precise chart requires an exact birth time. The records department in your birthplace should have that. If you can't get yours, a chart using sunrise on your birthday is an adequate substitute. To find out sunrise on a given day, see the Naval Observatory's free calculator: http://aa.usno.navy.mil/data/docs/RS_OneYear.html. You can receive your chart from me with a reading, class or transit report.

AREAS OF LIFE ASSOCIATED WITH THE TWELVE HOUSES

NATURAL RULERS

 1st House
Aries/Mars

 2nd House
Taurus/Venus

 3rd House
Gemini/Mercury

 4th House
Cancer/Moon

 5th House
Leo/Sun

 6th House
Virgo/Mercury

 7th House
Libra/Venus

 8th House
Scorpio/Pluto

 9th House
Sagittarius/Jupiter

 10th House
Capricorn/Saturn

 11th House
Aquarius/Uranus

 12th House
Pisces/Neptune

1 House of the Self, personality, outlook on life, outward behavior, self-awareness, self concern, mask ("persona"), build, health, appearance, vitality, individuality

2 Possessions, values, resources, personal financial security, how you make money or meet obligations, material and non-material resources, self-worth

3 Conscious mind, communications, near environment, short journeys, early education, how you learn, self-expression, siblings, neighbors, ground transportation

4 Roots, home, parents (particularly mother), heredity, traditions, subconscious, places of residence, real estate, property, conditions in early and late life

5 Creativity, personal self-expression, pleasures, objects of affection (children, pets, lovers), vacations, hobbies, games, speculation, talents, need for attention

6 Work, employment, co-workers or subordinates, working conditions, health, the work you do on your body, diet, hygiene, service, duties, daily tasks

7 Partnerships, relationships, marriage, close associates, concern for others, peers, agents, open enemies, contracts, close associates, negotiations, lower courts

8 Birth, death, reproduction, transformation, your money mixing with other people's money (credit, tax, insurance, joint finances, investment, inheritance), big business, sex, spirituality

9 Foreign environments and languages, long journeys, the Higher Mind, philosophy, religion, higher education, ethics, higher courts, publishing, in-laws, media, the internet

10 Public standing, reputation, status, worldly attainment, ambition, sense of mission, profession, career, responsibilities, authority, father, guardian, boss

11 Hopes and wishes, goals, ideals, humanitarianism, associates, acquaintances, groups, friends, business contacts, money made from career

12 Spirituality, subconscious, sleep, unseen or hidden causes, limitations, secrets, fears, need for withdrawal or privacy, hidden enemies, confinement, House of Self-Undoing

Everyone wants to live long, but no one wants to be called old.

Icelandic folk wisdom

DECEMBER 2011							JANUARY						
SU	M	TU	W	T	F	S	SU	M	TU	W	T	F	S
				1	2	3	1	2	3	4	5	6	7
4	5	6	7	8	9	10	8	9	10	11	12	13	14
11	12	13	14	15	16	17	15	16	17	18	19	20	21
18	19	20	21	22	23	24	22	23	24	25	26	27	28
25	26	27	28	29	30	31	29	30	31				

Moon in Capricorn • Void 5:37 am (P), 8:37 am (E)
Moon enters Aquarius 9:15 am (P), 12:15 pm (E)

26 MO 2

Morning brings many miscommunications. What you leave to others to handle runs into snags. Be careful if you decide to take over the wheel.

Boxing Day, Kwanzaa begins

Moon in Aquarius

27 TU 3

Start the day with an attitude of gratitude, even if you have to talk yourself into it. Soon friends get you smiling and leave you laughing.

Moon in Aquarius • Void 1:32 pm (P), 4:32 pm (E)
Moon enters Pisces 3:46 pm (P), 6:46 pm (E)

28 WE 3

Imagination and bright ideas solve problems and save the day when they have a practical slant. Get input from trusted colleagues or a mentor.

Moon in Pisces

29 TH 3

Sympathy and volunteering are put to good use making a difference this morning. Tonight conflicting aims send cooperation down the drain.

Moon in Pisces • Void 5:39 am (P), 8:39 am (E)

30 FR 2

Angry criticism erupts early. Later in the day, people mellow and lend a helping hand. After that, signals mix: half welcoming, half aloof.

Moon Void in Pisces • Moon enters Aries 1:49 am (P), 4:49 am (E)
First Quarter Moon (P)

31 SA 3

Brace yourself first thing for the unexpected, which may alter this evening's plans. Be flexible and defer to others if you're outvoted.

New Year's Eve

Moon in Aries • First Quarter Moon (E)

01 SU 3

You can't get what you want without speaking up. Go ahead and state your wishes. Then seek people who are able to support your desires.

New Year's Day

DEC. 26, '11–JAN. 01, '12 HIGHLIGHTS

Nothing stands out as a giant challenge this week. Maybe the planets are taking a holiday. The few difficult combinations occur very early in the morning or very late in the evening in North America, so they won't torment many of us. Still, planetary connections do color a day's ambiance for hours before or after they're exact, so you will spot some precautions in the daily messages.

Take your time with whatever you say or put in writing Monday. Lasting consequences hang in the balance. It's a good day to review the year and adjust your goals accordingly, if you can find a free moment for reflection. The Moon is very busy Monday to Wednesday nudging all the planets involved in the connections that occur this week. This keeps us hopping, too, and reinforces the suggestion to be circumspect in all you do. You'll get feedback quickly as to the wisdom of choices and actions.

The most potent factor comes mid-week when the Sun joins Pluto. We'll feel the intensity of the changes and decisions they generate as the Moon activates their union late Tuesday night and early Thursday. Their pairing happens once a year, signaling a need to bring resolve

to bear to remove something that may be outworn from our lives. It's a time for leaders to show they're capable of promoting positive changes. Individually and collectively, we're moved to take charge of financial matters. Some people might reveal confidences or have insights into what they've hidden from themselves.

The First Quarter Moon comes on New Year's Eve. The Moon in Aries (a sign of spring) wants us to get a move on toward something fresh. But it bangs heads with the stodgy Sun in Capricorn (a sign of winter), which prefers the familiar ways things have always been done. This is like the New Year baby dashing past the old man who stands for the year that's ending, a fitting way to shift from 2011 to 2012.

[Monday Mercury semisquare Saturn, Mercury conjunct North Node; Tuesday Venus semisquare Ceres; Wednesday Mercury sesquiquadrate Jupiter; Wednesday (P)/Thursday (E) Sun conjunct Pluto; Thursday North Node semisquare Saturn; Saturday Venus sextile North Node; Saturday (P)/ Sunday (E) Mercury square Mars; Sunday Mercury trine Eris]

FEBRUARY

SU	M	TU	W	T	F	S
				1	2	3	4
5	6	7	8	9	10	11
12	13	14	15	16	17	18
19	20	21	22	23	24	25
26	27	28	29			

2011-2012

December-January

If you're a little lonely, don't feel sorry for yourself. Pick up the phone and take the lead in contacting someone. Soon you'll be happier.

New Year's Day *(holiday observed)*

Moon in Aries • Void 12:08 pm (P), 3:08 pm (E)
Moon enters Taurus 2:17 pm (P), 5:17 pm (E)

★ **3 MO 02**

There are lots of balls to juggle! Get in a flow and handle them by instinct instead of intellect. You'll look like you really have it together.

Moon in Taurus

3 TU 03

The day starts off with a burst of energy but midday, we go flat and we can't figure out why. Something's not right. Tonight improves only a bit.

Moon in Taurus

3 WE 04

Many awake with an uneasy feeling left over from yesterday. A surprising turn early doesn't promise recovery. The situation may degenerate.

Moon in Taurus • Void 12:47 am (P), 3:47 am (E)
Moon enters Gemini 2:45 am (P), 5:45 am (E)

2 TH 05

It's better to tiptoe nimbly around barriers than to stay put. This evening, comrades pump up your self-worth. Still you see the down side.

Epiphany, Three Kings Day

Moon in Gemini

3 FR 06

Our minds are sharp, blending right and left brains well. We heal through caring and regenerate pride by the transformative power of love.

Orthodox Christmas

Moon in Gemini • Void 11:53 am (P), 2:53 pm (E)
Moon enters Cancer 1:06 pm (P), 4:06 pm (E)

★ **P 3 SA 07**

Despite unpredictability, we push for change from a place of sensitivity. With feet firmly planted, we open to new vistas with a sense of wonder.

Moon in Cancer • Full Moon (P) (Wolf Moon)

★ **2 SU 08**

Each month, the Moon passes by big, bright Jupiter. Many months, they're visible when most of us are asleep. At least one month each year, they're too near the Sun to be seen. Monday night, they're very close and easy to enjoy well before bedtime. Gaze in a south to southwesterly direction; there will be Jupiter below the Moon. Their monthly meeting usually increases appetites for a day or two before and after their team-up (the Moon rules eating and Jupiter is an expander). People who want to start dieting after the holidays will have an extra hurdle. Their sign, Taurus, loves to indulge in the senses, taste being an important one! Sweets and fatty dairy items are especially appealing.

Our confidence and sense of being in control are fine as the week begins, in fact, quite robust Tuesday. But they drop a notch Wednesday from self-doubt, only to turn around by Saturday. We gain an understanding then about why we were so skeptical and we set about repairing self-respect. Conversations perk and we're very active mentally all weekend. Some people figure out mysteries or have moments of genius. Midday Saturday is particularly fertile for giving form to ideas or dreams. Midday Sunday, the proverbial light bulbs go off in our heads. Such conditions

JANUARY 02-08, 2012 HIGHLIGHTS

are favorable for planning and outlining objectives for the coming year. Brainstorming with others yields good results.

Intensity builds all week, peaking at the very end. The Full Moon is Sunday night on the west coast (11:31 pm) and early next Monday morning (2:31 am) in the east. Within minutes, Eris turns Direct. As the planet of chaos, perhaps its disruptive nature is held at bay for this Full Moon since it is literally stopped in its tracks. A motionless planet's power is strong, though. Leave a wide berth for disorder.

[Monday Venus semisquare Uranus; Wednesday Sun semisquare Neptune; Wednesday (P)/Thursday (E) Mercury square Ceres; Friday Venus sextile Eris; Saturday Mercury sextile Saturn, Mercury sextile Neptune (Saturn and Neptune are trine within 1°), Venus semisquare Pluto, Sun semisquare Chiron; Saturday (P)/Sunday (E) Mercury enters Capricorn; Sunday Mercury trine Jupiter, Mercury square Uranus (Jupiter and Uranus are semisextile within 1°); Sunday (P)/Monday (E) Full Moon, Eris turns Direct]

We are the living links in a life force that moves and plays through and around us, binding the deepest soils with the farthest stars.

Alan Chadwick

Moon in Cancer • Full Moon (E) (Wolf Moon) • Void 6:26 pm (P), 9:26 pm (E)
Moon enters Leo 8:36 pm (P), 11:36 pm (E)

09 MO 3 ★

After an early morning interruption, the pace picks up. Answers to problems come from combining smarts and ESP. Help is there for the asking.

Mahayana (Buddist New Year)

Moon in Leo

10 TU 2

Slow down! You might miss important details or make errors in your haste. Others are too focused on their own goals to be of much assistance.

Moon in Leo

11 WE 2

Obligations demand attention when we'd rather follow a desire for fun. Perhaps a competitive activity can satisfy ambitions for achievement.

Moon in Leo • Void 12:24 am (P), 3:24 am (E)
Moon enters Virgo 1:45 am (P), 4:45 am (E)

12 TH 3

Productivity is more appealing than yesterday but can be impeded by a commotion involving someone's ego. Make any criticism constructive.

Moon in Virgo • Void 5:59 pm (P), 8:59 pm (E)

13 FR 4 P ★

Powerful communication is persuasive. People are motivated to act as long as you don't ask too much of them. Friendly teamwork aids all efforts.

Moon Void in Virgo
Moon enters Libra 5:29 am (P), 8:29 am (E)

14 SA 3 ★

Do your own thing or follow someone else's lead? A tough choice this morning, but later we're all about bonding and being best buddies.

Moon in Libra

15 SU 2

Our sense of balance seems off, leaning toward melancholy, feeling mistreated or on the short end of the stick. Seek solace.

World Religion Day

JANUARY 9-15 HIGHLIGHTS

This is no ordinary vanilla Full Moon kicking off the week [Monday 2:31 am (E)]. It belongs to a Moon Family* which began with a Solar Eclipse on July 11, 2010. The degree is close to the USA Sun so there's likely to be a lot of attention on the nation and the President. In individuals' lives, expect a peak in circumstances with roots going back about a year-and-a-half. Both that Eclipse New Moon and this Full Moon find the Sun and Moon rubbing Eris the wrong way, indicating disarray and rivalry (see last week's Highlights). The Cancer Full Moon accentuates emotions, including patriotism and protectionism. These are unlikely to express aggressively since Mars (the anger planet) connects nicely with the Sun and Moon. Instead, we can act in determined, disciplined and productive ways, when we're in the mood to. Still, this is not time to make great strides. Saturn is nearly motionless in January and February, turning Retrograde Feb. 7 (see the Star Pages). Work proceeds slowly with lots of frustration. The week begins with unpredictability and a jerky pace. Yet hopes are high and practical approaches come easily. Smart solutions are at hand, aided by cooperation. Several planets blend together to promote success for projects that have widespread benefits.

This weekend, Venus dances into Pisces, a sign where its sweet side shows strongly. Sympathy and a helpful attitude stimulate social and romantic interactions.

*A relationship between lunar phases forming a series, as noted and named by Dietrech J. Pessin (Lunar-Shadows.com). Nine months after a New Moon is a First Quarter Moon at nearly the same degree of the same sign, with a Full Moon nine months later and a Third Quarter Moon nine months after that, all near the same location in the zodiac. Events often unfold in a story with developments around these key points. (See page 69.)

[Monday (E) Full Moon, Eris turns Direct; Monday Mercury sextile Chiron; Wednesday (P)/Thursday (E) Sun square Eris; Thursday Sun trine Mars; Friday Venus trine Saturn, Mercury conjunct Pluto, Venus conjunct Neptune; Friday (P)/ Saturday (E) Venus enters Pisces; Saturday Venus sextile Jupiter]

 Read "Using This Planner" for the meaning of Moon Void and symbols ★, **MR**, **VR**, **P**.

FEBRUARY

SU	M	TU	W	T	F	S
				1	2	3	4
5	6	7	8	9	10	11
12	13	14	15	16	17	18
19	20	21	22	23	24	25
26	27	28	29

Friday the 13th was not always considered unlucky. Like many Goddess-worshipping traditions, this day was branded as "bad" by conquering patriarchal types (see the Star Pages).

January

A mellow morning eases us into the week. A dream may bring inspiration or a solution. Afternoon is transformative, maybe intense, but in a good way.

Martin Luther King, Jr. Day

Moon in Libra • Third Quarter Moon • Void 7:30 am (P), 10:30 am (E)
Moon enters Scorpio 8:35 am (P), 11:35 am (E)

4 MO 16

What seems clear early gets fogged up by tonight. Our sense of direction seems skewed and a disruption in the afternoon throws us off course.

Moon in Scorpio

★2 TU 17

Creative juices flow first thing and can be channeled well then. Later, we get scattered and have to sift between brilliant and crazy ideas.

Moon in Scorpio • Void 10:32 am (P), 1:32 pm (E)
Moon enters Sagittarius 11:30 am (P), 2:30 pm (E)

3 WE 18

Relationship concerns (involving victimization or selfishness) mar the morning. Then, pressure for a decision weighs on us. We fret about erring.

Moon in Sagittarius

★2 TH 19

There's a feeling of relief or a second chance after yesterday's hurdles. Afternoon brings cooperation. Evening smoothes out after a bump.

Sun enters Aquarius

Moon in Sagittarius • Void 1:50 pm (P), 4:50 pm (E)
Moon enters Capricorn 2:41 pm (P), 5:41 pm (E)

★4 FR 20

Strong motivation for productivity early on fades later. Many want to socialize day or night or both, but some withdraw to do their own thing.

Moon in Capricorn

3 SA 21

Words can be very problematic today. Watch yours and don't misconstrue what others say. Strive for clarity and leave ego out of the conversation.

Chinese New Year (Year of the Dragon) (P)

Moon in Capricorn • Void 5:39 pm (P), 8:39 pm (E)
Moon enters Aquarius 6:54 pm (P), 9:54 pm (E) • New Moon (P)

★2 SU 22

JANUARY 16-22 HIGHLIGHTS

Some fresh ideas planted in 2010 that sprouted in 2011 get a boost this week from two forward-leaning planets that teamed up before and now link nicely. Their liaison is exact Tuesday evening (see Star Pages) but more helpful when emphasized by the Moon Friday evening and by the Sun over the weekend, pushing us past prior limits in surprising ways. The Sun's entrance into Aquarius Friday enhances our drive for progress. It sets our sights on the future and opens us to experimentation and using technology more in the coming month. Yet the lunar cycle is dwindling, following Monday's Third Quarter Moon. This is not the week to initiate projects. Prod something further along or to a conclusion. For new ventures, wait until after the New Moon, Sunday night 11:40 pm (P).

You might not be able to get a health appointment on a holiday, but if you can, Monday's great for anything related to well-being. Engage in activities that create more harmony and balance in your life, whether that's improving a relationship (forgiveness is very healing) or de-cluttering and cleaning your living space for better Chi. Have a nice bath or give yourself a foot massage. Expressing creativity, enjoying entertainment or just relaxing also offers a good break from normal routines.

Mid-week, it's easy to slip into negative thinking, which gets you nowhere fast. Ghandi said, "There is nothing that wastes the body like worry," so don't undo all the good you did for yourself Monday! Thursday we are reminded of how difficult it is to decide whether to tighten the reins on an important situation or pull out all the stops. Optimism is pierced by a strong dose of reality. Obligations to a partner or teammate cause tension or perhaps provide motivation. In the end, be guided by practicality.

[Monday Venus conjunct Chiron; Tuesday Sun semisquare North Node, Mercury semisquare Neptune, Jupiter semisextile Uranus; Thursday Venus semisquare Eris, Ceres enters Aries, Sun square Saturn, Mercury semisquare Chiron; Friday Sun enters Aquarius, Venus sextile Pluto, Sun sextile Ceres; Saturday Sun sextile Uranus; Saturday (P)/Sunday (E) Sun square Jupiter; Sunday Mercury square Eris]

Freedom is the last, best hope of earth.
Abraham Lincoln

JANUARY							FEBRUARY						
SU	M	TU	W	T	F	S	SU	M	TU	W	T	F	S
1	2	3	4	5	6	7				1	2	3	4
8	9	10	11	12	13	14	5	6	7	8	9	10	11
15	16	17	18	19	20	21	12	13	14	15	16	17	18
22	23	24	25	26	27	28	19	20	21	22	23	24	25
29	30	31					26	27	28	29			

Moon in Aquarius • New Moon (E)

23 MO 3 ★

A strong urge to judge tempered by cool detachment and flexible live-and-let-live tolerance keeps trouble at bay. Talk things through.

Chinese New Year (Year of the Dragon)(E)

Moon in Aquarius

24 TU 3

To push toward more of what you desire, be assured it's not selfish to do so. Satisfying your wants puts you in a better position to share.

Moon in Aquarius • Void 12:34 am (P), 3:34 am (E)
Moon enters Pisces 1:12 am (P), 4:12 am (E)

25 WE 2

A wave of generosity rises early. Be realistic about what you can offer. People will take advantage of you if your boundaries aren't firm.

Robert Burns' Birthday

Moon in Pisces • Void 8:54 pm (P), 11:54 pm (E)

26 TH 2

A kiss of sweetness starts the day but stress soon mounts from high expectation and low appreciation. Complaints outweigh compliments.

Moon Void in Pisces
Moon enters Aries 10:29 am (P), 1:29 pm (E)

27 FR 3 ★

After a morning lull, minds and mouths buzz with bright ideas (sparked by friends or associates) that just might pay off. Keep a notepad handy!

Moon in Aries

28 SA 2 P

It's a frustrating day of conflicts where we're torn between helping others and pursuing our own agenda. Stubbornness and adaptability duke it out.

Moon in Aries • Void 10:09 pm (P)
Moon enters Taurus 10:29 pm (P)

29 SU 3

Work on becoming comfortable asserting yourself with confidence. Then it will be easier to convey your wants to those nearby or far away.

JANUARY 23-29 HIGHLIGHTS

The friction we experienced last Thursday is evident again as the week begins. Perhaps a situation causing anxiety then requires further attention or maybe a whole new set of problems will crop up. The planetary culprits are part of a challenging pattern formed by the Moon and Sun at the New Moon Monday morning [2:40 am (E)], propelling the difficulties forward over the coming four weeks (see Star Pages for Jan. 2). Relationships undergo growing pains and money issues involve questions of fairness. Many people want to handle things their own way and find compromise difficult. Obstinacy makes matters worse. A little relief may come from trying a new and unusual approach or from eliciting sympathy, though some will only feel it for a certain group instead of everyone.

The Aquarius New Moon is a time when brotherhood should shine forth and friendships flourish, yet we'll see some heated disagreements based on conflicting philosophies. Arguments should stay verbal and not progress to violence, since the planet of antagonism (Mars) is slowed to a stop, turning Retrograde Monday. Its strong connection then to the main planet of communication (Mercury) indicates a lot of talk, including some constructive criticism. Although inclined to be helpful, it's hard for some people to see past concerns in their immediate area and generalize to a bigger picture.

Tuesday the ruling planet of Aquarius, Uranus, is joined by Ceres, an influence that wants to help us bear fruit, in this case from our own uniqueness and ingenuity (see Star Pages for Jan. 19). They're in a harmonious connection with the Moon and Sun at the New Moon, adding to the urge to follow our own drumbeat. Aquarius also signals the power of the group. Joining forces with like-minded souls now is likely to be effective in bringing about positive changes.

[Monday Mercury trine Mars, Venus square Nodes, Mars turns Retrograde; Tuesday Ceres conjunct Uranus; Wednesday Mercury semisquare North Node, Venus sesquiquadrate Saturn; Friday Mercury square Saturn, Mercury enters Aquarius; Saturday Sun sesquiquadrate Mars, Venus semisquare Jupiter, Mercury sextile Uranus, Mercury square Jupiter; Sunday Mercury sextile Ceres]

MARCH

SU	M	TU	W	T	F	S
				1	2	3
4	5	6	7	8	9	10
11	12	13	14	15	16	17
18	19	20	21	22	23	24
25	26	27	28	29	30	31

January-February

The day dawns with hope but soon confusion and miscommunication snare us in a snag, which could easily lead to anger if cool heads don't prevail.

Moon in Taurus (P), in Aries (E) • Void 1:09 am (E)
Moon enters Taurus 1:29 am (E) • First Quarter Moon

P 2 MO 30

Stick to your principles and let intuition be your guide when an interrupter demands attention. It's better to be calm and kind than to criticize.

Moon in Taurus

3 TU 31

Making yourself understood causes strain today. First you need to be clear, and that's a problem, too. Slow down, then feel your way through.

National Freedom Day, Black History Month begins

Moon in Taurus • Void 11:07 am (P), 2:07 pm (E)
Moon enters Gemini 11:16 am (P), 2:16 pm (E)

1 WE 01

The pieces fall together and the picture is clearer than it's been for days. Say what comes naturally, as long as you don't step on others' toes.

Groundhog Day, Candlemas, Imbolc

Moon in Gemini

3 TH 02

You see the target but it seems like forces are conspiring to keep you from heading toward it. Rather than going in circles, find another route.

Moon in Gemini • Void 9:07 pm (P)
Moon enters Cancer 10:05 pm (P)

★ 2 FR 03

Early morning is the best time today. Seek tranquility or a source of inspiration. When people are pushy later, you'll be able to handle it.

Mawlid al-Nabi (Muhammad's Birthday)

Moon in Cancer (P), in Gemini (E) • Void 12:07 am (E)
Moon enters Cancer 1:05 am (E)

2 SA 04

Steer clear of those who would like to rub salt into your wounds or whose negativity brings you down. This evening offers support like a salve.

Superbowl Sunday

Moon in Cancer

2 SU 05

A tricky and troublesome web among three quick planets prompts putting your foot in your mouth more than once this week. Watch out for this at work as well as in personal relationships, especially those between opposite genders. People aren't on the same page and disagreements could be heated, particularly when values, money, possessions or feelings are involved. The pieces of the pattern are exact Monday and Wednesday, with the trio aggravated by the Moon Monday and again Friday. Monday's First Quarter Moon contributes extra inflexibility that could also impede peace. A sharp tongue cuts to the quick and while people might be tough Monday and let things slide Wednesday, they'll be sensitive and easily hurt Friday. It will take extra effort to iron out wrinkles after the fact so don't make waves in the first place, unless you have to fight for fairness. In any case, exercise diplomacy and give respect if you want to receive it.

The big astrological news is Neptune's entrance Friday into the sign it rules, Pisces. Though it tested these waters briefly from April to August of 2011, now it dives in for a long swim over the next 13-14 years. While there will be a new tide of developments affecting the world at

JAN. 30-FEBRUARY 05 HIGHLIGHTS

large (see the Star Pages), for individuals, this is a time to deepen your spiritual understanding and commitment, learn to appreciate nuance and what is unspoken, and see signs and signals of something bigger in everyday occurrences. Delve into art (including music, dance and poetry) or entertainment, spend time near the ocean or water, and learn from dreams or other means of tapping the subconscious (such as tarot or divination). Neptune and Pisces rule the feet, so be kind to your tootsies. This planet and sign are connected to volunteering, charitable activities and helping the underdog. Expect to see an uptick in these, which will be needed because another association is with misery and suffering.

[Monday Mercury semisquare Venus; Tuesday Sun sextile North Node; Wednesday Mercury sesquiquadrate Mars, Venus opposite Mars; Friday Mercury sextile North Node, Neptune enters Pisces]

Ideologies separate us. Dreams and anguish bring us together.

Eugene Ionesco

Moon in Cancer • Void 4:32 am (P), 7:32 am (E)
Moon enters Leo 5:25 am (P), 8:25 am (E)

06 MO **2**

You juggle changing conditions and navigate pulls in opposite directions. Good thing there's plenty of creativity and ingenuity at hand.

Moon in Leo • Full Moon (Storm Moon)

07 TU **1 P ★**

Personal wants compete or conflict with those of others. Amidst a lot of banter and finger-pointing, no one yields or even sees eye-to-eye.

Moon in Leo • Void 8:43 am (P), 11:43 am (E)
Moon enters Virgo 9:33 am (P), 12:33 pm (E)

08 WE **3 ★**

Keep your goals squarely before you and maybe you'll avoid the strong temptation to daydream or dawdle. Late afternoon is the most productive.

Moon in Virgo • Void 9:13 pm (P)

09 TH **2**

Don't let unchecked impulses compound mental overload, especially when shopping. People are very aggressive tonight (and tomorrow night, too).

Moon in Virgo, Void (P) • Void 12:13 am (E)
Moon enters Libra 11:55 am (P), 2:55 (E)

10 FR **2**

I want what I want. You want what you want. Can't we both have what we want? It doesn't work that way. Don't flinch. Take the lead to get an edge.

Moon in Libra

11 SA **2 ★**

Early risers are crabby but brighten up quickly. Later some people sulk, feeling dejected or off balance. They can turn to a mate for some TLC.

Moon in Libra • Void 1:10 pm (P), 4:10 pm (E)
Moon enters Scorpio 2:02 pm (P), 5:02 pm (E)

12 SU **3**

You sense a shift coming in your focus or purpose. You could proceed on instinct but it's wise to explore ideas and plans with a trusted advisor.

Lincoln's Birthday

FEBRUARY 06-12 HIGHLIGHTS

Interruptions and unexpected developments abound on Monday, possibly spawning arguments, especially if pride is involved. Everyone seems to be pushy and stubborn. The trend continues Tuesday, the roughest day of the week, which would be hard enough if it wasn't also a Full Moon [exact at 1:55 pm (P), 4:55 pm (E)]. We're painfully aware of how jumbled and mixed up circumstances are, and it seems to be "every man for himself" with cooperation nowhere in sight. The planet that normally helps us be civil is at a standstill, turning Retrograde Tuesday morning. It's a planet of karma, currently at the last degree of the sign of balance and partnership, presenting us with tests to see if we can be mature, committed and righteous (not self-righteous!) with our significant others. The planet of love and harmony is at the final degree of Pisces at the Full Moon, a degree famous for psychic connection, on the positive side, and suffering, on the low end of the scale. The generous Leo Moon should spur us to help anyone being harassed or to stand up for ourselves if we're the downtrodden one. This is supposed to be the time for Aquarian brotherhood and treating each other as friends. The key now is communication with – not at – one another, keeping a cool yet compassionate tone in discussions, foregoing purely selfish desires, and casting any criticism as helpful suggestions.

One of the best features of the week (strong Wednesday through Friday) is a fresh appreciation of yourself and your unique qualities. You may be able to use these to your advantage in situations where popularity is beneficial. But don't cross the line and engage in obnoxious bragging, which might be tempting, particularly Saturday evening. A significant shift in mental attitude or perspective arises Friday or Saturday, allowing you to see things in a clearer light, although it might feel more like reality slapping you in the face.

[Monday Sun semisquare Uranus, Mercury semisquare Uranus; Tuesday Mercury conjunct Sun, Saturn turns Retrograde; Tuesday (P), Wednesday (E) Venus enters Aries; Wednesday through Friday Finger of God: Mercury and Sun sextile Eris and all three quincunx Mars; Wednesday Mars quincunx Eris; Wednesday (P)/Thursday (E) Mercury quincunx Mars; Thursday Mercury sextile Eris, Mercury semisquare Ceres, Venus conjunct Uranus; Friday Sun quincunx Mars, Mercury semisquare Pluto, Sun sextile Eris; Saturday Sun quintile North Node and Jupiter (Quintile Triangle); Saturday (P), Sunday (E) Sun semisquare Ceres, Sun semisquare Pluto]

MARCH

SU	M	TU	W	T	F	S
				1	2	3
4	5	6	7	8	9	10
11	12	13	14	15	16	17
18	19	20	21	22	23	24
25	26	27	28	29	30	31

The final degree of a sign brings an intense dose of all the sign represents. Saturn hangs at Libra's last degree all February long, testing our relationships and commitments.

February

We're in a no-nonsense, get-down-to-business mood, ready to streamline or make changes. Tonight we want to relax but something pops up.

Moon in Scorpio

★ **3 MO 13**

If someone or something doesn't benefit you, part of you would just as soon leave. But your sympathetic side hangs in, hoping for the best.

Valentine's Day

Moon in Scorpio • Third Quarter Moon • Void 9:05 am (P), 12:05 pm (E)
Moon enters Sagittarius 4:57 pm (P), 7:57 pm (E)

★ **2 TU 14**

You're optimistic about getting more of what you want, even if that means working hard for it. Look for the right person to show you how.

Susan B. Anthony Day

Moon in Sagittarius

2 WE 15

Ideas are sprouting every which way, whether whimsical or practical. You start the day solo but later find support from those around you.

Moon in Sagittarius • Void 8:04 pm (P), 11:04 pm (E)
Moon enters Capricorn 9:04 pm (P)

4 TH 16

Put some of yesterday's great notions into practice, the sooner the better. By this evening, resolve fades and self-indulgence beckons.

Moon in Capricorn (P), Void in Sagittarius (E)
Moon enters Capricorn 12:04 am (E)

3 FR 17

Though you may happily help, obligations keep you from your own agenda. But that allows you time to see things from a different, clearer angle.

Sun enters Pisces (P)

Moon in Capricorn

★ **3 SA 18**

Find time to do what pleases you, especially anything related to arts or entertainment. You may have to attend to some chores first, though.

Sun enters Pisces (P)

Moon in Capricorn • Void 1:23 am (P), 4:23 am (E)
Moon enters Aquarius 2:59 am (P), 5:29 am (E)

★ **3 SU 19**

This time each year, the Sun shifts from Aquarius to Pisces. In many years, Mercury is nearby and does likewise. What's different this year is that when they change signs this week, each immediately passes Pisces' ruling planet, Neptune. This strengthens the importance of all the related associations of both sign and planet. Whereas Aquarius is outgoing and social, Pisces induces us to internalize and feel the effects of others' vibes. Neptune clouds our view of reality while helping us focus on the unseen realms and our connection to Divinity and the "other side." The need for rest or downtime increases. We may be very moved by music or art, or wish to participate in creative endeavors. Communication is unlikely to be straightforward and many people will skirt issues. This is a problem Tuesday evening in particular, just when lovers want assurances on Valentine's Day. Instead, they're likely to get little white lies to spare feelings. If you want to know the score in your relationship, ask Thursday night. Even then, it still might be served with a sugar coating.

The Third Quarter Moon in Scorpio midday Tuesday helps us process feelings in response to what we've learned over the past three weeks, especially at last week's Full Moon. See how much freer you will be if

FEBRUARY 13-19 HIGHLIGHTS

you can shed some negativity. Wednesday night, be careful not to go overboard in whatever you do. Irritation may bring you to a breaking point in matters of pride, values or finances. (In fact, expect a tough week fiscally, especially Tuesday morning and Friday afternoon.) Good can result from such stress, though, maybe even by Friday morning, if you discuss it with humor and put things in perspective. A calm and kind veneer coats the week, thanks to a lovely connection exact Tuesday and amplified Thursday, a day when words can be very healing.

[Monday Mercury trine Saturn, Mercury enters Pisces; Monday (P), Tuesday (E) Mercury conjunct Neptune; Tuesday Ceres square Pluto, Jupiter sextile Chiron; Tuesday (P)/Wednesday (E) North Node quintile Jupiter; Wednesday Venus square Pluto, Mars sesquiquadrate Jupiter, Venus conjunct Ceres; Thursday Mercury conjunct Chiron, Mercury sextile Jupiter; Thursday (P), Friday (E) Venus trine North Node; Friday Mercury semisquare Eris; Saturday Sun trine Saturn, Mercury sextile Pluto, North Node trine Ceres; Saturday (P), Sunday (E) Sun enters Pisces; Sunday Mercury square Nodes, Sun conjunct Neptune]

The soul should always stand ajar,
ready to welcome the ecstatic experience.
Emily Dickinson

FEBRUARY								MARCH					
SU	M	TU	W	T	F	S		SU	M	TU	W	T	F	S
			1	2	3	4					1	2	3
5	6	7	8	9	10	11		4	5	6	7	8	9	10
12	13	14	15	16	17	18		11	12	13	14	15	16	17
19	20	21	22	23	24	25		18	19	20	21	22	23	24
26	27	28	29					25	26	27	28	29	30	31

Moon in Aquarius

20 MO 3

Though you may enjoy socializing, you're happiest left to your own devices or at least calling the shots. You really don't need anyone else.

Presidents Day (US), Family Day (Canada)

Moon in Aquarius • Void 8:18 am (P), 11:18 am (E)
Moon enters Pisces 9:32 am (P), 12:32 pm (E) • New Moon

21 TU 3

A solid start of good cooperation disintegrates. After a detour to fix problems, boost a wounded ego or deal with misinformation, all ends well.

Mardi Gras

Moon in Pisces • Void 6:25 pm (P), 9:25 pm (E)

22 WE 2

We drift off course this morning. To achieve clarity, we must see through another's eyes and recognize a block. A disparity can lead to a clash.

Ash Wednesday, Washington's Birthday

Moon Void in Pisces • Moon enters Aries 6:49 pm (P), 9:49 pm (E)

23 TH 2

Antagonism or at least a healthy argument helps show all sides of an issue. If you must register disapproval, cushion it with compassion.

Moon in Aries

24 FR 3

Set fears aside. Be confident, trust intuition and pursue a creative approach to find answers. Exploration will prove fruitful.

Moon in Aries

25 SA 2 P

For some, hesitation and trepidation undermine the brave independence that is needed. Others are so self-assured, they're overbearing.

Moon in Aries • Void 4:53 am (P), 7:53 am (E)
Moon enters Taurus 6:31 am (P), 9:31 am (E)

26 SU 3

A morning that starts mellow soon sours and crabbiness or bossiness ruffles feathers. After some apologies, everyone has a good laugh.

FEBRUARY 20-26 HIGHLIGHTS

We're entering a strong period for spirituality, meditation, health and charitable activities, for going deep within and well beyond ourselves. This week's New Moon in Pisces [Tuesday 2:36 pm (P), 5:36 pm (E)] finds the Sun and Moon sandwiched between Pisces' ruler, Neptune, and the healing asteroid, Chiron. The luminaries so close to Neptune illuminate our shadow side, showing subconscious tendencies. Chiron offers insights for improvement. Imaginations work overtime in the next four weeks to envision innovations to aid those in need. If you're sluggish, revive through rest and a break from routines. A favorable tie between Mercury and Venus brings inspirational words and loving encouragement. Fiscal or romantic matters benefit from compassion and sharing. A positive link from Uranus highlights unique talents and a beneficial contact with Jupiter offers material support. This lunar cycle coincides with Lent, a time for prayer, repentance, charity and self-denial – all typical Pisces traits.

Pisces is associated with unconditional love and non-judgment. The opposite sign, Virgo, is concerned with separating good from bad. These approaches clash in a face-off between Mercury and Mars early Thursday (more apparent Wednesday night as the Moon passes Mercury). With Mars Retrograde, people may turn a critical eye toward themselves rather than attacking others. But oppositions are famous for confrontations and this pair can spell a doozy.

Multiple skirmishes this week (particularly Saturday) pit self-centered Aries energy against the selfless caring of Pisces, pointing to the eternal competition between individuals and the collective. Sometimes a strong spine keeps us from being swallowed up in the ocean of mankind; other times we must surrender ego for the good of all.

[Tuesday Venus semisquare Neptune, Mercury sesquiquadrate Saturn, Sun semisextile Uranus; Thursday Mercury opposite Mars, Mercury semisextile Venus; Friday Sun conjunct Chiron; Saturday Sun sextile Jupiter, Venus semisquare Chiron, Mercury semisquare Jupiter, Sun semisquare Eris; Sunday Venus conjunct Eris]

 Read "Using This Planner" for the meaning of
Moon Void and symbols ★, **MR**, **VR**, **P**.

APRIL

SU	M	TU	W	T	F	S
1	2	3	4	5	6	7
8	9	10	11	12	13	14
15	16	17	18	19	20	21
22	23	24	25	26	27	28
29	30					

February-March

We feel like we're on the right track. We cruise with good momentum, accomplishing a lot efficiently. Tonight, though, our rhythm is disrupted.

Moon in Taurus

3 MO 27

We gather input this morning. A little research should do the trick. Later we anticipate a shift coming and want to preserve gains prudently.

Moon in Taurus • Void 11:47 am (P), 2:47 pm (E)
Moon enters Gemini 7:28 pm (P), 10:28 pm (E)

3 TU 28

Problems come to light early on. Sidestep troublemakers and try to be smart about your liaisons without being too sensitive or selfish.

Leap Day

Moon in Gemini • First Quarter Moon

1 WE 29

Take a stand on what you think is the right course of action, especially if you run into stubborn resistance (which could be couched as humor).

Moon in Gemini

3 TH 01

Diplomacy goes awry when it encounters a burst of aggression. Sensitivity can lean toward either compassion or a feeling of mistreatment.

Moon in Gemini • Void 5:15 am (P), 8:15 am (E)
Moon enters Cancer 7:09 am (P), 10:09 am (E)

★ 3 FR 02

We're torn between giving people the benefit of the doubt and protecting ourselves from exploitation. Trust your gut about whom to believe.

Moon in Cancer

2 SA 03

It's hard to balance self-interest and mutual interests. Clarity is likely to be clouded by emotion. What would a loving mother recommend?

Moon in Cancer • Void 2:18 pm (P), 5:18 pm (E)
Moon enters Leo 3:19 pm (P), 6:19 pm (E)

P 1 SU 04

FEB. 27-MARCH 04 HIGHLIGHTS

"Life is too short," we always say. Once every four years, we get a bonus day. This Wednesday is it – enjoy! It coincides with the First Quarter Moon, time to round a bend and head in a different direction. With the Sun in Pisces, we operate primarily on feelings. With the Moon in rational Gemini, we want things to make sense. However we don't have full information yet (prior to the Full Moon's illumination) and we must continue using instincts. Still, the more data we collect, the more comfortable we'll be with decisions.

Venus is in the part of its Evening Star cycle where it's farthest ahead of the Sun (peaking on March 27). From Feb. 27 to April 16, they're in the only grating connection they ever make, a semisquare (45° apart), exact April 10. In the next six weeks, assess whether relationships and resources are working to your personal advantage. During this time, the Sun and Venus make harsh links to other planets simultaneously, at times forming pesky triangles that tip our scales. They do this midweek with the Moon's Nodes, indicators of the direction in which we need to head as well as what we need to release. This weekend, they interact with a frustrating clash between

Mars and Saturn (exact Friday) that makes us feel like we're driving with one foot on the accelerator and the other on the brake. The Moon aggravates the tangle Sunday afternoon, the toughest time of the week. With Mars in fussy, critical Virgo stirring up trouble with Saturn (nearing the end of its 3-year stay in Libra), the arena of close relationships is where petty arguments can occur. Equilibrium and tact are harder to muster when the Sun and Venus don't play nicely. So be good to yourself and your partner. The best use of this energy is to figure out together where you want to go and what holds you back from your goals. Then make a step-by-step plan.

[Monday (P), Tuesday (E) Sun sextile Pluto; Tuesday Sun square Nodes; Wednesday Venus sesquiquadrate North Node; Friday Mercury enters Aries, Mars semisquare Saturn; Saturday Sun opposite Mars, Venus sesquiquadrate Mars, Sun sesquiquadrate Saturn; Sunday Venus opposite Saturn]

We are what we pretend to be, so we must be careful about what we pretend to be.

Kurt Vonnegut, Jr.

Moon in Leo

05 MO 3 ★

Concerns about adequate supplies or resources worry us this morning but by tonight we're more comfortable that we have enough of what we need.

Moon in Leo • Void 5:28 pm (P), 8:28 pm (E)
Moon enters Virgo 7:28 pm (P), 10:28 pm (E)

06 TU 3

Confidence, or perhaps a dollop of chutzpah, propels us past power struggles. We didn't really want to fight anyway. At heart, we're mellow.

Moon in Virgo

07 WE 3

Whatever eats away at you first thing dissipates quickly, replaced by efficient productivity. Later you might get frustrated yet again.

Moon in Virgo • Full Moon (Chaste Moon) • Void 1:41 am (P), 4:41 am (E)
Moon enters Libra 8:51 pm (P), 11:51 pm (E)

08 TH 2

By setting big goals and high standards for yourself, you open the door to self-criticism that could undermine a sense of worth. Be realistic.

Purim

Moon in Libra

09 FR 2

Murphy's Law is evident at every turn and you feel like you're running into one wall after another. It might be easier to try an alternate route.

Moon in Libra • Void 7:10 pm (P), 10:10 pm (E)
Moon enters Scorpio 9:25 pm (P)

10 SA 2

A busy day of slapping band-aids on situations, hand-holding and compensating for imbalances leaves us little time for our own To Do list.

Moon in Scorpio (P), Void in Libra (E)
Moon enters Scorpio 12:25 am (EST)

11 SU 3 ★

An emotional start to the day intrudes on a relaxed mood. Good thing you feel patient and generous. Optimize the afternoon's high energy.

Daylight Saving Time begins

MARCH 05-11 HIGHLIGHTS

Venus prances through Taurus each year, bringing an appreciation for scents, sounds, tastes, beauty and all forms of touch. As it arrives Monday, it begins a decade of friendly contacts from Taurus to Neptune in Pisces. Together they offer healing and becoming closer to the Divine through the senses. Their liaison is exact on Tuesday and boosted by the Moon early Sunday – good times for meditation, creativity, a healing treatment, a moment in nature or lingering in bed with a lover. Late Tuesday night as the Moon accentuates them is another ideal chance to lose yourself in another's embrace, create beautiful crafts or art, or do something beneficial for your body. Mercury passes Uranus annually, too, also coming around on Monday. Their mentally stimulating yet jittery influence is quite noticeable late that night and early Friday as the Moon pushes their buttons. Since Mercury turns Retrograde March 12, this combination repeats (see Star Pages and Highlights for next week).

The Full Moon Thursday [1:41 am (P), 4:41 am (E)] pits the practical Moon in Virgo against the idealistic Sun in Pisces. Issues involve critical judgment versus unconditional acceptance. The outstanding pattern then is a wonderful Grand Trine in earth signs (joined by the Moon midday Wednesday), featuring quick Mars and a longer-lasting Jupiter-Pluto trine (see next week's Highlights). Material concerns flourish in such conditions. Take action to stimulate growth and progress in joint money matters or situations requiring transition. Chiron interacts with this pattern, adding innovation. Grand Trines are generally good but their main job is to grease wheels. This combination of forceful planets could bring a release of pent-up anger. A positive use of this energy is powerful physical activity or heavy lifting to clear away unwanted stuff.

[Monday Venus enters Taurus, Mercury conjunct Uranus, Ceres semisquare Neptune; Tuesday Venus sextile Neptune; Wednesday Moon forms Grand Trine with Jupiter trine Pluto, Venus semisquare Sun; Saturday Venus sextile Chiron; Sunday Sun quintile Pluto]

 Read "Using This Planner" for the meaning of Moon Void and symbols ★, **MR**, **VR**, **P**.

APRIL

SU	M	TU	W	T	F	S
1	2	3	4	5	6	7
8	9	10	11	12	13	14
15	16	17	18	19	20	21
22	23	24	25	26	27	28
29	30					

In most of Canada and the U.S. (except Arizona), Daylight Saving Time begins at 2:00 am on Sunday, March 11. Set clocks and watches ahead an hour.

A speedy response is needed before you even get going. It's hard to react quickly! Then calm ensues but doesn't last long. Tonight's intense.

Moon in Scorpio • Void 11:31 am (PDT), 2:31 pm (EDT)
Moon enters Sagittarius 11:55 pm (PDT)

MR ★ 3 MO 12

A hard-to-pinpoint worry sits to the side as we go about our business trying to be positive instead of irritated. A turn-around is imminent.

Moon in Sagittarius (P), Void in Scorpio (E)
Moon enters Sagittarius 2:55 am (EDT)

MR ★ 3 TU 13

Things are over the top, mostly but not entirely in a good way. We may expect too much from a situation and get discouraged at what's lacking.

Moon in Sagittarius • Third Quarter Moon

MR P 3 WE 14

Look for inspiration early to help you transcend interruptions midday. Tonight a shift in orientation lays groundwork for future success.

Moon in Sagittarius • Void 12:35 am (P), 3:35 am (E)
Moon enters Capricorn 3:25 am (P), 6:25 am (E)

MR 3 TH 15

It won't be easy but try to stay grounded and maintain focus as questions and doubts arise amidst the chaos of rapidly changing circumstances.

Moon in Capricorn

MR 2 FR 16

Get things straight with your mate or closest buddy. Then enjoy a social evening with lively chatter. Listen for smart ideas popping up.

St. Patrick's Day

Moon in Capricorn • Void 6:02 am (P), 9:02 am (E)
Moon enters Aquarius 9:13 am (P), 12:13 pm (E)

MR 3 SA 17

People are sensitive about how they feel different (and possibly inferior). Think twice before speaking. Be careful, even offering praise.

Moon in Aquarius

MR 2 SU 18

MARCH 12-18 HIGHLIGHTS

Mercury Retrograde starts pre-dawn Monday and in no time dishes out weird and unexpected goings-on due to its proximity to wacky Uranus (see Star Pages for March 5). Keep a loose schedule and have Plan B ready to implement. You'll likely need it at least one of these days: Monday, Tuesday, Thursday, Saturday or Sunday. We usually have to re-learn some lessons during Mercury Retrograde. As it backtracks from Aries into Pisces, its instruction will remind everyone: (1) you are just a drop in the ocean, not the center of everything, and (2) slow down and do a gut check to feel if you're on the right track instead of forcing an issue.

We're under pressure to examine if we're doing things in a way that serves our best interests or if we need to make adjustments. This relates to Mars's square to the Nodes, exact Thursday and emphasized by the Moon Tuesday evening and Friday night. Criticism that you don't know where you're going is irritating but may be true (at least partially). Look from a wider scope and chuckle at yourself.

Even when Mercury is Retrograde, slower planets can throw their weight around and gain traction – and everything's slower than Mercury (except for the Moon). We have a great opportunity this week to gain benefits through being well organized, tenacious and thorough, especially if we're smart and do our homework, courtesy of a helpful connection between Jupiter and Pluto (exact Monday night). Mars brings action, initiative and energy to our tasks as it elevates the Jupiter-Pluto link to a powerful Grand Trine Wednesday (loosely in effect at last week's Full Moon). As frosting on the cake, Venus passes Jupiter Tuesday night, adding fiscal wisdom and upside financial potential, and the Moon joins the party Thursday night when it cruises by Pluto. A quick pay-off is at hand for our hard work.

[Monday Mercury turns Retrograde, Sun biquintile Saturn; Monday (P), Tuesday (E) Jupiter trine Pluto; Tuesday Venus trine Pluto; Tuesday (P), Wednesday (E) Venus conjunct Jupiter; Wednesday Venus trine Mars, Mars trine Jupiter, Sun semisquare Jupiter, Mars trine Pluto; Thursday Mars square Nodes; Sunday Mercury conjunct Uranus]

Just remember, we're all in this alone.
Lily Tomlin

Moon in Aquarius • Void 1:32 pm (P), 4:32 pm (E)
Moon enters Pisces 5:06 pm (P), 8:06 pm (E)

19 MO 3 ★ MR

Begin the week pumped with confidence and strong resolve, bolstered by cooperation. Charge ahead because tonight, doubts start to creep in.

Spring Equinox, Ostara, Sun enters Aries (P)

Moon in Pisces

20 TU 2 ★ MR

Some self-questioning is good so you won't trip dashing forward with blind ambition. Let instincts guide you when it's time to make a turn.

Spring Equinox, Ostara, Sun enters Aries (E)

Moon in Pisces • Void 1:40 am (P), 4:40 am (E)

21 WE 2 MR

A good day to finish a project unless you're overrun by a mood of introspection. Balance self-criticism by remembering your best qualities.

Moon Void in Pisces • Moon enters Aries 2:58 am (P), 5:58 am (E)
New Moon

22 TH 3 MR

Do you want to be one of the heroes who rights the wrongs of the world, or at least those in your neck of the woods? Expect some chaos in the process.

Moon in Aries

23 FR 2 ★ MR

If you need sympathy or help today, you'll find people absorbed in their own concerns or lost in some other fog, reluctant to part with money.

Moon in Aries • Void 10:18 am (P), 1:18 pm (E)
Moon enters Taurus 2:44 pm (P), 5:44 pm (E)

24 SA 3 MR

An eye-opener shows us how what seems a personal matter reflects a wider trend, helping us appreciate our situation in a new perspective.

Moon in Taurus

25 SU 4 MR

Make good use of the large supply of patience, physical strength and endurance to be incredibly productive. Or simply revel in nature.

MARCH 19-APRIL 25 HIGHLIGHTS

This is going to be a weird week. Whenever crazy Uranus is a key player, allow for the unexpected. Since it's in the early degrees of Aries, naturally there's an emphasis on it as spring begins. The equinox occurs early in the week [Monday 10:16 pm (P)/Tuesday 1:16 am (E) – see Star Pages] with both the Sun and Mercury near Uranus. Mercury is Retrograde (reaching the halfway point of its backward jaunt Wednesday), adding an "X" factor; things can get screwy! The likely areas for difficulty are the two nearest our hearts: love and money. They're ruled by Venus, which sits in Taurus (a sensuous and finance-related sign) in a jarring position (semisquare) to the trio in early Aries. The Aries urge is to hurry while Venus in Taurus wants us to slow down and smell the roses, or at least be sure of our footing before we sprint. Taurus fosters bringing matters to conclusion, which is also smart before starting anything new. The equinox moon phase near the end of a lunar cycle also suggests we need to finish something up, trying not to rush it.

The New Moon Thursday [7:38 am (P), 10:38 am (E)] shares most features of the spring equinox chart, softened slightly by a mildly positive link to Neptune one sign from the Sun and Moon. Some of

Aries' usual self-centered focus is diluted by a concern for those less fortunate. The intense drive to take action is tempered by consideration of consequences or delayed by apprehension or lack of confidence. With Mars exactly across from Chiron, we might fear that being forward or pushy will backfire somehow. Mars is involved in three patterns (see Star Pages for March 19-20), making it a major player in the coming four-week lunar cycle and three-month season. At some point, taking a stance or launching into an endeavor can't be avoided. Choose what and when carefully.

[Monday Ceres semisquare Chiron; Monday (P), Tuesday (E) Ceres conjunct Eris, Sun enters Aries; Tuesday Chiron semisquare Eris; Wednesday Mercury semisquare Venus, Mars sesquiquadrate Ceres, Mercury conjunct Sun; Thursday Mars opposite Chiron, Mars sesquiquadrate Eris; Friday Mercury re-enters Pisces, Venus semisquare Uranus; Saturday Ceres sesquiquadrate North Node, Sun conjunct Uranus; Sunday Moon joins earth Grand Trine – see Star Pages for spring equinox]

MAY

SU	M	TU	W	T	F	S
		1	2	3	4	5
6	7	8	9	10	11	12
13	14	15	16	17	18	19
20	21	22	23	24	25	26
27	28	29	30	31		

Mars rules both anger and action.
If something makes you mad, get busy.
Do something to improve the situation.

Curb your impulses, even generosity, or at least pause to assess wisdom before acting. Let your strongest values be your measuring stick.

Moon in Taurus • Void 9:36 pm (P)

MR 2 MO **26**

It's easy to get sidetracked, especially with requests for help. An interruption could prove to be pleasant but more likely holds you back.

Moon in Taurus, Void (P) • Void 12:36 am (E)
Moon enters Gemini 3:44 am (P), 6:44 am (E)

MR ★ 3 TU **27**

You have a clear sense of direction but it's not necessarily a shared vision. Find common ground, even if that requires a compromise.

Moon in Gemini

MR ★ 2 WE **28**

Fertile minds play with ideas this morning, perhaps teasing or flirting a bit, followed by a serious afternoon and a mellow, relaxed night.

Moon in Gemini • Void 11:06 am (P), 2:06 pm (E)
Moon enters Cancer 4:08 pm (P), 7:08 pm (E)

MR 3 TH **29**

You can only repair or improve so much in one day. Strive for a good mix between competing interests: work, home life, and personal concerns.

Moon in Cancer • First Quarter Moon

MR 2 FR **30**

People are crabby to start the day but manage to shift to a brighter attitude by afternoon. Tonight an impetuous side clashes with maturity.

Moon in Cancer • Void 9:21 pm (P)

MR 2 SA **31**

Unbridled enthusiasm and inspired ingenuity lift spirits and lighten hearts, bringing joy. So much fun may leave some worn out by evening.

Moon in Cancer, Void (P) • Void 12:21 am (E)
Moon enters Leo 1:37 am (P), 4:37 am (E)

MR 3 SU **01**

April Fool's Day, Palm Sunday

Our thinking and communicating isn't at its best. Mercury Retrograde has a bad enough reputation. The current season is tainted by it with the further handicap of Mercury close to unpredictable Uranus at the spring equinox (see last week's Highlights). As of last Friday, Mercury backed into Pisces, where it prefers fantasy to reality and escapism to facing facts. This week another challenge comes from Mercury in a grating connection to Jupiter (exact Monday and most noticeable Thursday when the Moon slaps them around). Watch out for tall tales, blurting, exaggerating and leaping to conclusions. Fortunately, Venus in a friendly relationship with Mercury (exact Thursday) shows people are inclined to make allowances for one another in a good-natured way.

Tuesday finds tongues wagging, some off on a tangent, some pointedly sharp, and others cooking up smart ideas. Brains are on overdrive late into the night.

Watch out for a self-righteous and judgmental edge to some people's behavior, coming from the Sun's square to Pluto (occurring Thursday, with emphasis from the Moon Monday and Friday). Venus is still in a tough link to the Sun so it also bumps heads with Pluto this week

MARCH 26-APRIL 01 HIGHLIGHTS

(on Wednesday; also part of the Monday and Friday mishmashes with the Moon). Disagreements are likely to arise concerning values, possessions, finances and who's the boss. This is not a happy combination for real estate or business matters, though a turning point in negotiations could come with the First Quarter Moon Friday afternoon. Sunday afternoon is the brightest point of the week, great for fun, entertainment, creativity, travel or brainstorming next steps. The inner child emerges in all of us, which should make for some good April Fool's Day tomfoolery.

▶ Read "Using This Planner" for the meaning of Moon Void and symbols ★, **MR**, **VR**, **P**.

[Monday Mercury semisquare Jupiter; Wednesday Sun trine North Node, Saturn quintile Pluto, Venus sesquiquadrate Pluto; Thursday Mercury sextile Venus, Sun square Pluto; Friday Moon forms T-Square with Sun and Pluto]

MARCH							APRIL						
SU	M	TU	W	T	F	S	SU	M	TU	W	T	F	S
				1	2	3	1	2	3	4	5	6	7
4	5	6	7	8	9	10	8	9	10	11	12	13	14
11	12	13	14	15	16	17	15	16	17	18	19	20	21
18	19	20	21	22	23	24	22	23	24	25	26	27	28
25	26	27	28	29	30	31	29	30					

Moon in Leo

02 MO 2 MR

The TO DO list is too long! Your time may have to be divided, first fulfilling obligations to someone close to you before doing your own thing.

Moon in Leo • Void 6:48 am (P), 9:48 am (E)
Moon enters Virgo 6:54 am (P), 9:54 am (E)

03 TU 1 ★ MR

Early on, be careful not to offend someone's pride. The rest of the day is consumed with combatting chaos as you give or get help or healing.

Moon in Virgo • Void 10:38 pm (P)

04 WE 2 ★

Energy is highest this morning. We're productive throughout the day. Later, we fade more from mental than physical exhaustion.

Moon in Virgo, Void (P) • Void 1:38 am (E)
Moon enters Libra 8:33 am (P), 11:33 am (E)

05 TH 2

First, see what you can simplify. Later, the focus is on social interactions, which could take you away from what you prefer to pursue.

Moon in Libra • Full Moon (Seed Moon)

06 FR 1 P ★

Diplomacy and empathy might keep you from being hurt or hurting others on this tense day where balancing priorities takes a juggler's skills.

Good Friday

Moon in Libra • Void 3:16 am (P), 6:16 am (E)
Moon enters Scorpio 8:19 am (P), 11:19 am (E)

07 SA 3 ★

Start the day with a favor to someone deserving. Continue by making a difference in an area of need. It's not the time to go after what you want.

Passover Begins

Moon in Scorpio • Void 11:57 pm (P)

08 SU 1

Those pushing a personal agenda won't get any traction. There's a lot of resistance to change or anything untraditional. Stick to the same old.

Easter

APRIL 02-08 HIGHLIGHTS

For the next two months, Venus strays off the planets' ordinary path (see "out of bounds" in the Star Pages). Matters under Venus's purview (primarily relationships and finances) may go far afield in extraordinary ways so hold onto your heart and wallet. With Venus in Gemini for a full third of 2012 (see April 3 Star Pages), thoughts and discussions put an inordinate amount of attention on Venusian matters. Variety entices us and we seek stimulus from a wide circle of people and ideas. Venus begins its visit to Gemini with a jarring link to Neptune, prompting confusion about what's most important. Anxiety rises to a critical point by the Full Moon Friday [12:20 pm (P), 3:20 pm (E)], when the Sun, Moon and Mars are entangled with the Venus-Neptune snag. This presents an even bigger challenge for lovers or business partners than the usual early spring Full Moon in Libra opposite the Aries Sun does. We're supposed to meet significant others halfway, at the same time as we're spurred to promote or protect personal interests. If the sacrificing that Neptune signals doesn't seem fair according to Venus's reckoning, an ego could be offended and react with displeasure. Venus also forms a lovely triangle assisting us to give and receive respect, or walk away from liaisons where that ingredient is missing. Those tempted to act on secret attractions might be dismayed to find karmic consequences develop quickly.

This week and next, Venus briefly links to an irritating pattern already in place (see March 19-20 in the Star Pages about Mars) that signals difficulty in choosing a direction or finding hope in the midst of hurt and anger. In conflicting allegiances, there may be no totally good alternatives or win-win options. Selecting the route that offends the fewest may be the best solution.

[Monday Ceres opposite Saturn; Tuesday Venus enters Gemini; Wednesday Mercury turns Direct; Thursday Venus square Neptune; Friday Sun semisquare Neptune, Venus biquintile Saturn; Saturday Nodes square Chiron, Venus biquintile Pluto, Venus square Mars; Sunday Sun sesquiquadrate Mars]

 Read "Using This Planner" for the meaning of Moon Void and symbols ★, **MR**, **VR**, **P**.

MAY

SU	M	TU	W	T	F	S
	1	2	3	4	5	
6	7	8	9	10	11	12
13	14	15	16	17	18	19
20	21	22	23	24	25	26
27	28	29	30	31		

April 4, Mercury ends its first Retrograde of 2012. One down, two to go. The craziness isn't over, though. Mercury still has to pass Uranus one more time on April 22.

April

Despite an upbeat mood and friendly faces, energies scatter and the day is marred by floundering. Even the well intended veer off on a tangent.

Easter Monday

Moon in Scorpio, Void (P) • Void 2:57 am (E)
Moon enters Sagittarius 8:13 am (P), 11:13 am (E)

★ **2 MO 09**

Something that's been hidden is exposed. Maintain a sense of humor and a confident stance, but don't brag. That's asking for trouble.

Moon in Sagittarius

★ **2 TU 10**

You can't count on much today except confusion resulting in irritation. You can try to keep things straight; they'll still end up cock-eyed.

Moon in Sagittarius • Void 4:07 am (P), 7:07 am (E)
Moon enters Capricorn 10:03 am (P), 1:03 pm (E)

2 WE 11

There's only a slim silver lining in today's clouds and it comes from keeping your feet on the ground. Danger lurks unseen around corners.

Moon in Capricorn

1 TH 12

Be patient and keep your cool when someone or something infuriates you. Find a way to talk things through, listening with your heart.

Moon in Capricorn • Third Quarter Moon • Void 10:06 am (P), 1:06 pm (E)
Moon enters Aquarius 2:49 pm (P), 5:49 pm (E)

★ **2 FR 13**

After a heavy week, a jovial and cooperative mood lightens spirits through the day. But tonight's spoiled by stubborn or opinionated people.

Moon in Aquarius

3 SA 14

An unexpected turn of events this morning throws you off kilter but you're able to regain control, turning the day around to your advantage.

Orthodox Easter

Moon in Aquarius • Void 3:43 pm (P), 6:43 pm (E)
Moon enters Pisces 10:39 pm (P)

3 SU 15

APRIL 09-15 HIGHLIGHTS

When planets change direction, they hang out at their turning point (called a station) for days or even weeks (slower planets linger longer). Whatever they represent seems to either come to a halt or go to an extreme, demanding attention. Last week, normally quick Mercury was nearly motionless and now advances through the final degrees of sleepy Pisces; minds will still be fuzzy. This week, two planets are on station. The planet signifying everything outworn that should be shed (Pluto) stops in its tracks and turns tail Tuesday, right ahead of the planet of freshness and everything new (Mars) resuming forward motion Friday after going backwards most of the year thus far. Get the idea that something has to change? It's time to let go of whatever you've been hanging onto for far too long, whether physical items, opinions or emotions. Replacements will show up soon enough. The intense Third Quarter Moon Friday promotes this process. It urges us to round the bend from last week's Full Moon crest toward closure and preparation for a new cycle at next week's New Moon. The Moon and Sun both clash with Saturn (and others – see Star Pages), forcing us to see any limits we've exceeded or consider how to achieve better

balance or more fairness. With the Sun in Aries, many people are operating on a "me first" basis, which doesn't sit well with Saturn in Libra, the sign of putting your feet in the other guy's shoes.

Next Sunday (April 22) is Earth Day and to get us ready, this Monday Ceres, the little planet closest to Mother Nature's heart, enters the most luscious sign in the earth element, Taurus, remaining there until the first days of summer. This adds an extra dose of sensuality to our spring, especially for the four-week lunar cycle beginning at the next New Moon April 21, which occurs only three degrees away from Ceres.

[Monday Venus sextile Uranus, Ceres enters Taurus; Tuesday Pluto turns Retrograde, Venus semisquare Sun; Wednesday Sun conjunct Eris, Venus semisquare Eris, Sun sesquiquadrate North Node; Wednesday (P)/Thursday (E) Venus opposite North Node; Thursday Sun semisquare Chiron, Venus square Chiron; Friday Mars turns Direct; Sunday Sun opposite Saturn, Ceres sextile Neptune]

Fear nothing, for every renewed effort raises all former failures into lessons, all sins into experiences.

Katherine Tingley

Moon in Pisces (P), Void in Aquarius (E)
Moon enters Pisces 1:39 am (E)

16 MO 2 ★

Some people are eager to help, especially on improvement projects. Others coldly refuse requests for aid or offer only a modicum of support.

Moon in Pisces • Void 7:35 am (P), 10:35 am (E)

17 TU 3

Caring and sharing abound in certain corners yet self-concern or frugality blocks generosity elsewhere. Let worries roll off your back.

Moon Void in Pisces • Moon enters Aries 9:00 am (P), 12:00 pm (E)

18 WE 3

After a quiet morning, words fly fast and furious from afternoon through evening. Don't jump to conclusions until you hear the whole story.

Moon in Aries

19 TH 3 ★

There's too much on your mind! Slow down, stick to basics, then cover all your bases. Talk to someone you trust. Two heads are better than one.

Holocaust Remembrance Day, Sun enters Taurus

Moon in Aries • Void 12:36 pm (P), 3:36 pm (E)
Moon enters Taurus 9:06 pm (P)

20 FR 1

It's hard to shake a feeling you're off track or going in the wrong direction. You're left to your own devices. Only you can right your ship.

Moon in Taurus (P), Void in Aries (E)
Moon enters Taurus 12:06 am (E) • New Moon

21 SA 5 ★

Renewed confidence, based on a strong footing, sparks new activities. Some have lucrative potential. Solutions appear as if by magic.

Moon in Taurus • Void 10:11 am (P), 1:11 pm (E)

22 SU 3

Happily, the morning's good mood helps you laugh at the mishaps, mix-ups and interruptions that threaten to spoil the afternoon and evening.

Earth Day

APRIL 16-22 HIGHLIGHTS

The meteorological forecast is usually quite nice this time of year. This week's astrological "weather" is pretty good, too. Friday is the only ugly day. Both Mercury and Mars are cruising ahead again, and once Mercury returns to Aries Monday, they are in the signs ruled by each other (see Mutual Receptions in the Star Pages). This bodes well for progress in physical endeavors, health issues and all communication matters. Since the spring equinox, Mars has been in a challenging pattern (see the Star Pages). Difficulties ease now that it's in forward motion. With Mars across from two health indicators (Neptune and Chiron), this is an appropriate period for a procedure. (Mars rules injections, cutting and suturing. For major operations, check your chart or better yet, consult an astrologer before scheduling.) Mercury's third hook-up with Uranus Sunday (see Star Pages for March 5) offers opportunities to implement smart ideas conceived and researched or refined over the past six weeks.

The Sun enters Taurus Thursday, joined by the Moon at the New Moon Saturday [12:20 am (P), 3:20 am (E)]. Taurus is the natural time to attend to possessions, finances and whatever you value most. The Sun

and Moon soon pass Ceres, the planet related to harvests, a favorable harbinger for abundance. Meanwhile Ceres is in a fabulous Grand Trine pattern in earth signs with Mars and Pluto, lasting the next four weeks. This is a fortuitous period for material concerns, especially since this coincides with the four-week lunar cycle starting Saturday. No exact difficult connections are in place at this New Moon, a real rarity! Although the Full Moon in two weeks is rather tough, this cycle is still a good time to "make hay while the Sun shines" and increase your net worth as well as your overall enjoyment of life.

[Monday Venus sesquiquadrate Saturn, Mercury enters Aries; Thursday Mars trine Ceres, Mercury semisquare Jupiter, Sun enters Taurus; Friday North Node sesquiquadrate Eris; Sunday Sun sextile Neptune, Mercury conjunct Uranus]

 Read "Using This Planner" for the meaning of Moon Void and symbols ★, **MR**, **VR**, **P**.

JUNE

SU	M	TU	W	T	F	S
					1	2
3	4	5	6	7	8	9
10	11	12	13	14	15	16
17	18	19	20	21	22	23
24	25	26	27	28	29	30

The April 21 New Moon is the calmest of the year. In patient, persistent Taurus, it prods us to be centered and stick to our best habits, putting us on a path toward plenty.

April

Set your sights on a lofty goal – the sky's the limit (well, at least in your mind). Why not envision the best? Then take action on your dream.

Moon Void in Taurus
Moon enters Gemini 10:06 am (P), 1:06 pm (E)

3 MO 23

All synapses are firing as soon as you awake. It's a good day to solve a problem, especially in tandem. Tonight, be with someone special.

Moon in Gemini

2 TU 24

The competitive urge is strong. Rivalries go beyond a friendly contest. People bring their best effort and want the status of winning.

Administrative Professionals Day

Moon in Gemini • Void 1:32 pm (P), 4:32 pm (E)
Moon enters Cancer 10:43 pm (P)

2 WE 25

Despite a minor twist and turn, we feel comfortable that our labors are bearing good fruit, that our work matters and is making a difference.

Moon in Cancer (P), Void in Gemini (E)
Moon enters Cancer 1:43 am (E)

3 TH 26

It's a struggle to maintain optimism amid doubts and abrasion; no one seems to be pleased. Tonight someone's sense of superiority is a problem.

Moon in Cancer

2 FR 27

A kind, tender touch delivered with joy brightens the day (whether you give or receive the lift), especially if anyone feels unappreciated.

Moon in Cancer • Void 12:07 am (P), 3:07 am (E)
Moon enters Leo 9:12 am (P), 12:12 pm (E)

4 SA 28

Express gratitude and give credit where it's due. Everyone likes praise and being valued. Even a small gesture turns things for the better.

Moon in Leo • First Quarter Moon

4 SU 29

APRIL 23-29 HIGHLIGHTS

It's evident from the short list of planetary connections in the brackets below, a fairly calm week is on deck. Right from the start, we seem to have a good idea of where we're going and the will to stay on course. A comment arises late Monday that gives us pause for thought but by the next morning, we move past this adroitly. Relationships are the main topic Tuesday, whether with a significant other, a neighbor, a sibling or another family member. Something needs ironing out.

Wednesday begins with ruffled feathers. Words blurted hastily sting, even if they're true. What one person brushes off, another thinks should be taken seriously. Diplomacy comes to the rescue and by afternoon, a truce is negotiated. Thursday, emotional and financial security are the main items on the agenda: how to have what we want without sacrificing too much freedom to get it. "Where there's a will, there's a way" but you may have to think outside the box. The usual end-of-the-week cheer is lacking and people feel put upon and seem grumpy most of Friday, aside from a break in the afternoon. But the weekend should make up for that.

With the Moon in cheery Leo, fun is on the docket Saturday and Sunday. The only question might be how much to spend on a good time or how to find budget-friendly pleasures. Creativity is abundant and free! Either day is good for a party or get-together, however Saturday night there's competition about whose light shines brightest. Overall the mood is convivial. The First Quarter Moon early Sunday morning features the Moon and Sun in two signs from the "fixed" category (see Keywords on p. 98), signaling a stubborn face-off between playful and practical factions. This could as easily be a bone of contention in a person's internal dialogue as between two people.

[Monday Mercury trine North Node, Sun trine Mars; Wednesday Mercury square Pluto; Thursday Sun conjunct Ceres; Saturday Sun sextile Chiron; Sunday Sun trine Pluto]

The earth has enough for every man's need, but not for every man's greed.
Mahatma Gandhi

APRIL								MAY						
SU	M	TU	W	T	F	S		SU	M	TU	W	T	F	S
	1	2	3	4	5	6	7				1	2	3	4	5
8	9	10	11	12	13	14		6	7	8	9	10	11	12
15	16	17	18	19	20	21		13	14	15	16	17	18	19
22	23	24	25	26	27	28		20	21	22	23	24	25	26
29	30							27	28	29	30	31		

Moon in Leo • Void 7:18 am (P), 10:18 am (E)
Moon enters Virgo 4:03 pm (P), 7:03 pm (E)

30 MO 2

For the most part, people are fair, possibly even generous, but those who think they're superior have to learn some humility and perspective.

Moon in Virgo

01 TU 3

This should be a productive, profitable day unless you drift off course or get roped into helping someone. Even then, some good could result.

May Day, Beltane

Moon in Virgo • Void 3:59 am (P), 6:59 am (E)
Moon enters Libra 7:05 pm (P), 10:05 pm (E)

02 WE 2

Don't get discouraged by this nose-to-the-grindstone day of near drudgery with a draining load of details. But you wish things were simple.

Moon in Libra

03 TH 2

Start the day with a smile from a friend to make disruptions and irritations tolerable. Be grateful for the patience and tact you possess.

National Day of Prayer

Moon in Libra • Void 11:03 am (P), 2:03 pm (E)
Moon enters Scorpio 7:21 pm (P), 10:21 pm (E)

04 FR 3

Early today feisty people have their say, though in a palatable way. By explaining the rules, problems are averted and peace is maintained.

Moon in Scorpio • Full Moon (Hare Moon)

05 SA 2 P

Realizing negativity blocks progress, a shift in thinking precipitates a change in direction toward receptivity and optimism.

Cinco de Mayo

Moon in Scorpio • Void 5:15 am (P), 8:15 am (E)
Moon enters Sagittarius 6:40 pm (P), 9:40 pm (E)

06 SU 2

Throw off the shackles of excesses that have become burdensome, whether they're emotional or material. A light, free feeling follows.

April 30–MAY 06 HIGHLIGHTS

Sometimes Mercury really earns its nickname, quicksilver. (Only the Moon moves through the zodiac faster.) Because of its speed, it links to other planets frequently. It seems to be batted about a lot this week, making our heads spin, as intensity builds leading up to the Full Moon. Only one of its connections is a gentle one (Thursday night, to Venus) and even this has a drawback (Venus is misbehaving – see Highlights for April 2). We're refining how to express disagreement without being harsh and critical or selfish. If we can honor ethics and throw a little humor into the mix, we'll probably be able to avoid stepping in you-know-what or at least reverse the damages if we do. Friday (especially in the morning) is the most precarious time for communication, when we really need to mind our Ps and Qs.

The Sun and Moon as a pair are not strongly involved with the other planets at the Full Moon Saturday night (8:36 pm (P), 11:36 pm (E)). Just the Moon, though, is in a positive pattern promoting action to achieve more prosperity and/or a happier social or love life. Still, partners may not be of one mind and have trouble achieving a balance of power. Arguments are possible and miscommunication can have hurtful consequences, even if unintended. Respect and rules are likely bones of contention. Another area of disagreement might be which person does more for the other, especially if someone feels used. There's plenty of civility at hand; voices might not be raised and talk may be couched in sweet terms, but topics are serious nonetheless.

Another pattern favorable for material concerns (like finances and assets), in place since the New Moon two weeks ago (see Highlights), is kicked up a notch this week and next. Think outside the box for new sources of income or better uses of what you already have.

[Monday Venus semisextile Jupiter; Monday (P)/Tuesday (E) North Node trine Uranus; Tuesday Mercury semisquare Neptune, Ceres sextile Chiron; Wednesday (P)/Thursday (E) Ceres trine Pluto; Thursday Mercury sesquiquadrate Mars, Mercury sesquiquadrate North Node, Mercury sextile Venus; Friday Mercury conjunct Eris; Saturday Mercury semisquare Chiron, Mars square Nodes, Venus sextile Eris, Mercury opposite Saturn, Moon forms Quintile Triangle with Venus and Mars]

JUNE

SU	M	TU	W	T	F	S
					1	2
3	4	5	6	7	8	9
10	11	12	13	14	15	16
17	18	19	20	21	22	23
24	25	26	27	28	29	30

Mercury and Venus are in the signs ruled by one another May 9-24 (see Mutual Receptions in the Star Pages).

April-May

React quickly this morning to jump out of harm's way or to take advantage of a sudden change of events. Later, measure your words carefully.

Moon in Sagittarius

★ **2 MO 07**

A good blend of respect and affection aids frank discussions.
People open up and get things off their chest, facilitating closure on a topic.

National Teacher Day

Moon in Sagittarius • Void 6:35 pm (P), 9:35 pm (E)
Moon enters Capricorn 7:01 pm (P), 10:01 pm (E)

★ **3 TU 08**

We're busy. There's a lot to do! A distraction early pulls us off course.
By midday, we resume a productive pace, but some remain aggravated.

Moon in Capricorn

★ **3 WE 09**

An overarching mellow mood helps you forgive when annoyances and boundary violations crop up. You point out problems, but with kindness.

Moon in Capricorn • Void 12:12 pm (P), 3:12 pm (E)
Moon enters Aquarius 10:04 pm (P)

2 TH 10

People are friendly as the day gets going, even if they disagree. Later, they tend to withdraw and keep to themselves, maybe to avoid trouble.

Moon in Aquarius (P), Void in Capricorn (E)
Moon enters Aquarius 1:04 am (E)

★ **2 FR 11**

We want certainty and security though we know these are impossible in a rapidly shifting scenario. This evening, friends or loved ones perk us up.

Moon in Aquarius • Third Quarter Moon
Void 5:53 pm (P), 8:53 pm (E)

★ **3 SA 12**

A positive outlook and the belief you can head in a better direction boost confidence. Tonight, taking a flip comment seriously breeds doubt.

Mother's Day

Moon Void in Aquarius
Moon enters Pisces 4:43 am (P), 7:43 am (E)

★ **P 3 SU 13**

MAY 07-13 HIGHLIGHTS

Instability and volatility are problems this week. There's a shake-up between conservative and progressive factions, not only in politics. A jarring link exact late Monday is felt strongly Wednesday morning as the Moon magnifies it. New approaches meet with resistance from people more comfortable with what they've always done. This same theme at Saturday's Third Quarter Moon pits forward-thinking Aquarius against tried-and-true Taurus. Uranus throws some unpredictability or insurrection into the mix. Wednesday night and Thursday, critics are quick to point out everything that could go wrong instead of finding useful ways to incorporate fresh suggestions. Meanwhile, a combination of links exact this Friday and next week is spotlighted by the Moon Thursday. Being a stickler or acting self-righteous creates problems. Flexibility and warmth are required.

Saturday evening, a fleeting wonderful configuration in the social signs of the air element smoothes relations between people, making it a suitable time for business entertaining or a pleasurable gathering. The window is small, though [4-6 pm (P), 7-9 pm (E)], with a need to stroke egos beforehand and a potential breach of manners afterward.

Proceed carefully to make the most of the good moment in the middle. Sunday night, the Moon briefly joins a quick, friendly pattern formed by connections exact this week and next. The signs in the formation are primarily in the earth element, putting our focus mostly on material concerns. Yet there is a spiritual or healing piece, too. It's easy to be grounded for meditation and use visualization for abundance and/or health. This is one of the early peaks in a four-year period of improvements achieved by embracing trust to let go of old ways. Faith trumps skepticism.

[Monday Jupiter semisquare Uranus; Tuesday (P)/Wednesday (E) Mercury enters Taurus; Wednesday Mars sesquiquadrate Eris; Thursday Mercury sextile Neptune; Friday Saturn sesquiquadrate Chiron; Saturday Sun semisquare Uranus, Chiron sextile Pluto; Sunday Sun conjunct Jupiter, Mercury trine Mars, Mercury semisquare Venus; Sunday (P)/Monday (E) Mercury forms Kite with Mars, Chiron and Pluto]

Believe nothing, no matter where you read it, or who said it, no matter if I have said it, unless it agrees with your own reason and your own common sense. — Buddah

---

Moon in Pisces

14 MO 3

Faith gives you hope while your practical wisdom ensures you're smartly skeptical. As Ronald Reagan said, "Trust, but verify."

Moon in Pisces • Void 5:00 am (P), 8:00 am (E)
Moon enters Aries 2:47 pm (P), 5:47 pm (E)

15 TU 2 ★ VR

Information received isn't necessarily reliable. If something feels wrong, question it. Watch your tone so as not to offend by accusing.

Moon in Aries

16 WE 2 ★ VR

A surprise early starts the day hopping. You could be exhausted before lunchtime. Think twice before you bite off more than you can chew.

Moon in Aries • Void 2:45 pm (P), 5:45 pm (E)

17 TH 2 ★ VR

Personal interests beckon but you may have to forego them to meet others' needs, which could be irritating. Think of it as a karmic investment.

Moon Void in Aries
Moon enters Taurus 3:04 am (P), 6:04 am (E)

18 FR 3 VR

Today is calm and mellow, a welcome break after a couple of crazy days. Relax and recharge. Tonight, socialize with uplifting company.

Moon in Taurus

19 SA 4 VR

If you feel like working, attend to finances or your yard. But it's a great day to just enjoy life, especially nature and simple pleasures.

Armed Forces Day

Moon in Taurus • Void 5:36 am (P), 8:36 am (E)
Moon enters Gemini 4:06 pm (P), 7:06 pm (E) • Solar Eclipse New Moon

20 SU 2 ★ VR

Stubbornness begs to be goaded, even if it's just to play the Devil's Advocate. A mischievous side prompts teasing but that might backfire.

Sun enters Gemini

MAY 14-20 HIGHLIGHTS

About every year-and-a-half, we go through a period of forty days or so re-assessing values, inspecting finances and examining relationships as Venus backtracks. The planet of attraction, income, possessions and love turns Retrograde Tuesday morning. It's not recommended to marry, form a legal partnership or make major purchases while Venus is Retrograde. In fact, all monetary transactions should be conducted with extra caution. Since Retrogrades point a planet's energies inward, one of the key lessons now is to appreciate oneself. This Retrograde takes place in Gemini, indicating how important it is to speak from the heart or exhibit caring in communications. Doing so could have its challenges, though, because this spring Venus rubs the wrong way against antagonistic Mars (see Star Pages for April 7).

The Sun has barely entered Gemini on Sunday when the Moon cruises between it and the earth for a Solar Eclipse New Moon [4:48 pm (P), 7:48 pm (E)]. Gemini is the primary sign of learning, interest in community issues, travel around the local area and dealings with siblings, any of which may be important for you in the coming four weeks. Creative endeavors, particularly verbal talents, are strongly highlighted. This is a good period to compose lyrics or poetry, journal, or write a letter the old-fashioned way – almost a lost art! A lovely interaction between Mercury and Venus also makes this a perfect time to serenade your sweetheart.

Beware going overboard in activities or projects this week. Jupiter (which loves to expand everything it touches) makes trying links to two planets more concerned with keeping matters under control. Some hard decisions must be made. Wednesday is a prime candidate for dealing with excesses. Since the influences are in place at the Eclipse, there can be a continuation of the effects over the coming month or longer.

[Monday Mercury trine Pluto, Venus semisextile Sun, Mercury sextile Chiron, Sun sesquiquadrate Pluto; Tuesday Venus turns Retrograde, Mars semisquare Saturn; Wednesday Mars trine Pluto, Jupiter quincunx Saturn; Wednesday (P)/Thursday (E) Mars opposite Chiron; Thursday Mercury conjunct Ceres, Jupiter sesquiquadrate Pluto; Sunday Sun enters Gemini, Mercury semisquare Uranus, Solar Eclipse New Moon]

JUNE

SU	M	TU	W	T	F	S
					1	2
3	4	5	6	7	8	9
10	11	12	13	14	15	16
17	18	19	20	21	22	23
24	25	26	27	28	29	30

Usually a Mercury-Sun hook-up in Gemini is great for communication. But their union May 27 is in a jolting link to Eris. Bold or brash statements could provoke an argument or spark a rivalry.

Fertile minds generate brilliant ideas early. Later, misconstrued comments lead to hurt feelings but open a dialogue for improvements.

Victoria Day (Canada)

Moon in Gemini

VR 2 MO 21

You can say anything if it comes from a place of love or respect. Business meetings are fruitful. Review financials and revise, if necessary.

Moon in Gemini • Void 3:52 pm (P), 6:52 pm (E)

VR 4 TU 22

The serenity that starts the day disintegrates this afternoon due to doubt or distrust. People are on edge tonight, restless or rebellious.

Moon Void in Gemini • Moon enters Cancer 4:32 am (P), 7:32 am (E)

VR 2 WE 23

Take stock of your feelings. Seek the source of any pain or anxiety. Figure out what to say, then speak up to be better supported and more secure.

Moon in Cancer

VR ★ 2 TH 24

Relying only on your mind could lead you astray. Give credence to instincts as well as common sense and higher principles. Tonight, have fun!

Moon in Cancer • Void 7:35 am (P), 10:35 am (E)
Moon enters Leo 3:12 pm (P), 6:12 pm (E)

VR 2 FR 25

It's a good day for creative pursuits and self-discovery. Learn something new, perhaps in the arena of technology, history or metaphysics.

Moon in Leo

VR ★ 3 SA 26

Everyone wants attention. There's competition unless we take turns sharing the spotlight and appreciating each person's uniqueness.

Shavou'ot, Pentecost

Moon in Leo • Void 4:55 pm (P), 7:55 pm (E)
Moon enters Virgo 11:07 pm (P)

VR 3 SU 27

MAY 21-27 HIGHLIGHTS

Gemini is the chattiest sign. You'll find people with this sign strong in their charts who prattle on and on just to fill silence. During the Gemini Sun-sign time of year, everyone is more talkative. Gemini is about various forms of communication, whether paperwork, phone calls, news, books, articles or email. It's also the sign of curiosity, studying and teaching. These are all spotlighted currently. Gemini's ruling planet, Mercury ("messenger of the gods"), enters this sector of the zodiac Thursday morning. All week, it's very active, mostly in difficult ways. The quantity and quality of data is a key theme. Monday and Tuesday, watch out for "too much information," either secrets revealed or an overload of facts. Confusion or trust violations spur some sparring in the afternoon Wednesday. Mercury lies low then but the Sun in Mercury's sign confronts nebulous Neptune. Emotions impact communications adversely Wednesday night and midday Thursday. Friday, mixed signals, inconsistencies and maybe even intentional deception mar interactions. Saturday, there's a notion we need to put behind us and move on. If we don't, it's likely to trap us in some way. Sunday may be the craziest day of all. Some people will be stuck in their own minds, not hearing or seeing what's plain to others. Disruptions or surprises are very possible, though serendipity or a good ending might emerge.

Consequences from occurrences around the Solar Eclipse catch up with us this week, especially Thursday evening and Friday. Things said last week have a ripple effect now and it's hard to just let them go. Over the weekend, people from our past may be in touch with us again. There's a strong dose of challenging Neptunian energy Wednesday and Thursday evenings and all day Friday, also harking back to the Eclipse. Extra effort is required to communicate in an open and clear way.

[Monday Mercury semisextile Venus, Mercury sesquiquadrate Pluto; Monday (P)/ Tuesday (E) Mercury conjunct Jupiter; Wednesday Sun square Neptune; Thursday Venus sextile Eris, Mercury enters Gemini; Friday Mercury square Neptune, Sun conjunct South Node; Saturday Mercury conjunct South Node; Sunday Mercury conjunct Sun, Mercury semisquare Eris, Mercury sextile Uranus]

What would people think about if they were not taught what to think about?

Arthur Morgan

Moon in Virgo (P), Void in Leo (E)
Moon enters Virgo 2:07 am (E) • First Quarter Moon

28 MO 1 P VR

Stay alert. Chaos, surprises and mixed signals come at us from all directions, trying our patience. Humility and common sense will help.

Memorial Day

Moon in Virgo • Void 10:51 pm (P)

29 TU 3 VR

Some people aim to accomplish goals by throwing their weight around. The power of persuasion works better, especially based on compromise.

Moon in Virgo, Void (P) • Void 1:51 am (E)
Moon enters Libra 3:47 am (P), 6:47 am (E)

30 WE 2 VR

Even an off-hand comment can easily be misinterpreted as criticism. Respond to brusqueness with good manners and don't take it personally!

Moon in Libra • Void 6:32 pm (P), 9:32 pm (E)

31 TH 3 VR

Discussions today are amicable though not completely clear. Go ahead and ask questions. Tonight, being antagonistic tests social niceties.

Moon Void in Libra • Moon enters Scorpio 5:32 am (P), 8:32 am (E)

01 FR 3 VR

Resentment resulting from run-ins earlier in the week may seep through a veneer of acceptance. Dig deep to discover what needs to be released.

Moon in Scorpio

02 SA 2 VR

Energy, drive and persistence push you toward the goal line. Put a lid on obsessions and don't let anxiety unravel your achievement.

Diamond Jubilee of Queen Elizabeth II

Moon in Scorpio • Void 2:31 am (P), 5:31 am (E)
Moon enters Sagittarius 5:33 am (P), 8:33 am (E)

03 SU 2 VR

Be vigilant in considering words before you speak. Once the cat is out of the bag, you can't get it back in and diplomacy can repair only so much.

Orthodox Pentecost

MAY 28–JUNE 03 HIGHLIGHTS

It's a blessing Monday is a holiday, at least in the U.S. Conducting normal business is a challenge in the midst of a hodgepodge of planetary knots. Restaurants and travel or entertainment venues have no choice but to soldier through the day. A First Quarter Moon, generally innocuous, is infused with a jarring influence from Eris, the rabble-rouser, which incites disruption. (Saturn's stand-off with Eris – see May 26 Star Pages – could keep a lid on it to a degree.) With the Moon in Virgo, people are picky and quick to find fault. In early morning, the Moon is caught in a pattern where people don't know which way they're headed, spawning discomfort and distrust (see July 10 Star Pages). All afternoon and evening, the Moon adds to the ugly jumble of Sun and Mercury ties. Mercury in Gemini usually makes us mouthy. Its contact with suppressive Saturn might tone that down or it could add harsh judgment and haughty superiority to complaints instead. Throw in a bump from Chiron and hurt feelings result, though Chiron's high side may offer sympathy to balance an attack. A positive Sun-Uranus link helps some sidestep trouble by spotting agitators and keeping a distance. A lone nice Moon liaison (to Pluto) prompts us to process emotions and not hold on to resentment.

Tuesday and Wednesday, the Sun mimics Monday's difficult Mercury relations but without additional interference. Still, communication and cooperation are tough. A Mercury-Mars jolt Wednesday adds impatience and irritation that the harmonious Libra Moon tries to counter. The mood shifts toward sweet talk and teamwork with Mercury and Venus crossing paths Friday, highlighted by the Moon Thursday. Mercury ends the week with friendly bows to Eris and Saturn Sunday, but they're in their own battle (see above). All in all, you'll need Gemini's flexibility to dance to this week's disjointed tune.

[Monday Mercury sesquiquadrate Saturn, Sun semisquare Eris, Sun sextile Uranus, Mercury square Chiron; Tuesday Sun sesquiquadrate Saturn; Wednesday Sun square Chiron, Mercury square Mars; Friday Mercury conjunct Venus; Sunday Mercury sextile Eris, Mercury trine Saturn]

JULY

SU	M	TU	W	T	F	S
1	2	3	4	5	6	7
8	9	10	11	12	13	14
15	16	17	18	19	20	21
22	23	24	25	26	27	28
29	30	31				

An extraordinary event occurs June 5 that has astronomers and astrologers very excited: a "Venusian eclipse." It won't recur in our lifetime.

May-June

Search dreams or signs to get a sense of your place in the grand scheme. Then assess what's most important to you and how to further your aims.

Moon in Sagittarius • Lunar Eclipse Full Moon (Dyad Moon)
Void 10:09 pm (P)

VR ★ P 1 MO 04

Weave creativity into your productivity today. Leave room for the unexpected tonight. Be patient with those who are antsy or self-involved.

World Environment Day

Moon in Sagittarius, Void (P) • Void 1:09 am (E)
Moon enters Capricorn 5:32 am (P), 8:32 am (E)

VR ★ 2 TU 05

We push full steam ahead at first but soon get thrown off course. Later, order erodes as commotion envelopes us. Persistence may save the day.

Moon in Capricorn

VR 2 WE 06

It's too confining to stick to one particular goal when there's so much around to enjoy. People go off on their own, possibly shirking duties.

Moon in Capricorn • Void 5:39 am (P), 8:39 am (E)
Moon enters Aquarius 7:18 am (P), 10:18 am (E)

VR ★ 1 TH 07

We'd rather share ideas than buckle down to work. However, socializing stimulates creative juices, which are better used non-verbally.

Moon in Aquarius

VR 3 FR 08

A clash ensues this morning when opinions are foisted on those with different values. Later, flexibility prevails, fostering flip-flops.

Moon in Aquarius • Void 11:34 am (P), 2:34 pm (E)
Moon enters Pisces 12:23 pm (P), 3:23 pm (E)

VR 2 SA 09

You're better off to yield or dodge when determined people push, to be sure you don't get hurt. Selfish types want their way and are oblivious.

Moon in Pisces

VR 3 SU 10

JUNE 04-10 HIGHLIGHTS

What a way to begin a week! We hit the ground running, thanks to a Lunar Eclipse Full Moon early Monday [4:13 am (P), 7:13 am (E)]. It's time to raise the bar regarding where to head next. The primary directional indicator (the Moon's Nodes) nears a major turning point: a T-square with Neptune, exact July 10. Neptune is strongly sensitized now, turning Retrograde just hours after the eclipse. The configuration is close enough to exact to offer a glimpse of the next milestones. We have many chances to tune in to its messages over the coming month; the Moon highlights this interaction at least once a week, such as this Saturday night. For some, Neptune's influence dissipates resolve or sparks anxiety about the future. For others, the Retrograde represents a return to once-held hopes that faded and can now be revived. Other good times to seek messages from your High Self or guides are Tuesday morning and Friday and Saturday nights, when a nice link to Neptune from Mercury is activated.

Venus has its own sort of eclipse Tuesday – one that's much rarer and potentially more important – when it marches across the face of the Sun. This magnifies everything related to both the Sun and Venus, particularly where their influences converge: in the arts and creativity. Also in the spotlight are the popularity of leaders, hero worship, love of fathers and executive power over finances. Negative expressions are self-aggrandizement and craving attention. Difficulties come from the Sun and Venus in a harsh connection to Mars, adding elements of selfishness and antagonism which disturb the cooperation and tranquility one normally expects from a Venusian highpoint.

Look for important developments following Mercury's entry into Cancer Thursday. Mercury is associated with news and the doorway to any season-changing sign is a power point of the zodiac. Hot topics are water, families, food and the housing market.

[Monday Lunar Eclipse Full Moon, Neptune turns Retrograde, Venus square Mars; Tuesday Ceres semisquare Uranus, Venus conjunct Sun; Thursday Mercury enters Cancer, Ceres sesquiquadrate Pluto, Sun square Mars; Friday Mercury trine Neptune]

What is learned in the cradle lasts to the grave.
French saying

Moon in Pisces • Third Quarter Moon • Void 3:42 am (P), 6:42 am (E)
Moon enters Aries 9:22 pm (P)

11 MO 1 P ★ VR

What a commotion! Those who are easily upset are very vocal. Even people who normally let things slide are provoked enough to comment.

Moon in Aries (P), Void in Pisces (E)
Moon enters Aries 12:22 am (E)

12 TU 2 ★ VR

We try to recover from yesterday's melee but soothing words or apologies may not be enough. Wounds may be re-opened. Speak from the heart.

Moon in Aries • Void 8:10 pm (P), 11:10 pm (E)

13 WE 2 P VR

It takes effort to achieve cooperation amidst baiting and brawling between strong individuals. Be flexible and set fair ground rules.

Moon Void in Aries
Moon enters Taurus 9:23 am (P), 12:23 pm (E)

14 TH 3 VR

A whirlwind of activity early is draining. We're drawn off course to tend to others. Then, things slow down but we might perk up again tonight.

Flag Day

Moon in Taurus

15 FR 3 VR

Practicality prevails. Tackle accounting tasks, assess finances, plan for future needs, untangle snarls or finish up pending business.

Moon in Taurus • Void 5:10 am (P), 8:10 am (E)
Moon enters Gemini 10:25 pm (P)

16 SA 3 VR

This is not a good day for shopping or fiscal decisions; you'd make poor choices or overspend. Instead, enjoy good food and good company.

Moon in Gemini (P), Void in Taurus (E)
Moon enters Gemini 1:25 am (E)

17 SU 2 VR

We begin the morning groggy or disoriented, then snap into defense when challenged. Evening is nicer aside from stray discouraging words.

Father's Day

JUNE 11-17 HIGHLIGHTS

Monday, Jupiter (the planet of expansion) enters Gemini (a sign of mental pursuits and verbal exchanges), ushering in a year of increased communication that begins with bruises. Emotional conversations dominate the landscape that day. With the Third Quarter Moon in Pisces, some people will feel disrespected or infringed upon. If things go to extremes, there will be blow-back due to a rebellious edge that won't put up with power plays. A saving grace might come from tolerance or finding some humor in the middle of the hubbub. Dealing with pain is a main theme Tuesday as the "wounded healer" asteroid, Chiron, turns Retrograde. Over the coming four months, we may find that no one outside ourselves can console us the way we can on our own. Conversations pick up that afternoon where they left off the day before, this time with an eye toward ameliorating the situation. Still, those bound to have the last word or hammer their points home hard can reverse any progress. The mood mellows considerably by the end of the evening, replaced Wednesday by rivalry, which is the big issue morning and night. There can only be one kingpin and sharing the spotlight is tough. Midday, people give one another a little leeway

(perhaps grudgingly) but this doesn't last long.

We're very productive Friday, the best day of the week. Some people push themselves to do more than can be done in a day, maybe to make up for earlier in the week when we were distracted from our goals. On Saturday, energy is low with the Moon Void of Course all day and the lunar cycle winding down. Cruise on autopilot or complete projects ahead of next week's New Moon. We reach a crossroads Sunday with pressure to decide which way to turn, not that an answer is easy. It will take soul-searching and perhaps a little arguing (possibly with yourself). In the end, follow your heart.

[Monday Jupiter enters Gemini, Mercury square Uranus, Mercury opposite Pluto; Tuesday Chiron turns Retrograde, Mercury trine Chiron; Tuesday (P)/Wednesday (E) Mercury semisquare Ceres; Wednesday Sun sextile Eris, Sun trine Saturn; Saturday Mercury semisquare Jupiter, Venus square Chiron; Sunday Mercury sesquiquadrate Neptune; Sunday (P) Mercury sesquiquadrate North Node]

JULY

SU	M	TU	W	T	F	S
1	2	3	4	5	6	7
8	9	10	11	12	13	14
15	16	17	18	19	20	21
22	23	24	25	26	27	28
29	30	31				

Although the Summer Solstice is only one day after a New Moon, both the Sun and Moon change from Gemini to Cancer between these events, differentiating the influences.

June

Motivation is low on this uneventful day, a good time to finish projects. Energy picks up this evening. Maybe an argument gets a rise out of you.

Moon in Gemini

VR 2 MO 18

A fresh breeze ushers in excitement about new possibilities. We're inspired to pursue our dreams. Family members are warm and supportive.

Juneteenth

Moon in Gemini • New Moon • Void 8:03 am (P), 11:03 am (E)
Moon enters Cancer 10:35 am (P), 1:35 pm (E)

VR 4 TU 19

Differing points of view collide with a loud clang. Friends try to calm us down but can't keep emotions from erupting. Logic falls on deaf ears.

Summer Solstice, Litha, Sun enters Cancer

Moon in Cancer

VR ★ P 2 WE 20

Yesterday's arguments still sting this morning. By evening, they become a springboard to action that repairs damages or improves matters.

Moon in Cancer • Void 9:49 am (P), 12:49 pm (E)
Moon enters Leo 8:48 pm (P), 11:48 pm (E)

VR 3 TH 21

A great day for a meeting or party: people are congenial and cooperative, ready for fun or creativity. It's easy to brainstorm great ideas.

Moon in Leo

VR 4 FR 22

Unless we're mindful of spiritual principles, dramatic displays of displeasure or rebellion disrupt the evening. Be tolerant and polite.

Moon in Leo • Void 3:27 pm (P), 6:27 pm (E)

VR ★ 2 SA 23

Overactive imagination inflates a minor criticism into perceived mistreatment. Clarify motives instead of assuming bad intentions.

St. Jean-Baptiste Day (Quebec)

Moon Void in Leo • Moon enters Virgo 4:44 am (P), 7:44 am (E)

VR ★ 2 SU 24

JUNE 18-24 HIGHLIGHTS

What a busy week this is in astrology! Probably we'll be very busy, too. There's a New Moon Tuesday [8:03 am (P), 11:03 am (E)] and the Summer Solstice Wednesday. Sunday is the first of three instances of a key stand-off between two slow-moving planets both known for eliciting major changes. (We've already been feeling their effects (see Overview). They're not interconnected with other planets presently so their potency isn't as evident now as at other times.) While these big events loom large on the celestial landscape, a couple other heavy interactions are also in the works and cause some trouble for quick Mercury and Venus. The Sun, Moon and Mars manage to stay out of the fray, as does Ceres. She just chugs along minding her own business, entering Gemini Saturday (a little late to the party already in progress there). The New Moon is in the final degrees of Gemini, the sign where we had a New Moon eclipse last month at the first degree. Two cycles in a row commencing with the same sign doubles the importance of everything the sign represents (see Highlights for the weeks of May 14-20 and 21-27). The coming month will have a milder dose because it's not an eclipse.

Relationships and monetary matters seem like they're going in reverse, courtesy of Retrograde Venus. Its little collision with Chiron last Thursday is still in effect at the New Moon and Solstice. This propels their influence forward through the coming month and season. The challenge is to revise where we're headed in romance and finances. The good news is we're able to think outside the box to find solutions to our problems. A prime time for that is Friday morning to afternoon, when the Moon creates a lovely Kite pattern with Venus, the Nodes and Uranus. Friends or family offer inspiring ideas.

[Monday (E) Mercury sesquiquadrate North Node; Wednesday Mercury square Eris and Saturn (T-square), Sun enters Cancer, Venus sextile Uranus, Mercury semisquare Venus; Thursday Mercury sextile Mars, Mercury sesquiquadrate Chiron; Saturday Venus sesquiquadrate Saturn, Ceres enters Gemini, Sun trine Neptune; Sunday Uranus square Pluto, Venus semisquare Eris]

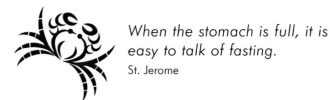

When the stomach is full, it is easy to talk of fasting.

St. Jerome

	JUNE							JULY					
SU	M	TU	W	T	F	S	SU	M	TU	W	T	F	S
					1	2	1	2	3	4	5	6	7
3	4	5	6	7	8	9	8	9	10	11	12	13	14
10	11	12	13	14	15	16	15	16	17	18	19	20	21
17	18	19	20	21	22	23	22	23	24	25	26	27	28
24	25	26	27	28	29	30	29	30	31				

Moon in Virgo

25 MO 2 ★ VR

Emotions are a bit much to handle this morning. Logic can't dispel an uneasy feeling. Don't berate yourself. Tonight, you'll be more certain.

Moon in Virgo • Void 3:54 am (P), 6:54 am (E) • Moon enters Libra 10:16 am (P), 1:16 pm (E) • First Quarter Moon

26 TU 4 VR

This is a great day for projects that call for teamwork. Cooperation is easy to achieve and smart ideas pay off when heads are put together.

Moon in Libra

27 WE 1 ★ VR

Don't get caught in a vicious cycle of one worry fueling another, especially if the concerns aren't your own. Let others solve their problems.

Moon in Libra • Void 1:23 am (P), 4:23 am (E)
Moon enters Scorpio 1:33 pm (P), 4:33 pm (E)

28 TH 3

Disagreements start the day on the wrong foot, with bad feelings in their wake. There's a turn-around by evening, perhaps after an apology.

Moon in Scorpio

29 FR 2 ★

Even though it's well-meaning, a push to do "something for your own good" could spark resentment. Try to take it in the best light and benefit.

Moon in Scorpio • Void 12:47 pm (P), 3:47 pm (E)
Moon enters Sagittarius 3:05 pm (P), 6:05 pm (E)

30 SA 2

People are touchy early this morning and evasive tonight. Midday, confidence is strong and we're very caring, with energy to spare and share.

Moon in Sagittarius

01 SU 1

We want to do our own thing, without encumbrances. Even if it miffs a mate, we need to take off for a little while to gain a sense of self-direction.

Canada Day

JUNE 25-JULY 01 HIGHLIGHTS

Relationships have been going through the wringer during Saturn's nearly three-year visit to Venus-ruled Libra. It's the sign affiliated with romance, business partners, clients, even "open enemies." Since February, Saturn spent its third lengthy backward jaunt in Libra, the final time in its current 30-year orbit. It forced us to look at and perhaps re-define expectations in interactions. Hopefully we learned what's okay or unacceptable by the end of the Retrograde Monday. The past six weeks may have been hardest with Venus also Retrograde, which is over Wednesday. In between, the First Quarter Moon in Libra Tuesday helps us adjust emotionally to changing conditions in our associations. Thursday, Venus and the Sun align cooperatively, reinforcing self-worth and promoting attention to and from significant others. We are indeed turning a corner but we're not done ironing out wrinkles. This weekend, Venus repeats difficult links it made last weekend as it inches forward through the degree it occupied then. We face similar issues about boundaries or selfishness. The added challenge now is from autonomy versus security. People want assurances in relationships but breathing room as well, with the freedom to be who they are and not be told how to act. Luckily, there's help from open mindedness and humor to smooth out the bumps.

There are doubts or fears to get past, as shown by a strong and trying connection (exact Monday and aggravated by the Moon Wednesday evening) between the planets of exaggeration and imagination, Jupiter and Neptune. Jupiter gets an additional push when the South Node passes it Wednesday and Mercury prods both gently Thursday and Friday. This marks a time to stop obsessing about what might have been or could come next. When we focus on the now, we gain a renewed feeling of freedom.

[Monday Jupiter square Neptune, Saturn turns Direct, Mercury enters Leo; Tuesday Mercury sextile Ceres; Wednesday South Node conjunct Jupiter, Venus turns Direct; Thursday Venus semisextile Sun, Mercury trine North Node; Friday Sun opposite Pluto and square Uranus (T-square), Mercury sextile Jupiter; Saturday Venus semisquare Eris, Sun trine Chiron; Sunday Ceres square Neptune, Venus sesquiquadrate Saturn]

AUGUST

SU	M	TU	W	T	F	S
			1	2	3	4
5	6	7	8	9	10	11
12	13	14	15	16	17	18
19	20	21	22	23	24	25
26	27	28	29	30	31	

Beginning July 3, Mercury forms a handful of Fingers of God in its upcoming Retrograde and related shadows (see the Star Pages).

June-July

We're comfortable with well-worn ideas until challenged to see things from a new angle. Then philosophical disagreements could get ugly.

Moon in Sagittarius • Void 3:22 pm (P), 6:22 pm (E)
Moon enters Capricorn 3:52 pm (P), 6:52 pm (E)

2 MO 02

Despite well-laid plans, an unexpected start to the day throws off the schedule. You recoup quickly enough and return to the business at hand.

Moon in Capricorn • Full Moon (Mead Moon)

★ 3 TU 03

People appreciate their space this morning. Later, there are needs that can't be handled individually, requiring a collective approach.

Moon in Capricorn • Void 5:26 am (P), 8:26 am (E)
Moon enters Aquarius 5:27 pm (P), 8:27 pm (E)

Independence Day (U.S.)

P 3 WE 04 ◯

We get along well, displaying a love of humanity, generosity and openness to others' ideas. Catch this wave early and ride it all day.

Moon in Aquarius

4 TH 05 ◯

Morning is a flurry of activity, establishing order where chaos encroached or straightening out waste made by haste. Then things calm down.

Moon in Aquarius • Void 8:50 am (P), 11:50 am (E)
Moon enters Pisces 9:30 pm (P)

2 FR 06

Unless we focus on intentions, we're apt to wander, dissipating energy on distractions. Midday we might muster some fruitful motivation.

Moon in Pisces (P), Void in Aquarius (E)
Moon enters Pisces 12:30 am (E)

2 SA 07

A good mood from the get-go carries us through the day. We're forward socially and seek out new knowledge or a stimulating interchange.

Moon in Pisces • Void 4:01 am (P), 7:01 am (E)

4 SU 08 ☽

JULY 02-08 HIGHLIGHTS

Politicians may not be the only Americans up on soapboxes this Independence Day. Discussions are dramatic with Mercury in Leo. Its sextile to Venus puts the focus on values, and Venus in Gemini promotes a love of talking. Tuesday and Wednesday, this pair is in a Finger of God pattern pointing to Pluto. It's the planet of shared resources and finances (including taxes), currently in Capricorn, the sign of systems and laws. People need to try to find common ground concerning where funding comes from and how it's dispersed. A second Finger of God involving Mercury and Pluto (together spawning transformative ideas), brings assistance in the form of empathy and fresh ideas from Chiron in Pisces. Emotions run high when the Sun is in Cancer, evoking strong instincts to take care of family, home and nation. A Full Moon is usually a peak of feelings, too, but cooler heads (even cold hearts?) prevail when it's in down-to-earth, practical Capricorn. This sign shows no qualms about setting rigid standards. The crest Tuesday [11:53 am (P), 2:53 pm (E)] finds the Sun and Moon in the grasp of the difficult ongoing Uranus-Pluto square (see Star Pages for June 24). Authoritarians are headed for a run-in with feisty, independent types.

Mars, the planet of conflict, has just entered Libra, normally non-confrontational. However this placement does foster fighting about fairness. Disparity begs to be addressed, particularly Saturday evening when the Moon highlights Venus, the primary planet of balance, as it grates against Chiron, showing where pain is paramount.

The best part of the week comes Thursday morning. The Moon weaves three favorable planetary connections (exact Wednesday) into a wonderful blend of innovation and collaboration, great for any gathering, whether purely social or with a mission in mind.

[Monday South Node conjunct Ceres; Tuesday Mars enters Libra, Venus quincunx Pluto; Tuesday (P)/ Wednesday (E) Mercury quincunx Pluto; Wednesday Mercury sextile Venus, Mercury trine Uranus, Venus sextile Uranus; Thursday Mercury quincunx Chiron; Saturday Venus square Chiron; Sunday North Node sextile Mars]

When childhood dies, its corpses are called adults.
Brian Aldiss

	JUNE							JULY					
SU	M	TU	W	T	F	S	SU	M	TU	W	T	F	S
					1	2	1	2	3	4	5	6	7
3	4	5	6	7	8	9	8	9	10	11	12	13	14
10	11	12	13	14	15	16	15	16	17	18	19	20	21
17	18	19	20	21	22	23	22	23	24	25	26	27	28
24	25	26	27	28	29	30	29	30	31				

Moon Void in Pisces • Moon enters Aries 5:15 am (P), 8:15 am (E)

09 MO 2

Exhibit quiet confidence, even if you're unsure. "Fake it 'til you make it."
Positivity is the best defense against negativity or hostility.

Moon in Aries • Third Quarter Moon

10 TU 1 ★

The day might start with a clear head but by afternoon, confusion surrounds
you and logic deserts you. Trust your heart and best instincts.

Moon in Aries • Void 2:24 am (P), 5:24 am (E)
Moon enters Taurus 4:32 pm (P), 7:32 pm (E)

11 WE 1

Try to avoid a tiff this morning by putting yourself in the other guy's shoes.
Then continue ongoing activities, especially solo projects.

Moon in Taurus

12 TH 3

Your feet are on stable ground today and you can make improvements
or steer things in a better direction. Tonight, stubbornness is a problem.

Moon in Taurus • Void 12:47 pm (P), 3:47 pm (E)

13 FR 2 ★

Stay calm and be persistent as the best approaches to handle extremes that
come your way. Looking for a silver lining or a good chuckle helps, too.

Moon Void in Taurus • Moon enters Gemini 5:28 am (P), 8:28 am (E)

14 SA 2 P ★ MR

Midday brings ramifications from a choice made Tuesday. Today's task
is to be bold without being brazen, assertive but not aggressive.

Bastille Day

Moon in Gemini

15 SU 2 MR

Social interactions thrive when based on a foundation of respect and
solid boundaries. Build on these with good listening and kind words.

JULY 09-15 HIGHLIGHTS

This is no week for sissies! The difficulties have nothing to do with Friday the 13th, though it might be blamed. Those low-numbered day ratings above show you nothing is going smoothly. Another Mercury Retrograde begins Saturday, just after Uranus turns Retrograde Friday. Talk about crazy screw-ups! Leave lots of room in your schedule for interruptions and do-overs; getting things right the first time will be darn near impossible. Maybe this is the week for vacation cause it sure would be good to get away from work!

A confrontation midday Monday starts as a civil debate. Responding with "big talk" could seem smart, but pushing buttons quickly triggers a surprisingly negative reaction. Tuesday is the peak of a pattern that's been coming on for months. When it finally arrives, the Moon greets it with a slap, forcing a decision that tests spiritual resolve. Will you live up to high principles or mutter lame excuses? The Third Quarter Moon in Aries calls for leadership to rise to the caretaking mission of the Sun in Cancer. Wednesday has not one positive planetary link. Happily, the friction is over early. Better lick your wounds Thursday when the greatest chance for repair and healing is at hand. That night, stress sets in again. As Uranus

begins its annual backtrack Friday, the Taurus Moon lassoes it and Pluto into a knot of stubborn defiance.

Although it's not harvest time just yet, symbolically the fruits of our labors are displayed this weekend. For some, the sight won't be pretty. A favorable pairing (exact Tuesday) that should yield bounty is tainted by a tough pattern, spoiling the crop. You'll need wisdom, tact and flexibility. The way to succeed is to communicate well and extend respect to deal deftly with demanding people. This will defuse the venom of adversaries.

[Monday Sun sesquiquadrate North Node and Neptune; Monday (P)/ Tuesday (E) Ceres conjunct Jupiter; Tuesday Nodes square Neptune; Friday Uranus turns Retrograde, Sun semisquare Jupiter; Saturday Ceres semisquare Eris, Sun square Eris, Mercury sextile Venus, Sun semisquare Ceres, Mercury turns Retrograde; Saturday (P)/Sunday (E) Sun square Saturn; Sunday Ceres sesquiquadrate Saturn]

 Read "Using This Planner" for the meaning of
Moon Void and symbols ★, **MR**, **VR**, **P**.

AUGUST

SU	M	TU	W	T	F	S
				1	2	3	4
5	6	7	8	9	10	11
12	13	14	15	16	17	18
19	20	21	22	23	24	25
26	27	28	29	30	31	

"Star Light, Star Bright, I wish I may, I wish I might have the wish I wish tonight." Beautiful Evening Star Venus shines at its peak of brilliancy July 10. Make your wish!

July

Don't undermine joint efforts by pushing yourself or others too hard. Innovative persuasion works better: paint a positive picture.

Moon in Gemini • Void 3:58 am (P), 6:58 am (E)
Moon enters Cancer 5:32 pm (P), 8:32 pm (E)

MR 3 MO 16

Energy is off the scales and needs careful channeling to be constructive. It's easy to over-do things. Know your limits and get some rest.

Moon in Cancer

MR ★ P 2 TU 17

Anything goes, every which way, on this crazy, draining day. Stay centered if you can. Instead of succumbing to emotions, master your moods.

Moon in Cancer • New Moon (P) • Void 9:25 pm (P)

MR ★ 1 WE 18

After a slightly off-kilter start to the morning, we set our sights on lofty goals. All the pieces fall into place and we're nearly invincible.

Moon in Cancer, Void (P) • New Moon (E) • Void 12:25 am (E)
Moon enters Leo 3:14 am (P), 6:14 am (E)

MR 4 TH 19

Sweet talk will get you far today. People are congenial and joy is in the air. Tonight, some may overstep boundaries or wear out their welcome.

Ramadan begins

Moon in Leo • Void 10:19 pm (P)

MR ★ 3 FR 20

The day is fairly lackluster, though some take fun seriously. This evening, we drift aimlessly and avoid anything that smacks of exertion.

Moon in Leo, Void (P) • Void 1:19 am (E)
Moon enters Virgo 10:25 am (P), 1:25 pm (E)

MR ★ 2 SA 21

Those who seek the center of attention may be sorry if that makes them a target for criticism. But most are lighthearted about any teasing.

Parents' Day, Sun enters Leo

Moon in Virgo • Void 5:45 pm (P), 8:45 pm (E)

MR ★ 2 SU 22

JULY 16-22 HIGHLIGHTS

That pesky clash between the planets of order and chaos is at it again! At the New Moon [Wednesday 9:25 pm (P)/Thursday 12:25 am (E)], the Moon and Sun in Cancer create a T-square with Saturn and Eris (see Star Pages for May 26). Eris is extra troubling since it turns Retrograde Wednesday. In the coming four weeks, we'll battle the natural forces of entropy and human-created disruptions, testing our ability to be kind and caring. Even tougher is another T-square at the New Moon and carried forward over the next month. Tuesday to Wednesday, brash and hasty Mars bumps heads with Uranus and Pluto (see June 24 Star Pages). The Moon inflates this into a brief but potent Grand Cross midday Tuesday. Whenever Mars assaults Uranus, we're impulsive and accident-prone. Some relief comes from the favorable Ceres-Jupiter pairing (see July 10 Star Pages) which assuages Mars and Uranus; an inventive or cutting edge approach can be very fruitful.

Saturn approaches its fifth and final rough connection to Chiron (see July 29 Star Pages). Harshness can be hurtful but getting organized is very healing. Last week when they tangoed with Eris, it was hard to stay on top of things. This week, they grate against the Ceres-Jupiter combo,

diminishing the return on investments of mental energy. Jupiter's difficult links to Eris (this Tuesday) and Chiron (next Tuesday) amplify the chance for harmful bedlam. Be vigilant as the Moon aggravates this interwoven mess Wednesday afternoon and overnight Saturday.

Thank heaven for the saving grace of the Quintile Triangle Tuesday to Thursday between Mars, Neptune and the Sun (and Moon at New Moon). This puts out the fires of anger, stokes the coals of compassion and provides a spark for creativity and cooperation on the home front.

[Monday Sun sesquiquadrate Chiron, Ceres sextile Uranus; Tuesday Mars trine Jupiter, Mars square Pluto, Jupiter semisquare Eris; Tuesday (P)/ Wednesday (E) Sun quintile Mars; Wednesday Ceres square Chiron, Jupiter quincunx Pluto, Sun biquintile Neptune, Eris turns Retrograde, Mars opposite Uranus; Thursday Mars biquintile Neptune; Friday Jupiter sesquiquadrate Saturn; Saturday (P)/Sunday (E) Jupiter sextile Uranus, Mercury sextile Ceres; Sunday Sun enters Leo, Mercury sextile Mars]

It is better to be a lion for a day than a sheep all your life.
"Sister" Elizabeth Kenny

JULY						
SU	M	TU	W	T	F	S
1	2	3	4	5	6	7
8	9	10	11	12	13	14
15	16	17	18	19	20	21
22	23	24	25	26	27	28
29	30	31				

AUGUST						
SU	M	TU	W	T	F	S
			1	2	3	4
5	6	7	8	9	10	11
12	13	14	15	16	17	18
19	20	21	22	23	24	25
26	27	28	29	30	31	

Moon Void in Virgo • Moon enters Libra 3:39 pm (P), 6:39 pm (E)

23 MO 3 MR

It's hard to maintain focus most of the day and easy to waste time catching up or re-doing. Tonight is perfect for networking or social fun.

Moon in Libra

24 TU 3 P ★ MR

With eyes wide open, you see both what's harmful and helpful. Team up and take action to rein in what's gone too far. Aim in a better direction.

Moon in Libra • Void 8:23 am (P), 11:23 am (E)
Moon enters Scorpio 7:30 pm (P), 10:30 pm (E)

25 WE 2 MR

To fix a problem, two heads are better than one – unless they argue, making matters worse. To prevent meddling, give bossy big-mouths a task.

Moon in Scorpio • First Quarter Moon
Void 8:39 am (P), 11:39 am (E)

26 TH 3 MR

As you talk over a situation, release pre-conceived notions. Be open to others' wisdom. Think of what you can apply from your own experience.

Moon Void in Scorpio • Moon enters Sagittarius 10:19 pm (P)

27 FR 2 MR

Suppressing negative feelings to avoid confrontation doesn't keep the peace. They fester under the surface unless purged or channeled.

Summer Olympics begin

Moon in Sagittarius (P), Void in Scorpio (E)
Moon enters Sagittarius 1:19 am (E)

28 SA 3 P MR

Enthusiasm has you raring to go this morning. Curb the impulse. Consider consequences or you'll end up wondering, "what was I thinking?"

Moon in Sagittarius • Void 2:02 pm (P), 5:02 pm (E)

29 SU 3 ★ MR

You're excited about your own ideas but take time to examine different suggestions, as well. Respectful give-and-take benefits everyone.

JULY 23-29 HIGHLIGHTS

Our society is obsessed with growth and progress. We believe "bigger is better," though it's not always true. Jupiter, the largest planet, is called a "benefic" (helpful influence), but expansion causes difficulties on occasion. This week, Jupiter is in two tough interactions. Tuesday is the first of three occurrences, stretching into next year, of a trying link to Chiron, indicator of pain or a weakness. They're accentuated by the Moon, turning up the volume on emotional reactions, midday Tuesday and Saturday afternoon. Snarled up with Saturn then as well (see last week's Highlights), the importance of playing by the rules and knowing limitations is stressed. Circumstances get worse before they get better, and might not improve any time soon. We nudge things along with the help Tuesday to Thursday from Mercury turning the current Jupiter-Pluto quincunx (see July 18 Star Pages) into a Finger of God. This type of triangle is famous for one crazy thing leading to another, finally ending up okay. The Mercury-Pluto involvement hints that a change in outlook is required to find the gift in strange circumstances. Thursday morning's First Quarter Moon in Scorpio seconds the need for release; ego attachments may impede the process of moving on.

As this week ends and rolls into the next, we get some relief regarding the challenges to relationships (including rivalries) and associated boundary issues that we've been experiencing for a while. Venus connects nicely to both sides of the Saturn-Eris opposition, taking some of the sting out of it temporarily. It helps us reach compromises more easily or call a truce in squabbles. Sunday afternoon, the Moon in cheery and flexible Sagittarius links harmoniously to all three, briefly creating a "Mystic Rectangle." This aids tolerance of differences and reminds us that even if we're on competing teams, we're playing in the same game.

[Monday Mars trine Ceres; Tuesday Jupiter square Chiron, Sun trine North Node, Mercury sextile Jupiter, Mercury quincunx Chiron; Wednesday Mercury trine Uranus; Thursday Mercury quincunx Pluto; Saturday Mercury semisquare Venus, Mercury conjunct Sun; Sunday Venus sextile Eris, Saturn sesquiquadrate Chiron]

 Read "Using This Planner" for the meaning of Moon Void and symbols ★, **MR, VR, P.**

SEPTEMBER

SU	M	TU	W	T	F	S
						1
2	3	4	5	6	7	8
9	10	11	12	13	14	15
16	17	18	19	20	21	22
23	24	25	26	27	28	29
30						

Usually it's good to be positive and think big, though extremes in that regard can backfire or have unexpected results (see July 24-26 Star Pages). Keep things in perspective.

July-August

We know hard work and sacrifice are needed to reach that better day we believe in. There's frustration when sudden turns throw us off course.

Moon Void in Sagittarius
Moon enters Capricorn 12:30 am (P), 3:30 am (E)

MR 3 MO 30

Stay centered in the midst of distraction and discord. Maintaining tight control is tempting but going with the flow will work out better.

Moon in Capricorn • Void 4:32 pm (P), 7:32 pm (E)

MR 2 TU 31

Strive to be innovative and involve others in what you do. If there's a chip on someone's shoulder, allow a venting and then offer some humor.

Moon Void in Capricorn • Moon enters Aquarius 2:57 am (P), 5:57 am (E)
Full Moon (Corn Moon)

Lammas, Lughnassad, Civic Holiday (Canada)

MR 2 WE 01

Whatever cooperation is possible comes in the morning and even then may take some cajoling. Tonight you might be happier keeping a distance.

Moon in Aquarius

MR 3 TH 02

A sour mood through midday has people singing the blues or evading the source of their misery. If you face the music, you can dance to it.

Moon in Aquarius • Void 12:25 am (P), 3:25 am (E)
Moon enters Pisces 6:59 am (P), 9:59 am (E)

MR 2 FR 03

It seems like you're drowning in a sea of too much information. Just pay attention to what you deem valuable and let the rest float on by.

Moon in Pisces

MR 2 SA 04

The day begins with a need to stroke someone's ego. By evening, people feel good about themselves and seek excitement or entertainment.

Friendship Day

Moon in Pisces • Void 10:57 am (P), 1:57 pm (E)
Moon enters Aries 2:00 pm (P), 5:00 pm (E)

MR 3 SU 05

JULY 30-AUGUST 05 HIGHLIGHTS

We all like to feel appreciated and validated for our individuality. This is especially true when the Sun (representing the Self) is in the sign it rules, Leo. It would be nice to be treated like royalty! The Full Moon Wednesday [8:29 pm (P), 11:29 pm (E)] is in Aquarius, a sign of our uniqueness as well as our common humanity. At the Full Moon, a positive configuration involving Aquarius's ruler, Uranus, with the Sun, Moon and Jupiter, pumps up egos and puts us in our best light. The Moon and Jupiter are in another favorable triangle (a Grand Trine) with Mars, a planet of confidence. Sounds good, but there are a couple snags.

These are the most independent planets (aside from the Moon, which can be very clingy), so you can see the potential conflict. We want to be admired but not required. Mars loses a measure of its freedom in Libra; personal wants bow to others' needs. Mars is also in a difficult pattern (coming to a head Friday) with Neptune and the South Node, signaling self-sacrifice or paying a karmic debt. Meanwhile, Venus is in the only tough relationship it can have with the Sun, straining any weak link in self-esteem. Instead of feeling different and special, some

may fear they're weird and unlovable. It's important to be able to laugh at our foibles and forgive any human weaknesses. An offsetting influence arises from a helpful trine between Venus in Gemini and Saturn in Libra (exact Tuesday and elevated to a Grand Trine by the Moon Thursday night). Re-assurance comes from significant others, family and possibly neighbors. The week concludes with a brief uplifting Grand Trine Sunday afternoon that prods us toward pride. Healthy self-interest from the Moon in Aries reinforces the optimism of the North Node in Sagittarius. Together they bolster the ability to shine (at least in one's own mind) of Mercury in Leo. Maybe we're pretty regal after all.

[Monday (P)/Tuesday (E) Sun trine Uranus; Tuesday Venus trine Saturn; Wednesday Mars semisquare North Node and sesquiquadrate South Node; Thursday Sun sextile Jupiter, Venus semisquare Sun; Thursday (P)/Friday (E) Mars sesquiquadrate Neptune]

You cannot play the game of life with sweaty palms."
"Dr. Phil," Phillip C. McGraw

JULY								**AUGUST**					
SU	M	TU	W	T	F	S		SU	M	TU	W	T	F	S
1	2	3	4	5	6	7						1	2	3	4
8	9	10	11	12	13	14		5	6	7	8	9	10	11
15	16	17	18	19	20	21		12	13	14	15	16	17	18
22	23	24	25	26	27	28		19	20	21	22	23	24	25
29	30	31						26	27	28	29	30	31

Moon in Aries

06 MO 4 MR

Leave room for something unanticipated to start the day. Soon it's smooth sailing with an upbeat outlook. Send cheer to those at a distance.

Civic Holiday (Canada)

Moon in Aries • Void 1:05 pm (P), 4:05 pm (E)

07 TU 1 MR ★

Frustration mounts on this stop-and-go day. Brusque comments might be hurtful, and it's hard to connect with the people you need to reach.

Moon Void in Aries • Moon enters Taurus 12:29 am (P), 3:29 am (E)

08 WE 4 ★

We take time to appreciate nature, art and one another, going out of our way to be of help. We can have a good time making a difference in some way.

Moon in Taurus • Third Quarter Moon • Void 11:56 am (P), 2:56 pm (E)

09 TH 3

Unsettling insecurities that crop up during the day are pacified this evening by love and unconditional support. Express your gratitude.

Moon Void in Taurus • Moon enters Gemini 1:12 pm (P), 4:12 pm (E)

10 FR 3

We're sluggish much of the day until a refreshing breeze awakens our senses. Conversation picks up and we get excited to pursue new ideas.

Moon in Gemini

11 SA 2 ★

Someone challenges assertions. There is information that turns out to be incorrect, causing a problem early on that clears up by afternoon.

Moon in Gemini • Void 2:51 pm (P), 5:51 pm (E)

12 SU 3 ★

An independent streak this morning sends people their own way. Later, teamwork is needed and you may have to speak up to enlist participation.

AUGUST 06-12 HIGHLIGHTS

The end of Mercury Retrograde comes none too soon on Wednesday, the day named for Mercury (Mercredi in French and Miercoles in Spanish). As it turns Direct, it clangs clumsily against Ceres, showing difficulty communicating nurturing needs or a hard time dealing with children. There could be negative news about agriculture or the food supply, and you should check the expiration date on old food in your fridge. Hours earlier, Tuesday morning, Venus enters Cancer. For the next month, our enjoyment of eating increases and we treat one another with extra TLC.

The Third Quarter Moon Thursday features two stubborn "fixed" signs. The Leo Sun encourages us to handle matters with the innocent creativity of a child while the Taurus Moon wants us to hang on to ingrained habits that are hard to change. Experience and common sense will tell you where you need to be more open and innovative.

Our horizons are definitely brightening, at least a bit. Jupiter, planet of optimism, is untangling from a web of difficult connections (see Highlights for July 23-29). Saturday night, it's joined by one of the thousands of asteroids between Mars and Jupiter. The second-largest and brightest, Vesta, is goddess of the hearth in mythology. It circles the zodiac in 3-1/2 years and has been approaching Jupiter for weeks. Vesta is related to the housing industry and market, safety and security, and insurance and investments. Vesta's union with Jupiter should show signs of improvement in these areas. On a personal level, Vesta, is associated with focus, devotion and sacrifice (especially on behalf of a cause). It's also linked to sexual expression, sometimes intentional abstention. (The Vestal Virgins, keepers of the sacred flame, were not allowed to marry.) This could be a period of increased commitment to whatever inspires you.

[Monday (P)/Tuesday (E) South Node biquintile Pluto; Tuesday Venus enters Cancer, Mercury semisquare Ceres; Tuesday (P)/Wednesday (E) Mercury turns Direct; Wednesday Sun sextile Ceres; Wednesday (P)/Thursday (E) Mercury semisextile Venus; Thursday Venus trine Neptune; Saturday Chiron semisextile Uranus, Mars opposite Eris; Saturday (P)/Sunday (E) Vesta conjunct Jupiter; Sunday Mars sesquiquadrate Chiron]

SEPTEMBER

SU	M	TU	W	T	F	S
						1
2	3	4	5	6	7	8
9	10	11	12	13	14	15
16	17	18	19	20	21	22
23	24	25	26	27	28	29
30						

Janet's Plan-its doesn't usually discuss asteroids (other than Chiron, which is more than an asteroid, really). Occasionally, one can't be ignored, such as Vesta now.

It seems everyone is sympathetic from morning through afternoon, granting favors freely. Later, though, strange strings are attached.

Moon Void in Gemini • Moon enters Cancer 1:29 am (P), 4:29 am (E)

3 MO 13

Strong characters assert their power. Competition among them is fierce. Innocent bystanders may suffer. Stand back, poised to escape harm.

Moon in Cancer

2 TU 14

Face reality about what is and isn't effective, or even possible, to handle troublesome people. Come from a place of respect and discipline.

Assumption Day

Moon in Cancer • Void 1:22 am (P), 4:22 am (E)
Moon enters Leo 11:06 am (P), 2:06 pm (E)

★ P 2 WE 15

Grant others the freedom to be who they are and they're likely to allow you to be you, too. A friendly, joyful, caring attitude builds bridges.

Moon in Leo

3 TH 16

Give credit where it's due but take no blame for what's not your doing. You can make great strides toward a goal by sticking to a schedule.

Moon in Leo • New Moon • Void 10:56 am (P), 1:56 pm (E)
Moon enters Virgo 5:34 pm (P), 8:34 pm (E)

3 FR 17

Think before you speak and be careful how you frame what you have to say. Don't be flip in serious matters or unmoved when tenderness is needed.

Moon in Virgo • Void 4:27 pm (P), 7:27 pm (E)

2 SA 18

This is a fairly calm day unless you permit over-analyzing to produce anxiety. Focus on something harmless, whether it's productive or fun.

Eid al-Fitr

Moon Void in Virgo • Moon enters Libra 9:46 pm (P)

★ 2 SU 19

AUGUST 13-19 HIGHLIGHTS

With a new lunar cycle starting this week in Leo (ruled by the Sun), you'd think our solar system's star would be the center of attention. Instead pushy little Pluto gets that honor. It's involved in three important patterns, all in effect at the New Moon Friday [8:55 am (P), 11:55 am (E)], extending their influence over the next four weeks. We'll be required to let go of something and move on, to turn the page and start a new chapter. Quite possibly, a personal relationship won't survive the shift. If that's the case, the bond was not strong enough.

First up is a configuration that brings luck or accentuates talent. It's been brewing since early August, greasing wheels for greater clarity or cooperation in systems or organizations (see Aug. 19 Star Pages). Wednesday, Mars participates in the arrangement, getting things moving. The Moon joins in midday Thursday, which could be a good time to make progress on an ongoing project with assistance from people with whom you've networked. However, simultaneously the second formation gums up the works. Venus turns the ongoing Uranus-Pluto standoff (see June 24 Star Pages) into a troublesome T-square, bringing a turning point. Watch out for a surprise from a key player with whom you've had a conflict. If

cajoling fails to achieve common ground, someone may walk away. A better time to make good things happen is next Wednesday, when Mercury slides into the favorable position the Moon occupies this Thursday, bringing creative communication to the process. Since this is after the New Moon, there's a better chance for forward momentum. The third configuration Saturday opens up discussion about what needs to be done to bring about healing changes. Still, improvement plans will go through twists and turns before their value can be realized.

[Monday Mercury semisquare Ceres; Tuesday Sun sesquiquadrate Pluto, Sun trine Eris; Wednesday Venus opposite Pluto, Mars conjunct Saturn, Sun sesquiquadrate Uranus; Quintile Triangle Wednesday: Mars biquintile South Node and quintile Pluto; Wednesday (P)/ Thursday (E) Venus trine Chiron, Venus square Uranus; Thursday South Node biquintile Saturn; Friday Sun sextile Saturn; Finger of God: Friday (P)/ Saturday (E) Mercury quincunx Pluto and Saturday Mercury quincunx Chiron; Saturday Mercury trine Uranus; Sunday Saturn quintile Pluto]

Look for a long time at what pleases you, and longer still at what pains you.
Colette

AUGUST						
SU	M	TU	W	T	F	S
				1	2	3	4
5	6	7	8	9	10	11
12	13	14	15	16	17	18
19	20	21	22	23	24	25
26	27	28	29	30	31	

SEPTEMBER						
SU	M	TU	W	T	F	S
						1
2	3	4	5	6	7	8
9	10	11	12	13	14	15
16	17	18	19	20	21	22
23	24	25	26	27	28	29
30						

Moon in Libra (P), Void in Virgo (E)
Moon enters Libra 12:46 am (E)

20 MO 2

Interpersonal issues mar the early part of the day but the storms blow over quickly. Then beware of over-optimism. Take only calculated risks.

Moon in Libra

21 TU 2

Stay centered in a harmonious mindset and you'll weather the turbulence of others' angst around you. Concentration and commitment pay off.

Moon in Libra • Void 12:14 am (P), 3:14 am (E)
Moon enters Scorpio 12:55 am (P), 3:55 am (E)

22 WE 4 ★

Your thoughts are well organized, you see with depth and precision and your words strike a healing chord. Tackle hard tasks and do good work.

Sun enters Virgo

Moon in Scorpio • Void 2:35 am (P), 5:35 am (E)

23 TH 2 ★

A serene morning descends into aggravation when complications arise. The more you try to keep things under control, the crazier they get.

Moon Void in Scorpio • Moon enters Sagittarius 3:51 am (P), 6:51 am (E)
First Quarter Moon

24 FR 1 P ★

After pervasive confusion and trust issues spark arguments and finger-pointing, there might be a truce or friendly overture by evening.

Moon in Sagittarius • Void 11:40 pm (P)

25 SA 2

Don't stuff resentment inside and stew. Resolution is possible only if you speak up, expose the problems and find something to laugh about.

Moon in Sagittarius, Void (P) • Void 2:40 am (E)
Moon enters Capricorn 7:00 am (P), 10:00 am (E)

26 SU 3

Fun takes a back seat as people feel responsible for conditions affecting everyone and find useful applications for their compassion.

Women's Equality Day

AUGUST 20-26 HIGHLIGHTS

The week gets off to high-spirited start Monday with two important connections involving Mars, the planet of get-up-and-go. It plays nicely with the Sun, inspiring us to follow our hearts with a sense of purpose. But it rubs Jupiter the wrong way; whatever we do, we over-do. We expect bigger results for our efforts than is realistic. With Jupiter in Gemini, many people talk a good line but don't back it up with action.

Pay attention to what you see, read, hear and say Wednesday, a big day for little Mercury, planet of the mind and senses. The Sun enters Virgo (one of two signs ruled by Mercury) that day, beginning an eight-day energy exchange with Mercury, currently in Leo, ruled by the Sun (see Mutual Receptions at the beginning of the Star Pages). Mental creativity is at a high point as are will power and self-oriented thinking (which isn't always bad). Also Wednesday, Mercury forms a magical Quintile Triangle with Pluto and Saturn (which were quintile last Sunday). This brings the right words to promote getting one's act together and figuring out where all the pieces of the puzzle fit. We can lighten our load by making good decisions about what to keep and what to discard.

The First Quarter Moon Friday prods us to take a wide-angled view. While the Sun in Virgo obsesses over minor details, the Moon in Sagittarius paints with broad strokes. Rather than suffer from negative thinking, seek the best in any situation, which won't be easy. Both the Sun and Venus have problems with Neptune that day. Be on the lookout for misunderstandings, bruised egos, money-handling mistakes, lovers' quarrels and escapist fantasies. To make matters worse, a long-term ugly link that spells trouble is exact Friday, too, bumped by the Moon that evening. Be clear about intentions and stick to them or you could become engulfed in someone else's quagmire.

[Monday Sun sextile Mars, Mars sesquiquadrate Jupiter; Wednesday Mercury biquintile Pluto, Sun enters Virgo, Mercury quintile Saturn, Mercury sextile Jupiter; Wednesday (P)/Thursday (E) Sun square Nodes; Thursday Mars enters Scorpio, Venus sesquiquadrate North Node; Friday Chiron semisquare Eris, Sun opposite Neptune, Mercury semisextile Venus, Venus sesquiquadrate Neptune; Sunday Mars trine Neptune]

OCTOBER

SU	M	TU	W	T	F	S
	1	2	3	4	5	6
7	8	9	10	11	12	13
14	15	16	17	18	19	20
21	22	23	24	25	26	27
28	29	30	31			

August-September

Penetrating insights point to needed changes. While hard to swallow, you know they're true. Still, it hurts when others confirm them.

Moon in Capricorn

1 MO 27

Morning offers smart, and probably strange, ideas or realizations but now isn't time to implement them. Everything's an uphill battle.

Moon in Capricorn • Void 3:34 am (P), 6:34 am (E)
Moon enters Aquarius 10:40 am (P), 1:40 pm (E)

2 TU 28

A positive, can-do attitude guides us in whatever we do. We make good decisions and practical alterations, resulting in a sense of pride.

Moon in Aquarius

★ **4 WE 29**

Endeavor to be kind and loving to yourself and others, especially when things get gallingly discombobulated. Accept rather than judge.

Moon in Aquarius • Void 10:49 am (P), 1:49 pm (E)
Moon enters Pisces 3:32 pm (P), 6:32 pm (E)

P 2 TH 30

If you get off on the wrong foot, the day will go downhill. Institute an attitude adjustment and focus on your highest values as motivation.

Moon in Pisces • Full Moon (Harvest Moon)

★ **1 FR 31**

It's hard to see through the mental fog permeating the whole day. Handle personal needs early before you give your time to benefit others.

Moon in Pisces • Void 1:03 pm (P), 4:03 pm (E)
Moon enters Aries 10:38 pm (P)

★ **2 SA 01**

An extreme level of energy should be channeled into productive activity or dissipated through physical exertion. Otherwise it may erupt in anger.

Moon in Aries (P), Void in Pisces (E)
Moon enters Aries 1:38 am (E)

2 SU 02

AUGUST 27-SEPT. 02 HIGHLIGHTS

As the week begins, mixed signals make matters harder than they have to be. Between Monday and Tuesday, Mercury is involved in two configurations, one benign, the other choppy. Attempts to confront what needs to be addressed, even when broached nicely, ruffle feathers. Only restraint and decorum prevent eruption into a brawl. Greater clarity emerges Wednesday and Thursday, but not without someone being upset. Friday we see the need to re-orient our outlook and direction, but there's still confusion Saturday. Maybe Sunday we'll get that fight we've been needing all week to clear the air.

There comes a point regularly in the Sun-Venus cycle when these two ordinarily nice planets clash and it's harder for people to like themselves or others much. This peaks just ahead of the Full Moon [Friday 6:59 am (P), 9:59 am (E)], which infuses extra agitation into the situation. The Moon's sign is Pisces, the height of sensitivity and feeling misunderstood or mistreated. The analytical and critical traits of the Sun in Virgo rub salt in the tender wounds of Venus in Cancer and the Moon in Pisces. Even a casual comment can spawn tears. All three planets bump into the current difficult connection between Chiron and Eris (see Aug. 24 Star Pages).

Domineering people try to steamroll those who are weaker or can't defend themselves. Relationships and financial matters, Venus's arenas, suffer unless some kind of a healing turn-around comes from people taking a mature, caring approach to matters. Things come to a head between Thursday and Friday morning, although repercussions roil next Monday as Venus and the Sun tango with Saturn. We need to tread lightly because of the karmic implications of our choices and actions. This is the Harvest Moon – what crop will our labors yield? If all we see is imperfection and disappointment, we could end up on the compost heap.

[Monday Ceres sextile Eris, Mercury sesquiquadrate Pluto; Tuesday Mercury trine Eris, Mercury sesquiquadrate Uranus, Mercury sextile Ceres; Wednesday Sun trine Pluto, Mercury sextile Saturn; Thursday Sun opposite Chiron, Venus sesquiquadrate Chiron, Sun sesquiquadrate Eris, Venus square Eris; Friday Venus semisquare Sun, Mercury enters Virgo, Mercury square Nodes; Saturday Mercury opposite Neptune, North Node enters Scorpio/South Node enters Taurus]

Kindness is more important than wisdom, and the recognition of this is the beginning of wisdom.

Theodore Isaac Rubin

AUGUST						
SU	M	TU	W	T	F	S
				1	2	3	4
5	6	7	8	9	10	11
12	13	14	15	16	17	18
19	20	21	22	23	24	25
26	27	28	29	30	31	

SEPTEMBER						
SU	M	TU	W	T	F	S
						1
2	3	4	5	6	7	8
9	10	11	12	13	14	15
16	17	18	19	20	21	22
23	24	25	26	27	28	29
30						

Moon in Aries

03 MO 3 P

Set your sights on what can be done, not what can't. Suspend disbelief, envision the life you want and take responsibility for creating it.

Labor Day (US & Canada)

Moon in Aries • Void 4:07 am (P), 7:07 am (E)
Moon enters Taurus 8:42 am (P), 11:42 am (E)

04 TU 2

Priorities are skewed this morning. Events take a decided turn for the better midday. Later, if evening hands you a disappointment, let it go.

Moon in Taurus • Void 11:56 am (P), 2:56 pm (E)

05 WE 3

There's been plenty to ponder and discuss. Now sift through suggestions to select those most worth implementing. Simplicity is appealing.

Moon Void in Taurus • Moon enters Gemini 9:11 pm (P)

06 TH 2 ★

Feelings are shifting. Something's ending; something bigger is about to begin. It's uncomfortable but resisting change makes it harder.

Moon in Gemini (P), Void in Taurus (E)
Moon enters Gemini 12:11 am (E)

07 FR 2

Freedom and confidence emerge when you voice and dispel your fears by dissecting their components. Figure out how to have the upper hand.

Moon in Gemini • Third Quarter Moon

08 SA 1

Don't blow an issue out of proportion or let little pieces block your view of the big picture. Strive for less mental chatter and more laughter.

Moon in Gemini • Void 4:00 am (P), 7:00 am (E)
Moon enters Cancer 9:50 am (P), 12:50 pm (E)

09 SU 3

Hidden gems surface when you take time for a heart-to-heart chat about what really matters. Find ways to support pursuing important dreams.

Grandparents Day

SEPTEMBER 03-09 HIGHLIGHTS

This is the week to put smart thinking into action and make significant repairs or improvements. There's a great interweaving of planets from Monday to Thursday. (It's amplified by the Moon overnight Tuesday into Wednesday, if you're inclined to sacrifice some sleep for brilliant ideas then.) The likely target areas are projects, products, finances and health. Dig down to the root of a situation to see what's out of whack and needs to be brought back to the center. Cleaning brings fresh chi. Whatever is old and outdated should be discarded. Did you know the principles of *feng shui* can be applied to any surface (dresser top, table, desk)? Creating better order will make you feel more in control, just don't become rigid in a need to be on top of everything. You'll benefit by learning to strike a balance between having a goal and surrendering to spontaneity.

Challenges in partnering and self-acceptance from last week continue. Venus and the Sun remain in a tough connection, this week linking awkwardly first with Saturn, then with Jupiter. There's ample evidence that relationships need extra attention and work. It's not easy to straighten matters out, though. Some people hold back on giving

affection while others are too demonstrative. The obstacles are more internal than external. A wider perspective is needed to help start moving things in a better direction. The Third Quarter Moon Saturday shows how much we've been stuck in our own views and points out the errors in our assessments. We have to admit mistakes, whether to ourselves or others, before we can correct them. The trick is to do this without creating bad feelings. At least, Venus leaves hypersensitive Cancer for joyous Leo Thursday. Try expressing any angst you're feeling about your liaisons through art, maybe by journaling, drawing or even singing the blues.

[Monday Venus square Saturn, Mars sextile Pluto, Sun semisquare Saturn, Mars trine Chiron; Tuesday Mercury trine Pluto, Mercury opposite Chiron, Mercury sesquiquadrate Eris; Wednesday Mercury sextile Mars; Thursday Chiron sextile Pluto, Venus trine North Node, Venus enters Leo, Venus semisquare Jupiter; Thursday (P)/Friday (E) Mercury semisquare Saturn; Friday Sun square Jupiter; Saturday Mercury square Jupiter; Sunday Mars sesquiquadrate Ceres]

OCTOBER

SU	M	TU	W	T	F	S
		1	2	3	4	5	6
7	8	9	10	11	12	13
14	15	16	17	18	19	20
21	22	23	24	25	26	27
28	29	30	31			

The Moon's Nodes have changed signs, bringing fresh challenges for our development and a new emphasis from eclipses over the next 18 months (see Sept. 1 Star Pages).

September

Healthy self-care begins by putting yourself first. This is not selfish; rather, it recognizes you can't help others if your needs aren't met.

Moon in Cancer

3 MO 10

An upsetting, chaotic morning tilts us off balance. Afternoon is consumed by attempts to calm those who are upset and to re-establish order.

Patriot Day

Moon in Cancer • Void 3:00 pm (P), 6:00 pm (E)
Moon enters Leo 8:02 pm (P), 11:02 pm (E)

2 TU 11

Cooperation is attainable early on. Later, disagreements predominate, even if for the sake of argument, but more likely to promote change.

Moon in Leo

★ 3 WE 12

Bright hopes start the day, however they don't last. Strong leadership is required to quell a kerfuffle about the way things are being done.

Moon in Leo • Void 10:15 pm (P)

2 TH 13

If you compare how things are to how they "should be" and become disparaged, get busy overhauling. Any sort of cleanup is a good place to start.

Moon in Leo, Void (P) • Void 1:15 am (E)
Moon enters Virgo 2:32 am (P), 5:32 am (E)

2 FR 14

The day begins with an awkward moment of openness or too much information. Later, focusing on outcomes motivates people to cooperate.

Moon in Virgo • New Moon

3 SA 15

Early morning offers an inspiring glimpse of ways to make a difference. Evening finds people bending over backward to avoid confrontation.

Mexican Independence Day

Moon in Virgo • Void 4:27 am (P), 7:27 am (E)
Moon enters Libra 5:56 am (P), 8:56 am (E)

★ 2 SU 16

SEPTEMBER 10-16 HIGHLIGHTS

Refining thought processes and means of communication are appropriate this week as Mercury finishes its visit to Virgo. Begin Monday with the timeless adage inscribed at the entry to the Oracle at Delphi: "Know thyself." It's easy to get so busy that there's no time for self-reflection. Then life may become a series of reactions rather than intentions. In this self-examination (a strong theme Tuesday and Wednesday morning, as well), be reminded of what you appreciate about yourself and the praise you receive from others. Enumerating faults and berating yourself is tempting but unproductive. A good understanding of what makes you tick, what you want and don't want, your limitations and strengths acts as a foundation for decisions and prioritizing. Clear thinking is yours for the claiming. You'll need it to handle the myriad of details at hand, Saturday in particular, but over the next four weeks, too, since that's the day of the New Moon [7:12 pm (P), 10:12 pm (E)]. The Moon and Sun are only five degrees from Mercury, all in Virgo, so this sign's traits are strongly emphasized for the coming cycle. On the plus side, these include health consciousness, service to others and a focus on work and productivity. On the down side are tendencies to criticize, nitpick and lose the forest for the trees. By the time Mercury arrives at Libra's doorstep Sunday, we'll be glad to get it out of Virgo!

Look for progress on the financial front and/or in relationships midweek as the planet in charge of both these areas forms a potent pattern with the indicators of alterations and improvements. Things may take strange twists and turns before arriving at a better place, but wheels are in motion in a better direction. Let resistance to change melt away, replaced by excitement about starting over.

[Monday Mercury conjunct Sun; Tuesday Mercury semisquare Venus; Wednesday Finger of God: Venus quincunx Chiron & quincunx Pluto; Wednesday (P)/ Thursday (E) Venus trine Uranus; Saturday Mercury square Ceres, Mercury semisextile Saturn, Saturn trine Ceres; Sunday Mercury sextile North Node, Mercury enters Libra]

Whoever loves true life, will love true love.
Elizabeth Barrett Browning

		SEPTEMBER								OCTOBER				
SU	M	TU	W	T	F	S		SU	M	TU	W	T	F	S
						1			1	2	3	4	5	6
2	3	4	5	6	7	8		7	8	9	10	11	12	13
9	10	11	12	13	14	15		14	15	16	17	18	19	20
16	17	18	19	20	21	22		21	22	23	24	25	26	27
23	24	25	26	27	28	29		28	29	30	31			
30														

Moon in Libra

17 MO 2 ★

We're scattered early but at least people get along. Later, interactions deteriorate. Self-protection supersedes the need to connect.

Constitution Day (Citizenship Day), Rosh Hashanah

Moon in Libra • Void 4:31 am (P), 7:31 am (E)
Moon enters Scorpio 7:47 am (P), 10:47 am (E)

18 TU 3 ★

Conversations probe private topics. Use your gut to know how much to reveal or conceal; the main goal is to heal. Light-hearted play may help.

Moon in Scorpio

19 WE 1 ★

Those in a rush might brush off something serious as trivial. Stop, look and listen to discover what most deserves attention or needs work.

Moon in Scorpio • Void 6:12 am (P), 9:12 am (E)
Moon enters Sagittarius 9:35 am (P), 12:35 pm (E)

20 TH 2

Be careful with your thoughts and words. Unless they come from a loving and hopeful place, they're more likely to do damage than assist.

Moon in Sagittarius

21 FR 3

This morning, prioritize to avoid a sea of information flotsam. Then be adventurous, learn something or enjoy interesting, fun people.

International Day of Peace

Moon in Sagittarius • Void 9:46 am (P), 12:46 pm (E)
Moon enters Capricorn 12:22 pm (P), 3:22 pm (E) • First Quarter Moon

22 SA 3 ★

We have a strong sense of commitment to and responsibility for those about whom we care the most, aiming not to resent any required sacrifice.

Autumn Equinox, Mabon, Sun enters Libra

Moon in Capricorn

23 SU 2

The day starts with a dose of disorder or dissension that could devolve into discouragement. Be diligent and delve into a useful project.

SEPTEMBER 17-23 HIGHLIGHTS

Autumn begins Saturday at 7:50 am (P), 10:50 am (E). The shifting of seasons is always an important time to round the bend and head in another direction. Often there's important news around a solstice or equinox. This one comes with an extra thrust, occurring within days of a powerful planetary turning point. And, like the summer solstice, it's close to one of five instances of the toughest link this year and next, the Uranus-Pluto square (see June 24 Star Pages). Pluto, the primary planet of clearing the decks, ends its annual backward jaunt Monday, priming us for progress in transformations we want in our lives. Uranus sparks reform in sudden and surprising ways. In its current clash with Pluto, changes no longer come slowly but rather arise quickly and are often instituted rashly. With Uranus in Aries, the tendency is for one person or party to instigate change, however the Sun in the teamwork and partnering sign of Libra should bring a buy-in from all those affected by alterations.

Because trading markets are related to Pluto, its long-term square with Uranus has produced a prolonged period of volatility. This week is no exception. There may be stagnation as the week begins, but

Wednesday and Thursday both look crazy. Be careful communicating trading orders then; even though Mercury is not Retrograde, it makes a nasty pattern Thursday, accentuated by the Moon late Wednesday. The jump is likely to be to the plus side on Thursday when Venus, a money planet, is in a favorable connection to Jupiter, planet of expansion. This boost might repeat Friday when the Moon highlights their tie; however another factor in place works against prospects for a fruitful day. Still, the Moon does stimulate the positive Venus-Jupiter association near the close of trading and that could raise the indexes. This also means Friday night is good for socializing.

[Monday Mercury semisquare Mars; Monday (P)/Tuesday (E) Pluto turns Direct; Tuesday Venus semisquare Ceres; Tuesday (P)/Wednesday (E) Uranus square Pluto; Thursday Mercury opposite Uranus and square Pluto (T-square), Venus sextile Jupiter; Friday Sun sextile North Node, Sun square Ceres; Saturday Sun enters Libra]

NOVEMBER

SU	M	TU	W	T	F	S
				1	2	3
4	5	6	7	8	9	10
11	12	13	14	15	16	17
18	19	20	21	22	23	24
25	26	27	28	29	30	

Some form of completion is typical when a slow planet is in the final degree of a sign. Saturn is finishing its time in Libra, marking an end or a final obligation in a relationship.

All day, we slog away dutifully without much joy. Then we realize that by thinking differently, it's possible to enjoy the evening after all.

Moon in Capricorn • Void 2:20 pm (P), 5:20 pm (E)
Moon enters Aquarius 4:34 pm (P), 7:34 pm (E)

2 MO 24

Rare is the person who can be gregarious when so many are stubborn, selfish and pushy. You might as well please yourself. Who else will?

Moon in Aquarius

P 2 TU 25

We need to stick together amidst overwhelming demands that create a sense of chaos. Watch out for over-thinking, thus missing the obvious.

Yom Kippur

Moon in Aquarius • Void 8:34 pm (P), 11:34 pm (E)
Moon enters Pisces 10:25 pm (P)

★ P 2 WE 26

Address needed improvements or repairs with sensitivity. A playful approach may be tempting but not appropriate for serious matters.

Moon in Pisces (P), Void in Aquarius (E)
Moon enters Pisces 1:25 am (E)

2 TH 27

We get distracted early or wander from task to task, completing nothing. Energy picks up later and persistence leads to accomplishment.

Native American Day

Moon in Pisces • Void 7:36 pm (P), 10:36 pm (E)

3 FR 28

There's resistance to change and nearly a rebellion against anyone trying to force the issue. People will fight for their own interests.

Moon Void in Pisces • Moon enters Aries 6:15 am (P), 9:15 am (E)
Full Moon (Blood Moon)

P 1 SA 29

A nonjudgmental or charitable attitude counterbalances selfish desires. Loving acceptance can turn the tide and bring a positive shift.

Moon in Aries

2 SU 30

SEPT. 24-30 HIGHLIGHTS

As Mars moves through Scorpio (a sign it ruled prior to Pluto's discovery), it urges us to be pro-active in renovating some aspect of our lives. Tuesday, it passes through the degree of the upcoming Nov. 13 Solar Eclipse and sets wheels in motion to impact subsequent events. Certainly you can take action with this intention. Also on Tuesday (the weekday named for Mars, easily heard in the French version, mardi), Mars connects to the current Uranus-Pluto square, reiterating the impulse for taking matters into our own hands. The caution, though, is to aim for a balanced approach or one that considers others. Mars is typically self-oriented. This week, it clashes with the primary planet of sharing and teamwork, Venus, which is also interacting with Uranus and Pluto on Tuesday and Wednesday, ahead of its tango with Mars on Thursday. The Moon accentuates all four planets Wednesday morning, the first of two intense peaks this week (the other being Saturday night).

The Mars-Venus self-other competition is significant because these are the ruling planets of Aries and Libra, the signs of Moon and Sun at the Full Moon Saturday night [8:20 pm (P), 11:20 pm (E)]. The first Full Moon of autumn always features this polarity and prompts us to find ways to be in relationship and still maintain our individuality. It's not impossible to look out for number one while also taking good care of numbers two and beyond. Because the Uranus-Pluto square urges us to revise how we've always done things, we must find new ways to walk that fine tightrope of balancing our own needs and desires with those of the people with whom we're closest. This will be a very intense Full Moon! Saturday the Moon joins Uranus while the Sun forms a forceful T-square with it and Pluto. Be ready for surprises and not necessarily pleasant ones. To use the energy constructively, dig into a cleanup or organization project.

[Monday Mercury semisquare North Node; Monday (P)/Tuesday (P) Mars sesquiquadrate Uranus; Tuesday Mars semisquare Pluto, Venus sesquiquadrate Uranus; Wednesday Ceres enters Cancer, Venus sesquiquadrate Pluto, Mercury sesquiquadrate Neptune, Mercury trine Jupiter, Venus trine Eris; Thursday Venus square Mars; Saturday Sun opposite Uranus, Mercury sesquiquadrate Chiron, Sun square Pluto; Sunday Mercury opposite Eris, Ceres trine Neptune]

Peace is such a precious jewel that I would give anything for it but truth.
Matthew Henry

○ Moon in Aries • Void 3:33 pm (P), 6:33 pm (E)
Moon enters Taurus 4:27 pm (P), 7:27 pm (E)
01 MO 3

We rush from morning 'til afternoon but manage to stay on track, reacting quickly when necessary. Tonight a calm, mellow mood refreshes us.

World Habitat Day, Sukkot begins

○ Moon in Taurus
02 TU 4

We prioritize, easily setting clear goals and finding cooperative assistance. Persistence and ambition push us toward accomplishment.

 Moon in Taurus
03 WE 1 ★

Frustrations mount as people drag their feet (when you wish they'd get going) or try to wiggle out of their duties, even if you offer to help.

 Moon in Taurus • Void 12:45 am (P), 3:45 am (E)
Moon enters Gemini 4:48 am (P), 7:48 am (E)
04 TH 2 ★

While some seem obsessed and on a mission, others are non-committal or off on a tangent, slowing progress. Turn to a caring colleague or friend.

 Moon in Gemini • Void 2:09 pm (P), 5:09 pm (E)
05 FR 3 ★

You could miss a key piece of the puzzle scratching the surface when you should dig deeper. Look twice and follow instincts to find the answer.

 Moon Void in Gemini
Moon enters Cancer 5:46 pm (P), 8:46 pm (E)
06 SA 4 ★

Feelings are easily expressed or detected, even if you wanted to keep them private. Tonight, tender support makes a positive difference.

Moon Void in Cancer
07 SU 2

There's a surprise snag this morning. Laudable intentions to help someone are misconstrued and backfire. "No good deed goes unpunished."

OCTOBER 01-07 HIGHLIGHTS

A lot of activity centers on our favorite topics, love and money, most of the week. The planet in charge of both, Venus, is very busy, including a move into a different sign Wednesday, when we relinquish a creative or playful attitude and get down to business. We're serious about partnering and finances, seeking ways to reap benefits from the work we're willing to put into them. We should be careful not to project expectations onto others and instead accept the reality of current circumstances. This is very challenging Wednesday to Saturday, especially Thursday morning when Jupiter in Gemini turns Retrograde. Be cautious with long-distance relationships or monetary transactions, which could suffer from bad information or mistrust. At the end of the week, communication is jumbled or goes awry and it's hard to reach the people with whom we want to connect.

A signal that a change in direction is needed comes Monday when we have to walk a tightrope between our own values and those of others close to us. Thursday, the scales tip in favor of the greater good and we're spurred to act on everyone's behalf. If we can benefit individually as well, all the better, but a personal sacrifice is likely required.

A somber and mature mindset commences Friday when Mercury and Saturn enter Scorpio hand-in-hand. This combination is great for research, psychology and investments, boosted by a sixth sense as both planets beeline for a trine to Neptune. Saturday night, the Moon joins them in a brief Grand Trine in water signs. Psychic wavelengths are magnified then but people may be upset by the intensity of their emotions. Mars trots into Sagittarius at the same time, immediately jarring Neptune, which could result in blunt, insensitive words or actions. An upset or hurt in the wallet or the heart closes the week as Venus clashes with Chiron.

[Monday Venus square Nodes; Tuesday Venus sextile Saturn; Wednesday Venus enters Virgo, Venus opposite Neptune; Thursday Venus sextile Ceres, Jupiter turns Retrograde, Mars conjunct North Node; Friday Mercury conjunct Saturn, Mercury enters Scorpio, Saturn enters Scorpio, Mercury trine Neptune, Sun sesquiquadrate North Node and semisquare South Node; Saturday Mercury sesquiquadrate Jupiter, Mercury trine Ceres, Mars enters Sagittarius; Sunday Mars square Neptune, Venus opposite Chiron]

NOVEMBER

SU	M	TU	W	T	F	S
				1	2	3
4	5	6	7	8	9	10
11	12	13	14	15	16	17
18	19	20	21	22	23	24
25	26	27	28	29	30	

Are you ready for another Mercury Retrograde? Mercury is in its backtracking range October 18 to December 14. You might want to make holiday plans and reservations before 10/18.

October

We're in a fog this morning and have trouble being understood. Later we're emotionally vulnerable or caught up in someone else's drama.

Moon in Cancer • Third Quarter Moon
Void 12:34 am (P), 3:34 am (E)

1 MO 08

Columbus Day, Thanksgiving Day (Canada)

Stand on principles and stick to your guns in handling a chaotic or imbalanced situation. Dig down to the root causes but do so with tenderness.

Moon Void in Cancer • Moon enters Leo 4:56 am (P), 7:56 am (E)

3 TU 09

Hopes are bright and you believe anything is possible, especially since your determination is so strong. Yet tonight something goes wrong.

Moon in Leo • Void 2:41 pm (P), 5:41 pm (E)

★ 3 WE 10

You're pulled in opposing directions early. Afternoon is magical, but it's not just luck. Partly it's your hard work, even if it's unappreciated.

Moon Void in Leo • Moon enters Virgo 12:25 pm (P), 3:25 pm (E)

3 TH 11

Analytical skills are prominent and productive. We click on all cylinders today, accomplishing a lot. This evening, a block stymies us.

Moon in Virgo • Void 4:49 pm (P), 7:49 pm (E)

3 FR 12

You're sensitive to even a hint of a social slight, taking criticism to heart. Seek uplifting, supportive company to help you laugh at life.

Moon Void in Virgo • Moon enters Libra 4:03 pm (P), 7:03 pm (E)

2 SA 13

Unfriendly competition and angry outbursts mar get-togethers. Some escape confrontation to calm down. Maintaining perspective helps.

Moon in Libra

2 SU 14

OCTOBER 08-14 HIGHLIGHTS

As the week begins, some people may be haunted by self-doubt or insecurity; any of us could question an aspect of our lives. We're not sure whether to rely on hunches, use logic or try to blend the two. Early Monday, the Third Quarter Moon pits the ESP of the Cancer Moon against the Libra Sun's rationality. Each is in a tough connection to confusing Neptune; we question the veracity of vibrations we pick up. However with adequate grounding, we're unlikely to succumb to worries.

All month, Venus travels in a positive link to Mercury (exact twice: next Tuesday and Thursday the week after). They promote peaceful communication and offer plenty of opportunities to collaborate. Venus in Virgo values riding herd on details. Mercury in Scorpio enjoys figuring out puzzles. Combined, they blend common sense and instinct. Early in the week, they're in two interesting configurations. They form half of a Star of David via friendly ties to Chiron and Pluto (already in harmony – see Sept. 6 Star Pages), good for problem-solving or finding resources for improvements. The other pattern is not as smooth. A Finger of God with Uranus yields circumstances that, while sudden or strange, ultimately result in good ideas or insights after a little head-scratching.

We're in a period of a few weeks when our antennae tune in well to the unseen realm. Pay attention to your dreams midweek; they might be precognitive or their symbolism can reveal important messages from your subconscious. An innate understanding of where we can be of assistance and make a difference unites with a strong dose of compassion to pitch in. Our efforts have an immediate pay off Thursday afternoon into the evening. Rushing and impatience pose problems on the weekend, when you should be especially cautious outdoors around water.

[Monday Sun sesquiquadrate Neptune, Venus quincunx Uranus; Monday (P)/Tuesday (E) Sun trine Jupiter, Mercury trine Chiron; Tuesday Venus trine Pluto, Venus sesquiquadrate Eris, Mercury quincunx Uranus, Sun semisquare Mars; Wednesday Mercury sextile Pluto, Saturn trine Neptune; Saturday Sun sesquiquadrate Chiron; Sunday Mars square Chiron, Sun opposite Eris]

Love is the only thing that we can carry with us when we go, and it makes the end so easy.
Louisa May Alcott

Moon in Libra • New Moon • Void 5:04 am (P), 8:04 am (E)
Moon enters Scorpio 5:07 pm (P), 8:07 pm (E)

15 MO 3 ★

An independent impulse supersedes the urge to cooperate. We prefer the middle of the road, but have to be flexible in the midst of extremes.

Moon in Scorpio • Void 7:24 pm (P), 10:24 pm (E)

16 TU 3 ★

Don't sweat the small stuff. There are bigger issues that require your intellect. You find a new dimension when you probe past a cursory look.

Moon Void in Scorpio
Moon enters Sagittarius 5:27 pm (P), 8:27 pm (E)

17 WE 2

Persistence keeps us on course all day. Tonight, distractions veer us in another direction, either seeking diversion or a break to recharge.

National Boss Day

Moon in Sagittarius

18 TH 2

You have a lot of energy at first but want a say in how to expend it. Later, you learn the hard way how limitations take a toll on possibilities.

Moon in Sagittarius • Void 1:28 pm (P), 4:28 pm (E)
Moon enters Capricorn 6:42 pm (P), 9:42 pm (E)

19 FR 4

A cheery, easy-going day is followed by a smooth evening that would be great for a fundraiser or being supportive and helpful in some way.

Moon in Capricorn

20 SA 1

The right words are hard to find for the difficult, perhaps shocking, message you must convey. Just spit it out rather than dodge with a white lie.

Sweetest Day

Moon in Capricorn • First Quarter Moon • Void 8:33 pm (P),
11:33 pm (E) • Moon enters Aquarius 10:03 pm (P)

21 SU 3

A morning chat seems to set things straight, but not for long. The scene shifts when obligations necessitate conceding to others' priorities.

OCTOBER 15-21 HIGHLIGHTS

"It's the economy" – both micro (your wealth) and macro (the collective fiscal health) – at center stage now. A long-term connection (exact Monday) that forces conversations about finances gets bumped up a notch by a quick nudge (exact Tuesday) from Venus, the main planet of money. Venus is also part of another more harmonious triangle early in the week pointing us in the direction of greater prosperity. Both are in effect at the New Moon Monday morning [5:04 am (P), 8:04 am (E)], stretching their influences through the coming four weeks. This is the lunar cycle in which US elections take place so of course a lot of the hype will be about economics. Individuals examine household budgets, aiming to trim. Likely targets are costs for education and communications (such as mobile and internet service).

Minds are sharp all month with an acute ability to understand assets, liabilities and trends. We engage in deep discussions about values and what's most important to us. The emphasis on material concerns doesn't necessarily equate to greed. We also feel a strong responsibility to help those who can't take care of themselves, possibly including relatives (see Star Pages for Oct. 10). There will no doubt

be people who care only about their piece of the pie. The main thrust of a Libra New Moon is to be other-oriented. But the Moon and Sun stand exactly across from rabble-rouser Eris in the opposite sign, Aries, which can be selfish. In some circles, there's a belief that "every man for himself" is nature's way of "survival of the fittest."

The week concludes with a First Quarter Moon Sunday night. The Moon at the final degree of Capricorn turns a cold shoulder to the best efforts toward meaningful liaisons of the Sun at the last degree of Libra. The balance of power in a relationship is apt to shift if agreement isn't reached to share control.

[Monday Mars trine Uranus, Jupiter sesquiquadrate Saturn, Venus quintile Ceres; Tuesday Mercury sextile Venus, Venus square Jupiter, Venus quintile North Node, Mars sesquiquadrate Eris; Tuesday (P)/Wednesday (E) Venus semisquare Saturn; Thursday Mercury sesquiquadrate Ceres; Saturday Mercury sesquiquadrate Uranus; Sunday North Node biquintile Ceres, Mercury semisquare Pluto]

NOVEMBER

SU	M	TU	W	T	F	S
					1	2	3
4	5	6	7	8	9	10
11	12	13	14	15	16	17
18	19	20	21	22	23	24
25	26	27	28	29	30	

A strong and mostly helpful triangle is in place for much of the fall (see Highlights below). Its peak comes at the Oct. 29 Full Moon, when the Sun and Moon join in the pattern.

October

A pleasant surprise starts the day with a good mood. Criticism or fussiness could spoil that this afternoon. Tonight we're upbeat again.

Sun enters Scorpio

Moon in Aquarius (P), Void in Capricorn (E)
Moon enters Aquarius 1:03 am (E)

★ **3** MO **22**

Approach all communication with care and caution. Problems can arise if you're cool and glib when it would be better to be warm and sensitive.

Moon in Aquarius • Void 6:28 pm (P), 9:28 pm (E)

2 TU **23**

It's a blessing to give or to receive (without a receiver, there can't be a giver). People go out of their way to help, sewing seeds of good karma.

United Nations Day

Moon Void in Aquarius
Moon enters Pisces 4:01 am (P), 7:01 am (E)

4 WE **24**

Know your limitations or you'll have to learn them the hard way. If someone requests more than you can offer, saying no is hard but may be best.

Moon in Pisces

★ **3** TH **25**

This is the day to ask for or grant favors. Everyone's caring and receptive, knowing the right words. Be on the alert for money-making ideas.

Eid al-Adha

Moon in Pisces • Void 8:05 am (P), 11:05 am (E)
Moon enters Aries 12:32 pm (P), 3:32 pm (E)

★ **4** FR **26**

If you're speedy with comments or decisions, you may need to reverse them just as quickly. Even with good intentions, harm might result.

Make A Difference Day

Moon in Aries • Void 6:33 pm (P), 9:33 pm (E)

3 SA **27**

A burst of energy early sets the pace for an active day. The question is: who chooses what to do? Compromises are likely needed to keep the peace.

Moon Void in Aries • Moon enters Taurus 11:16 pm (P)

★ **2** SU **28**

OCTOBER 22-28 HIGHLIGHTS

An ostensibly "nice" configuration – which may be a bit much – began a couple weeks ago and lasts well into November (see Star Pages for Oct. 10). It's a strong conduit for emotions. Maybe you've noticed greater sympathy and more nurturing, tears or expressions of feelings than usual, in others or yourself. If not, pay attention this week. The Sun, known for bringing conditions "to light" (into consciousness), enters Scorpio Monday. It joins the pattern throughout the week. The Moon accentuates the formation Wednesday, the best day to see the flood of feelings in action. Scorpio is associated with deep emotions, though often these are kept private or shared only in an intimate setting. Now they're brought out into the open. If that's painful, be consoled that the result will be a form of healing. Wounds don't improve by being covered up; they need air. In astrology, air equates with communication. The primary planet of communication, Mercury, helps us get in touch with and express our feelings this week. A connection it makes Thursday night (reinforced by the Moon Tuesday night and Saturday afternoon) repeats twice over the next six weeks (see Oct. 25 Star Pages). You'll have more chances to identify and transform what lies deep within your soul. Friday morning, gentle, assuaging planetary liaisons offer a good opportunity to address hurts with tenderness.

Intensity builds throughout the week as next Monday's Full Moon approaches. Adding to the increasing energy level, Sunday Mars (the planet of dynamism) lines up opposite Jupiter, the exaggerator (felt strongly when the Moon prods them Thursday morning). Mars is in the sign Jupiter rules, pushing us to do things in a big way or even over-do them. The ability to act effectively is compromised if you overload your schedule. Don't spread yourself too thin!

[Monday Sun enters Scorpio; Tuesday Sun trine Neptune, Sun sesquiquadrate Jupiter; Thursday Sun conjunct Saturn, Mercury sextile Venus; Thursday (P)/Friday (E) Venus sextile North Node, Mercury conjunct North Node/opposite South Node; Friday Sun trine Ceres; Saturday Sun trine Chiron; Sunday Mars opposite Jupiter, Venus enters Libra; Sunday (P) Mercury enters Sagittarius]

The penalty that good men pay for not being interested in politics is to be governed by men worse than themselves.

Plato

OCTOBER							NOVEMBER						
SU	M	TU	W	T	F	S	SU	M	TU	W	T	F	S
	1	2	3	4	5	6						1	2	3
7	8	9	10	11	12	13	4	5	6	7	8	9	10
14	15	16	17	18	19	20	11	12	13	14	15	16	17
21	22	23	24	25	26	27	18	19	20	21	22	23	24
28	29	30	31				25	26	27	28	29	30	

Moon in Taurus (P), Void in Aries (E) • Moon enters Taurus 2:16 am (E)
Full Moon (Snow Moon) • Void 2:03 pm (P), 5:03 pm (E)

29 MO 3 ★

It's time for some changes. Seek a happy middle between common sense and inspiration from your guides or Higher Self about your direction.

Moon Void in Taurus

30 TU 2

Your need for security is heightened but you're not sure who's reliable or shares your concerns. You may have to break out of your comfort zone.

Moon Void in Taurus
Moon enters Gemini 11:41 am (P), 2:41 pm (E)

31 WE 2 ★

The support or pay-off you'd thought safe to expect is not forthcoming. You have to dance to a different tune by first altering your mindset.

Halloween, Samhain, All Hallows' Eve

Moon in Gemini

01 TH 2 ★

Morning is frustrating; staccato pacing breaks the rhythm. Later someone's unexpected behavior results in amusement or encouragement.

All Saints' Day, Dia de los Muertos

Moon in Gemini • Void 2:23 am (P), 5:23 am (E)

02 FR 2

The day begins with grumpy or feisty comments triggering abrasive dialogue. Stand up for yourself. Tonight, telling your tale is cleansing.

All Souls' Day

Moon Void in Gemini
Moon enters Cancer 12:44 am (P), 3:44 am (E)

03 SA 2

Pleasantries abound early but erode before long if good manners are outweighed by pushy selfishness. A friendship could be in jeopardy.

Moon in Cancer • Void 1:38 am (PDT), 3:38 am (EST)

04 SU 1

Give yourself a good pep talk or get one from someone trustworthy. Otherwise it's easy to drown in sorrows and become your own worst enemy.

Daylight Saving Time ends

OCT. 29-NOVEMBER 04 HIGHLIGHTS

Sunsets come earlier and nights are longer as we head into the middle of autumn. The Full Moon [exact Monday at 12:51 pm (P), 3:51 pm (E)] illuminates the evening sky this week, perfect for cavorting on Halloween, the mid-fall holiday. It allows us to disguise ourselves and pretend, which is very Neptunian. Appropriately, a strong connection to Neptune (exact Monday) is emphasized by the Moon Wednesday afternoon. Acting a part can be cathartic and healing, which are also Neptunian experiences. What character will you unearth from your psyche this Halloween? Mexicans celebrate the "Day of the Dead," an apt name for the quintessential holiday in Scorpio, the sign associated with death and transformation. Right on cue, the Scorpio Sun links nicely Tuesday to the sign's ruling planet, Pluto, bringing us awareness of what we need to release.

Venus plays into the hands of Pluto's long-term bout with Uranus Thursday through Saturday; there may be shocks or barbs in relationships and finances. Venus in Libra doesn't like to fight but will if someone doesn't play fair. Venus also has a run-in with Ceres as the dwarf planet turns Retrograde Wednesday (more noticeable midday Tuesday when the Moon

jostles them). Just when you wish someone had your back, you have to look hard to find comfort. Mercury in optimistic Sagittarius (and still in harmony with Venus) could lift your spirits enough that you won't feel abandoned. It's about to turn Retrograde, though (next Tuesday) and is shoved around by Neptune, breeding doubt. Mars is in Sagittarius, too, in a grating tie to somber Saturn in Scorpio. Try as we might to make light of serious topics, we know that's just a coping mechanism. Luckily, Mars and Venus are in a special pattern beginning Thursday (see Star Pages) that helps lovers console one another. The Full Moon in Taurus is great for hugs, too. We'll all need some this week as feelings peak.

Sunday, set your clocks back one hour for the end of Daylight Saving Time.

[Monday (E) Mercury enters Sagittarius; Monday Mercury square Neptune; Tuesday Sun sextile Pluto; Wednesday Venus square Ceres, Ceres turns Retrograde; Thursday Mars semisquare Saturn, Mars quintile Neptune, Venus opposite Uranus; Friday Venus biquintile Neptune; Saturday Venus square Pluto; Sunday Venus quintile Mars; Sunday (P) Ceres trine Saturn]

DECEMBER

SU	M	TU	W	T	F	S
						1
2	3	4	5	6	7	8
9	10	11	12	13	14	15
16	17	18	19	20	21	22
23	24	25	26	27	28	29
30	31					

October-November

It helps to talk through any moodiness and see issues from another's viewpoint. Then examine goals, set intentions and plan your attack.

Guy Fawkes Day

Moon Void in Cancer
Moon enters Leo 11:40 am (PST), 2:40 pm (EST)

3 MO 05

By looking past personal issues to the bigger picture, people hope for brighter prospects. But the conflict of values makes many cynical.

Election Day (US)

Moon in Leo • Third Quarter Moon

MR ★ 2 TU 06

You're enthusiastic about what you can do but feel stymied by circumstances beyond your control, possibly involving others' resources.

Moon in Leo • Void 7:28 am (P), 10:28 am (E)
Moon enters Virgo 8:36 pm (P), 11:36 pm (E)

MR 2 WE 07

People are cautious and hesitant this morning when information is unclear or incorrect. Attitudes improve midday but wither by evening.

Moon in Virgo

MR 3 TH 08

Partners who poke holes in potentials and seesaw between expecting the best and dreading the worst should just appreciate what they have.

Moon in Virgo • Void 4:28 pm (P), 7:28 pm (E)

MR 3 FR 09

Keep your wits about you and tiptoe carefully amidst multiple karmic booby-traps. The key is to maintain equilibrium. A sense of humor helps.

Sadie Hawkins Day

Moon Void in Virgo • Moon enters Libra 1:36 am (P), 4:36 am (E)

MR ★ P 1 SA 10

It's hard to decide what to say. You want to make someone feel better. Revealing the truth won't do that, but concealing it isn't wise, either.

Veterans Day (US), Remembrance Day (Canada)

Moon in Libra • Void 9:14 pm (P)

MR ★ 1 SU 11

NOVEMBER 05-11 HIGHLIGHTS

Trouble is brewing on the home front. Someone may feel stifled or fed up with rules and restrictions. Another possibility is more physical: something in need of repair or replacement or an incident involving fire, electricity or garbage. A key domestic indicator, Ceres, in the sign of family or property matters, Cancer, is in range of creating a T-square with Uranus and Pluto. (The configuration is not exact until next May, but hints of difficulties to come are evident.) The Libra Moon expands the formation into an aggravating Grand Cross Saturday. Despite a desire for peace, strain might erupt into arguments. That day, the Sun begins participating in the melee, lasting into next week; ego and pride issues enter the fray.

Relationships are pretty smooth the first half of the week, mostly due to increased passion and empathy. The weekend is more trying for mates. Things look hopeful Thursday night but by Friday night, confusion and insecurity arise. We don't know what to believe as Neptune slows to a halt to change direction Sunday.

The biggest event of the week is Mercury turning Retrograde on Tuesday, which is election day in the US. In the past 50+ years, Mercury was Retrograde for three US Presidential elections. In a close, hotly contested election in 1960, voter fraud was evident in Illinois for both Kennedy's and Nixon's benefit. An alleged conspiracy between the Reagan campaign and Iran to hold American hostages until after the election helped defeat Jimmy Carter in 1980, though the vote was not close. The historic intrusion of the US Supreme Court into state's electoral affairs in the 2000 vote count controversy in Florida gave the White House to George W. Bush. In 2012, Mercury is slowed to a stop, turning Retrograde late in the day on Election Day. What kind of controversy will we encounter with this election?

[Monday (E) Ceres trine Saturn; Tuesday Mars trine Eris, Venus biquintile Chiron, Mercury turns Retrograde, Venus semisquare North Node; Wednesday Mars quintile Chiron; Friday Venus trine Jupiter, Venus sesquiquadrate Neptune; Saturday Sun sesquiquadrate Ceres; Saturday (P)/Sunday (E) Neptune turns Direct; Sunday Mercury semisquare Venus, Sun sesquiquadrate Uranus]

*Sad soul, take comfort, nor forget
that sunrise never failed us yet.*
Celia Layton Thaxter

OCTOBER						
SU	M	TU	W	T	F	S
	1	2	3	4	5	6
7	8	9	10	11	12	13
14	15	16	17	18	19	20
21	22	23	24	25	26	27
28	29	30	31			

NOVEMBER						
SU	M	TU	W	T	F	S
				1	2	3
4	5	6	7	8	9	10
11	12	13	14	15	16	17
18	19	20	21	22	23	24
25	26	27	28	29	30	

Moon in Libra, Void (P) • Void 12:14 am (E)
Moon enters Scorpio 3:11 am (P), 6:11 am (E)

12 MO 4 MR

Relief comes from putting old feelings to rest, perhaps using ritual.
Those in a damaging situation should lay down the law or withdraw.

Moon in Scorpio • Solar Eclipse New Moon

13 TU 1 ★ MR

See if you can do no harm nor be harmed by inequality or incivility,
avoid domination of or by a group, and believe without being gullible.

Moon in Scorpio • Void 2:40 am (P), 5:40 am (E)
Moon enters Sagittarius 2:53 am (P), 5:53 am (E)

14 WE 1 ★ MR

Resentment is self-destructive. Mend buried heartaches by exhuming
and re-examining them. Then apply forgiveness and acceptance.

Moon in Sagittarius

15 TH 2 ★ MR

A stand-off between rivals tests their mettle and pushes each to be stronger.
As long as ground rules are followed, a battle may be positive.

Al-Hijra/Muharram (Islamic New Year)

Moon in Sagittarius • Void 1:45 am (P), 4:45 am (E)
Moon enters Capricorn 2:37 am (P), 5:37 am (E)

16 FR 3 ★ MR

Attempts to institute improvements efficiently get interrupted and
a re-start might be required. Perhaps instructions need revision.

Moon in Capricorn • Void 9:55 pm (P)

17 SA 3 P MR

Reflect on your intentions and direction. Persistence is admirable but
not if inflated into an obsession. Tonight, refrain from arguments.

Moon in Capricorn, Void (P) • Void 12:55 am (E)
Moon enters Aquarius 4:11 am (P), 7:11 am (E)

18 SU 3 MR

People are congenial though a bit distant. Some do their own thing while
others join in group endeavors. But no one wants to be told what to do.

NOVEMBER 12-18 HIGHLIGHTS

In an ideal world, relationships would run smoothly. People would put themselves in others' shoes and strive to meet halfway in any conflicts. In reality, personal (even selfish) concerns trump cooperation and sharing, and competitive urges spur a desire to triumph rather than reach win-win solutions. Such difficulties are more prevalent when a planet in Libra is across from disruptive Eris in Aries. The Moon and Sun occupied that position at last month's New Moon (see Oct. 15-21 Highlights). Thursday Venus is in the hot seat, throwing partners into dilemmas that could have painful consequences. Chiron, equally famous for inflicting wounds or healing us from hurts, is in a rough link all year with Eris (see March 20 Star Pages), tangling Venus in its clutches Tuesday. In between, the Moon messes with all three on Wednesday, just as Chiron is extra potent changing direction. The goal is to combine independence and strength (the best Aries traits) with compassion and helpfulness (Pisces' gifts) to achieve the fairness and harmony aims of Libra. Saturn in a supportive connection to Chiron brings maturity and a sense of responsibility to the table.

Fortunately, we don't have to achieve an idyllic balance immediately –

it's probably impossible to! The presence of these factors at Tuesday's Solar Eclipse New Moon [2:09 pm (P), 5:09 pm (E)] widens their influence over the coming six months to several years. Also poised for an extended impact is a Mercury-Neptune tie (see Nov. 6 Star Pages) that could either cloud our vision with cock-eyed optimism or inspire us to communicate without judging. However, another factor at the New Moon points to a lot of pointless babbling. As for action, some may go too far in pushing their principles zealously, especially if religion's involved. This may affect either personal or international relations.

[Tuesday Chiron semisextile Uranus, Solar Eclipse New Moon, Venus sesquiquadrate Chiron, Mercury square Neptune; Tuesday (P)/Wednesday (E) Mercury re-enters Scorpio; Wednesday Sun semisquare Pluto, Chiron turns Direct; Thursday Venus opposite Eris, Saturn quincunx Uranus; Friday Saturn trine Chiron, Mars enters Capricorn; Saturday Mercury conjunct North Node, Mars sextile Neptune, Mercury conjunct Sun, Sun conjunct North Node, Mercury semisextile Venus]

DECEMBER

SU	M	TU	W	T	F	S
						1
2	3	4	5	6	7	8
9	10	11	12	13	14	15
16	17	18	19	20	21	22
23	24	25	26	27	28	29
30	31					

We're in another "eclipse season," with the greatest intensity Nov.13 to 28. Eclipses occur in pairs or trios about six months apart, providing the impulse for important beginnings and peaks.

Examine impulses before taking action. Avoid verbal or written commitments, if you can. Anything said today is quickly subject to revision.

Moon in Aquarius

MR 1 MO 19

Extending the benefit of the doubt will probably work out okay, but it's best to know people's history or motives. Don't be afraid to ask.

Moon in Aquarius • First Quarter Moon • Void 6:33 am (P), 9:33 am (E) • Moon enters Pisces 8:56 am (P), 11:56 am (E)

MR 3 TU 20

While you're busy giving someone the shirt off your back, be careful your pocket's not picked. It's your fault if you're generous to a fault.

Sun enters Sagittarius

Moon in Pisces • Void 10:33 pm (P)

MR ★ 2 WE 21

Everyone is more accident-prone or klutzy than usual, and most are in a bit of a mental fog today, too. Slow down and pay attention in all you do.

Thanksgiving (US)

Moon in Pisces, Void (P) • Void 1:33 am (E)
Moon enters Aries 5:13 pm (P), 8:13 pm (E)

MR 2 TH 22

Continue on alert. You may have to take care of a mishap from yesterday or comfort somebody who suffered one. This evening is OK for travel.

Moon in Aries • Void 5:36 pm (P), 8:36 pm (E)

MR 3 FR 23

Watch out for wise guys who like to stir up trouble and don't fall prey to their pranks. Take the upper hand or be the adult in the situation.

Ashura

Moon Void in Aries

MR 3 SA 24

It makes such a difference when love and support surround you. Wrongs are righted, hurts are healed and things just seem to fall into place.

Moon Void in Aries • Moon enters Taurus 4:19 am (P), 7:19 am (E)

MR 4 SU 25

NOVEMBER 19-25 HIGHLIGHTS

While you should always be careful around traffic – whether you're a pedestrian, driver, or bus or bike rider – this week take extra caution. The main planets related to ground transportation (Mercury) and speed (Mars) are in a difficult connection (exact Thursday) and both interact in rough ways with the volatile and potentially destructive Uranus-Pluto square. The danger begins Monday at the start of the busiest travel week of the year (due to Thanksgiving) and continues through next Tuesday. The worst times are this Monday evening, Thursday afternoon and night, early Friday morning and next Monday night to Tuesday morning. Plan your travel to avoid the roads at these times, if possible. Air travel is not as much of an issue, though there is a chance for a snag overnight Wednesday, especially from fog or wet weather. The same indicators that point to problems getting around can also mean trouble from thoughtless blurting, so watch your mouth, as well.

The Sun leaves Scorpio for Sagittarius Wednesday, which usually lifts moods. However, within hours Venus shifts from easy-going Libra into intense Scorpio. Some people will experience emotional vulnerability while others could undergo a healing of their feelings. Thursday Venus and the Sun interact with each other and both connect to Neptune, increasing psychic connections between lovers as well as fears about romance or finances. Over the long weekend, Venus joins the ongoing Grand Trine in water signs (see Oct. 10 Star Pages). It's time to address the solidity of relationships, especially Sunday when the Moon expands the pattern into a Kite formation. The Moon in Taurus is known for patience and warmth, providing a comfortable context for confirming commitment or finding commonality in what people consider most important to them.

[Monday Mercury semisquare Pluto; Monday (P)/Tuesday (E) Mars opposite Ceres; Tuesday Venus sesquiquadrate Jupiter; Wednesday Sun enters Sagittarius, Venus enters Scorpio; Wednesday (P)/ Thursday (E) Sun square Neptune; Thursday Venus trine Neptune, Venus semisextile Sun, Mercury sesquiquadrate Uranus, Mercury semisquare Mars; Friday Mars square Uranus, Venus trine Ceres, Mars sextile Chiron; Saturday Mars sextile Saturn; Sunday Venus trine Chiron]

Education consists mainly in what we have unlearned.

Mark Twain

	NOVEMBER							DECEMBER					
SU	M	TU	W	T	F	S	SU	M	TU	W	T	F	S
				1	2	3							1
4	5	6	7	8	9	10	2	3	4	5	6	7	8
11	12	13	14	15	16	17	9	10	11	12	13	14	15
18	19	20	21	22	23	24	16	17	18	19	20	21	22
25	26	27	28	29	30		23	24	25	26	27	28	29
							30	31					

Moon in Taurus • Void 4:58 pm (P), 7:58 pm (E)

26 MO 3 ★ MR

Things are wacky but with a little luck, not in such a bad way. Still, you might have to do some damage control tonight. Stick to your principles.

Moon Void in Taurus
Moon enters Gemini 4:59 pm (P), 7:59 pm (E)

27 TU 3

The force of habit is strong this morning when a new routine is sorely needed. This evening, people are so free-floating you can't pin them down.

Moon in Gemini • Lunar Eclipse Full Moon (Oak Moon)
Void 5:05 pm (P), 8:05 pm (E)

28 WE 2 ★

By yielding too much, you could allow pushy people to get their way. It works better to show them the mutual benefits of your desired approach.

Moon Void in Gemini

29 TH 3 ★

A superficial glance, especially in haste, underestimates the importance of a situation. Investing time shows respect and earns points.

Moon Void in Gemini
Moon enters Cancer 5:56 am (P), 8:56 am (E)

30 FR 3

Early on, feathers get ruffled in disputes about values, followed by inspiration that could be lucrative. A brief mix-up later spurs support.

Moon in Cancer • Void 10:56 pm (P)

01 SA 3

Tenderness and maternal-style nurturance abound and may be too touchy-feely for those who want to buckle down and focus on concrete goals.

AIDS Awareness Day

Moon in Cancer, Void (P) • Void 1:56 am (E)
Moon enters Leo 5:58 pm (P), 8:58 pm (E)

02 SU 1

To get family members comfortable so they'll open up about sensitive topics, make a game out of it. Once the dam breaks, a flood ensues.

First Sunday of Advent

NOV. 26-DEC. 02 HIGHLIGHTS

The theme of examining "the ties that bind" couples continues from last week. Besides a strong inclination toward being serious, there's also a desire to refresh any situation that's grown stale and to seek variety and stimulation. The answer may lie in a change of venue, a little trip either literally or figuratively (such as being transported into another world through music, poetry, fiction or a movie). A sense of comfort and security is reassuring but may not feed the hunger for newness. Feelings ride a high tide for days before and after the Lunar Eclipse Full Moon Wednesday [6:47 am (P), 9:47 am (E)]. Partnerships probably won't be split asunder; it's more like they need a breath of fresh air. How that's achieved may involve a bumpy path (beginning as soon as Monday). An abrupt revelation or turn of events sparks conversations showing where work needs to be done. There might be issues involving maturity, respect, and the reliability of what is said. This is not the time for the silent treatment. Turn to humor to cushion the process and be forgiving if words don't convey what the heart is trying to say. If a fight happens, there's plenty of passion for an exciting make-up!

The same factors that spell a bit of a trying time for lovers can also translate into ripples in finances. Since emotions factor strongly into market moves, look for bigger than usual ups or downs in the indexes this week, especially impacted by news from foreign corners. For the most part, the astrological indicators are more positive than negative so hopefully this means a spike. Sometimes Full Moons are crests. This one in Gemini should help stocks related to the communications industry (including computer technology). On a personal level, a home repair or generosity in helping those in need could tug you off your budget.

[Monday Sun trine Uranus, Jupiter biquintile Saturn, Sun square Chiron, Mercury turns Direct, Venus biquintile Jupiter, Venus conjunct Saturn; Tuesday Mars conjunct Pluto; Wednesday Sun sesquiquadrate Eris, Lunar Eclipse Full Moon, Venus sextile Pluto; Thursday Venus sextile Mars; Friday Mars semisquare North Node; Friday (P)/Saturday (E) Mercury sesquiquadrate Uranus; Saturday Ceres trine Neptune; Sunday Sun opposite Jupiter]

JANUARY

SU	M	TU	W	T	F	S
				1	2	3	4	5
6	7	8	9	10	11	12
13	14	15	16	17	18	19
20	21	22	23	24	25	26
27	28	29	30	31

November-December

We start the day stubborn and stand-offish. By evening, we open up, becoming jovial and more generous, yet still careful about money.

Moon in Leo

2 MO 03

A little harmless frenzy this morning is easily laughed off. Later, the tone is serious. What begins as a question can escalate into a fracas.

Moon in Leo • Void 2:09 pm (P), 5:09 pm (E)

★ 2 TU 04

Some lick their wounds from yesterday's upsets. Others burrow into work to ignore any pain. Tonight, assistance is available for the asking.

Moon Void in Leo • Moon enters Virgo 3:53 am (P), 6:53 am (E)

2 WE 05

There's plenty of energy to accomplish a lot and yet, still more needs to be done. Good teamwork helps. Don't hold back on what needs to be said.

Moon in Virgo • Third Quarter Moon

3 TH 06

Multi-tasking to juggle multiple requests is tempting but ineffective and draining as your drive droops. Social plans change last-minute.

Pearl Harbor Remembrance Day

Moon in Virgo • Void 2:37 am (P), 5:37 am (E)
Moon enters Libra 10:36 am (P), 1:36 pm (E)

1 FR 07

Something's off balance early, at the "too much" end of the scale. Later, we want to avoid anything remotely like work and just be entertained.

Moon in Libra • Void 4:38 pm (P), 7:38 pm (E)

2 SA 08

After an inconsiderate slap or a shallow dig, kind words bring a smile to your face and tenderness makes a positive difference in the day.

Hannukah begins

Moon Void in Libra
Moon enters Scorpio 1:52 pm (P), 4:52 pm (E)

3 SU 09

DECEMBER 03-09 HIGHLIGHTS

It's a light-weight week astrologically. We need to catch our breath after last week's eclipse, not that there won't be at least a little insanity. The planet of unpredictability (Uranus) is slowing to a stop, turning Direct next week. Whenever a planet is motionless, it wields more power from its position. In this case, it pushes against the degree of a potent Lunar Eclipse featuring Pluto on June 26, 2010. Don't be surprised if events now have some connection to what was going on at that time, either in your life or in the news. (Headlines then included G20 summit leaders discussing deficit reduction and a Supreme Court ruling that Chicago's ban on handguns was unconstitutional.) Friday Venus has a run-in with Uranus, provoked by the Moon that evening (as well as Tuesday morning), bringing bumps in romances and finances. Watch out for an urge to spend impulsively.

Intense discussions that could change your views on a subject are sparked by a Mercury-Pluto clash, exact Wednesday. They're aggravated by the Moon Tuesday evening and Saturday morning, additional times when hidden or repressed information might be uncovered. Mercury passes the North Node Thursday, prodding us to look down the road to see if we're on the right (or best) path. Ceres leaves the zero degree of Cancer Tuesday, backtracking into Gemini until next April (see Nov. 29 Star Pages). Attention turns to the cost and value of an education and what rewards are likely from expenditures on it. Thursday's Third Quarter pits the Moon in Virgo against the Sun in Sagittarius, catching us in the net of the perennial forest/trees dilemma. A Mars-Neptune scrape Friday, emphasized by the Moon Saturday afternoon, dissipates our energy or distracts us from our goals. The week concludes with a luscious link Sunday afternoon from the Scorpio Moon to Neptune in Pisces – perfect for a relaxing, restorative bath, nap or massage.

[Monday Venus sesquiquadrate Ceres; Tuesday Ceres re-enters Gemini; Wednesday Mercury semisquare Pluto; Thursday Mercury conjunct North Node; Friday Mars semisquare Neptune, Venus sesquiquadrate Uranus]

*Believe those who are seeking
the truth; doubt those who find it.*
Andre Gide

NOVEMBER						
SU	M	TU	W	T	F	S
				1	2	3
4	5	6	7	8	9	10
11	12	13	14	15	16	17
18	19	20	21	22	23	24
25	26	27	28	29	30	

DECEMBER						
SU	M	TU	W	T	F	S
						1
2	3	4	5	6	7	8
9	10	11	12	13	14	15
16	17	18	19	20	21	22
23	24	25	26	27	28	29
30	31					

Moon in Scorpio

10 MO 3 ★

A good day for research, investigation or checkbook reconciliation, but tough for eliciting sympathy. People are matter-of-fact and cool.

Human Rights Day

Moon in Scorpio • Void 5:09 am (P), 8:09 am (E)
Moon enters Sagittarius 2:23 pm (P), 5:23 pm (E)

11 TU 3

Connect with others in a deep, supportive way but avoid probing into personal business. Their answers may be disguised to protect a secret.

Moon in Sagittarius

12 WE 2

Morning is hectic with too much to do. As the day proceeds, we get in the driver's seat, take firm control of matters and show who's the boss.

Moon in Sagittarius • New Moon • Void 12:43 am (P), 3:43 am (E)
Moon enters Capricorn 1:44 pm (P), 4:44 pm (E)

13 TH 2 ★

Even if you think you're keeping a lid on it, smoldering anger or agitation is poised to erupt. Then you might have to confess and ask forgiveness.

Moon in Capricorn

14 FR 1

Optimism is fine, but don't gloss over the gravity of a situation in need of straightening or repair. An ingenious solution is possible.

Moon in Capricorn • Void 1:16 pm (P), 4:16 pm (E)
Moon enters Aquarius 1:54 pm (P), 4:54 pm (E)

15 SA 2 ★

Ambition is strong and competition could get ugly. Tough talk is probably only that but someone might go a step further, becoming physical.

Moon in Aquarius

16 SU 2

Finding the right words is hard. You could say too little or (more likely) too much. Don't over-think; trust instinct and speak from the heart.

DECEMBER 10-16 HIGHLIGHTS

The Sun has been in Sagittarius for a couple weeks but the other quick planets are bringing up the rear. Both pass through the final degree of Scorpio (often indicating a difficult push for change or a time of deep emotional release) and emerge into the usually cheery light of Sagittarius, Mercury on Monday and Venus on Saturday. However, the day after entering this buoyant sign, each immediately has a tough encounter with nebulous Neptune that could burst their balloon. The Moon adds discomfort to uncertainty Tuesday evening and waits until next Monday night to increase insecurity, unrealistic expectations or a sense of suffering about love or money matters. Those who try to clarify the direction of their relationships and/or finances Tuesday (as Venus passes the North Node) find it's quickly subject to change. This is the end of a lunar cycle, a time for disintegration, allowing us to be open to the next impulse.

The New Moon Thursday [12:43 am (P), 3:43 am (E)] just hours before Uranus resumes forward motion, has a restless, nervous feel to it. In Sagittarius, it inspires us to go where we have not gone before. However the ordinary bravado of this risk-loving sign is defused by an abrasive connection to Saturn; we want to be more certain. We can achieve important changes or improvements in the coming month but only by taking careful steps and looking well before leaping. Expect twists and turns along the way, courtesy of a Finger of God coming into play (see Star Pages for Dec. 20).

The weekend seems booby-trapped to snare us in a fight. From Friday night through Sunday, a chip on a shoulder or an impatient, disagreeable mood impedes conversation. One person might be flip when most everyone else is way too serious. The final straw Sunday night is a rebellious "see if I care" attitude. Things don't smooth over until the middle of next week.

[Monday Venus semisquare Pluto, Mercury re-enters Sagittarius; Tuesday Mercury square Neptune, Venus conjunct North Node; Wednesday (P)/ Thursday (E) Sun trine Eris; Thursday Uranus turns Direct, Mars semisquare Chiron; Friday Mercury trine Uranus, Sun semisquare Saturn, Mercury square Chiron; Saturday Mars square Eris, Mercury sesquiquadrate Eris, Venus enters Sagittarius; Sunday Mercury semisquare Mars, Venus square Neptune]

JANUARY

SU	M	TU	W	T	F	S
		1	2	3	4	5
6	7	8	9	10	11	12
13	14	15	16	17	18	19
20	21	22	23	24	25	26
27	28	29	30	31		

An important Finger of God between slow planets peaks Dec. 20 to Dec. 26 (see the Star Pages). It's punctuated by Venus on Dec. 22, a key time for realizations about relationships.

December

Though people are friendly and warm, something's lost in translation; we talk past each other instead of with one another. Tonight's a blur.

Moon in Aquarius • Void 10:13 am (P), 1:13 pm (E)
Moon enters Pisces 4:49 pm (P), 7:49 pm (E)

2 MO 17

In planning action steps toward your goals, you imagine you're able to do more than is realistic. Consider downsizing your expectations.

Moon in Pisces

2 TU 18

A vision of what can be sparks creativity, inspiring you to experiment, with productive results. Later, information overload is confusing.

Moon in Pisces • First Quarter Moon (P) • Void 9:20 pm (P)
Moon enters Aries 11:44 pm (P)

3 WE 19

Being quick and nimble helps you seize the moment but you might miss something subtle and sublime, or of more enduring value, along the way.

Moon in Aries (P), in Pisces (E) • First Quarter Moon (E)
Void 12:20 am (E) • Moon enters Aries 2:44 am (E)

★ 2 TH 20

Speak up! Your strength and independence may seem daunting to others but it feels better than acquiescing and pushes you to rise to the top.

Winter Solstice, Yule, Sun enters Capricorn, Mesoamerican Long Count Calendar begins Baktun 13

Moon in Aries

★ 1 FR 21

Calm self-assurance and belief in your mission help you make your point and shine in a respectful light. This evening's social plans take a turn.

Moon in Aries • Void 4:58 am (P), 7:58 am (E)
Moon enters Taurus 10:26 am (P), 1:26 pm (E)

★ 3 SA 22

Examining what's most important to you versus what others revere exposes a needed re-orientation. Be judicious without being judgmental.

Moon in Taurus

2 SU 23

DECEMBER 17-23 HIGHLIGHTS

The acerbic exchanges that put a damper on the end of last week continue as this week begins. Monday night may bring a misunderstanding between partners or a disagreement over principles. Hostilities come to a head midday Tuesday. People are especially sensitive to barbs then and may construe any comments as cutting. This is already a stressful time of year so be extra considerate. A friendlier mood arrives Wednesday, and Thursday brings some healing, though it takes effort. In the midst of this mildly improving atmosphere, the First Quarter Moon Wednesday night finds us flexible and reasonably accepting. Despite questioning, we at least try to be open-minded. However, we're not so lenient as to let selfishness or rude behavior slide without a comment. Troublemakers will pay the price by Friday night, when patience runs out.

Friday is the Winter Solstice long awaited (dreaded by some). The Long Count of the Mayan/Aztec calendar completes the thirteenth Baktun (period of 144,000 days, equivalent to 394.25 years) since their count began more than five thousand years ago. They start counting with Baktun Zero, so we're entering Baktun Thirteen. It's not the "end of time," but rather the beginning of a new era. Thirteen was a sacred number for the Mesoamericans so we should consider this auspicious. Fortunately, the aggravating interplay between planets accounting for recent friction subsides by the Solstice. It's replaced by a placating connection between the Sun and Neptune, cooling us off and calming us down. We're more inclined to excuse trespasses. The Moon in Aries could contribute a combative tone, though you can use its drive to sustain a high energy level, helping you be active rather than sluggish this winter. This weekend is a time to address imbalances or extremes by applying sage wisdom or common sense.

[Monday Mercury opposite Jupiter; Tuesday Sun opposite Ceres, Mars sesquiquadrate Jupiter, Mars sextile North Node; Wednesday Venus trine Uranus; Thursday Venus square Chiron, Jupiter quincunx Pluto; Friday Sun enters Capricorn, Venus sesquiquadrate Eris; Friday (P)/Saturday (E) Sun sextile Neptune; Saturday Jupiter quincunx Saturn, Venus opposite Jupiter; Sunday North Node semisquare Pluto]

The tragedy of old age is not that one is old, but that one is young.
Oscar Wilde

Moon in Taurus • Void 9:59 pm (P)
Moon enters Gemini 11:14 pm (P)

24 MO 3

Just put one foot in front of the other and trudge through this slightly crazy day. Have clear goals in sight and don't quit 'til you hit them.

Christmas Eve

Moon in Gemini (P), in Taurus (E) • Void 12:59 am (E)
Moon enters Gemini 2:14 am (E)

25 TU 2 ★

There's a palpable buzz in the air if not a downright din, possibly including thoughtless comments midday that are soon graciously excused.

Christmas

Moon in Gemini • Void 10:51 pm (P)

26 WE 4 ★

After some early grumbling, the day and evening are very pleasant. People regale with tales of triumph and pump one other up with compliments.

Boxing Day, Kwanzaa begins

Moon in Gemini, Void (P) • Void 1:51 am (E)
Moon enters Cancer 12:08 pm (P), 3:08 pm (E)

27 TH 1

Logic lapses this morning, then instincts prevail. Don't let a profusion of data obscure the salient points. Your third eye can pierce the fog.

Moon in Cancer • Full Moon (Wolf Moon)
Void 6:44 am (P), 9:44 am (E)

28 FR 2

Emotions crest and can't be suppressed. At least, they let you know where you stand. Channel the intensity into making your home more orderly.

Moon Void in Cancer • Moon enters Leo 11:46 pm (P)

29 SA 2 ★

Chaos runs amok this morning but you don't have to let it get the better of you. Later you can take charge and steer in your desired direction.

Moon in Leo (P), Void in Cancer (E)
Moon enters Leo 2:46 am (E)

30 SU 3

Impatience or excitement pushes you to do more and act quickly, adding your own imprint. Slow down a little. You want to be proud of the outcome.

DECEMBER 24-30 HIGHLIGHTS

Usually there's a big rush as we approach the Christmas holiday, followed by a lull afterward. Since energy builds ahead of a Full Moon, this year there may not be that relaxed feeling in the vacation week for schools and many in the workforce. Last-minute shoppers midday Monday will find great deals in the midst of the frenzied hubbub. Early-birds will make some strange choices but oddly, those will be acceptable the next day. Mars, the planet of action and energy, is at the final degree of hardworking Capricorn Monday night, assisted by the Moon at the end of persistent Taurus. Those who waited to the last minute to get everything ready can burn the midnight oil and accomplish the task, at the price of some grogginess Tuesday morning. That evening, a jovial influence lightens the mood even if there's a clash about who's top dog. Outspoken comments are seen as refreshing and amusing. People are accepted when they display their individuality thanks to Mars entering Aquarius, though there might be a small, brief repercussion early Wednesday. The best time of the week is Wednesday afternoon into evening (with a similar refrain Sunday), excellent for examining goals, putting forth proposals and suggesting improvements.

Though the Winter Solstice moment managed to narrowly avoid a choking grasp from the Uranus-Pluto square, this week's Full Moon [Friday 2:22 am (P), 5:22 am (E)] is snagged in its trap. While you may stoically insist you're on track to handle what seems to be out of control (or even unmanageable), the little voice inside is quite concerned and uncomfortable. Fight the urge to act impulsively; doing so will not get you closer to your goals. Arm yourself with as much data as you need for an informed decision and then stick to a smart plan (with some flexibility built in). There's bound to be an unexpected detour but it's quite possible you can implement your ideas.

[Tuesday Mars enters Aquarius, Sun square Uranus, Mercury trine Eris; Wednesday Saturn sextile Pluto, Sun sextile Chiron; Thursday Mercury semisquare Saturn, Mercury opposite Ceres; Friday Ceres sesquiquadrate Saturn; Saturday Sun quincunx Jupiter, Sun semisquare North Node; Sunday Sun conjunct Pluto, Sun sextile Saturn]

FEBRUARY

SU	M	TU	W	T	F	S
					1	2
3	4	5	6	7	8	9
10	11	12	13	14	15	16
17	18	19	20	21	22	23
24	25	26	27	28		

December-January

2012-2013

Spontaneity and fun are on the docket! Be flexible: there may be a last-minute change in plans. Be on the lookout for some big news to end the year.

New Year's Eve

Moon in Leo • Void 1:53 pm (P), 4:53 pm (E)

★ **3** MO **31**

An infusion of inspiration and creativity begs to be put to practical use, perhaps in pursuit of a favorite hobby or visualizing future plans.

New Year's Day

Moon Void in Leo
Moon enters Virgo 9:36 am (P), 12:36 pm (E)

3 TU **01**

Honor awaits those who take advantage of an opportunity to show their abilities and shine, especially if doing so makes a difference in some way.

Moon in Virgo

4 WE **02**

Interruptions break the flow of your work. People may disappoint you if you rely on them for information, cooperation or support. Be firm.

Moon in Virgo • Void 4:16 am (P), 7:16 am (E)
Moon enters Libra 5:12 pm (P), 8:12 pm (E)

1 TH **03**

Get busy early: brilliant ideas emerge in a burst of activity that could benefit many. Later, walls go up, blocking effective collaboration.

Moon in Libra • Third Quarter Moon

P **2** FR **04**

If you set boundaries politely when someone wants all the attention this morning, you can turn a situation around. Later, everyone gets along.

Moon in Libra • Void 3:14 pm (P), 6:14 pm (E)
Moon enters Scorpio 10:10 pm (P)

★ **2** SA **05**

The power of thought to affect what manifests is evident today. You achieve what you believe, for good or ill. Therefore, picture only the best.

Epiphany, Three Kings Day

Moon in Scorpio (P), Void in Libra (E)
Moon enters Scorpio 1:10 am (E)

3 SU **06**

DEC. 31,-JAN. 06, 2013 HIGHLIGHTS

We made it through 2012 – that's something to celebrate! The mood is festive New Year's Eve with the Moon in Leo and an "anything goes" freewheeling Mars-Uranus link. People will really let loose. Although Mercury enters Capricorn that morning (ordinarily an influence that zips lips), an overnight link to Neptune loosens the grip. When inhibitions lift, secrets may spill out. The leak could continue into the afternoon of New Year's Day, especially if confiding is helpful in some way. Then it's back to work or school for most people Wednesday, when the Virgo Moon puts us in a buckle-down-to-business mood. It's likely to be the most productive time of the week, particularly in the morning, a striking contrast to Thursday, when the Moon is Void all day. Griping, nagging and fault-finding make it hard to get along then.

Friday morning, communication and cooperation abound and a high level of energy is at hand, in need of a focus. Without a goal, an opportunity for accomplishment could dissipate into idle conversation. That evening, harmony is hard to come by and it takes restraint to avoid an argument. Although the Third Quarter Moon Friday night is in approachable Libra, it grates against the cold shoulder of the Sun in Capricorn; people may

be stand-offish or brusque. A better time to socialize is Saturday evening, when the Moon is still in Libra and salutes Venus nicely. A serious tone ensues Sunday with the Moon in Scorpio. Mercury joins Pluto for the last hurrah of the current Finger of God (see Jan. 5, 2013 Star Pages). Discussions go to the heart of the matter and confidentiality may be required. Respect and integrity create an atmosphere for laying one's soul bare. Still, some people may eschew exposure, due either to fear or simply evasiveness (a tentative Sun-Neptune connection is the culprit). But digging deep can unearth an important treasure.

[Monday Mercury enters Capricorn, Venus semisquare Mars, Mars sextile Uranus; Monday (P)/Tuesday (E) Mercury sextile Neptune; Wednesday Venus trine Eris; Thursday Mercury square Uranus, Venus opposite Ceres; Friday Mars trine Jupiter, Mercury sextile Chiron, Venus semisquare Saturn, Mars sesquiquadrate Ceres; Saturday Mercury quincunx Jupiter, Mercury semisquare North Node; Sunday Sun semisquare Neptune, Mercury conjunct Pluto, Mercury sextile Saturn]

2012 On a Page

Janet's Plan-its™

Dates based on North American time zones. May differ from calendars using Greenwich Mean Time.

AR	Aries
TA	Taurus
GE	Gemini
CN	Cancer
LE	Leo
VI	Virgo
LI	Libra
SC	Scorpio
SG	Sagittarius
CP	Capricorn
AQ	Aquarius
PI	Pisces

RETROGRADE MOTION

As we spin, the signs along the zodiac belt and the planets appear to move east to west hour by hour. But over time, the planets move through the signs west to east. The Moon takes two to three days to traverse a sign while Pluto takes over a decade! Each planet (other than the Sun or Moon) appears to stop and reverse its direction from time to time. This is an optical illusion called "Retrograde" motion. Later, it stops a second time and resumes forward (Direct) motion. It hangs out longer at the degrees of these stopping points, called "stations." When that planet, or even another planet, later makes connections ("aspects") to the station degrees, issues that emerged during that Retrograde period are re-visited. Matters associated with the planet are more difficult during the Retrograde phase and are more intense for a few days around the stations.

Planets move through the Retrograde range three times. First they proceed forward through the range of degrees where the backtracking will occur. This is called the entry "shadow" (shaded on the graph). Next, they back up over that degree range in the Retrograde portion of the cycle (marked in black on the graph). Finally, they go forward again through the backtracking range in the exit "shadow" (shaded). Related events can occur during these three phases. We don't feel the effect of the shadows as much as we do the Retrograde itself, but we often sense the slow-down at the stations.

Many people notice the Retrograde of Mercury since it's linked to mix-ups in all forms of communication and local transportation. Anything begun then (or in the entry shadow) is subject to mistakes or revisions. A safer time for contracts, major decisions or beginning new activities is when Mercury is not in the entry shadow or Retrograde. There's less likelihood for revision later for activities initiated during the exit shadow.

Looking at the 2012 Retrograde chart, you can see there is usually one planet (or more) in Retrograde motion. Shadows are always in progress (which is typical). Times of "least resistance" are when no planets are Retrograde, only three weeks: 1/1-1/22. Just one planet is Retrograde 1/23-2/6. After that, two or three are Retrograde until 5/14. The rest of the year, three or more are Retrograde, the most being six 7/18-8/8, 10/31-11/5 and 11/12-11/14, and seven: 11/6-11/11. Progress is most impeded then. (Note: these numbers include Eris, not shown on the bar chart.)

MOON GROOVES

The degree of New and Full Moons repeats for a period of about six months, moving through consecutive signs. (I coined the term "moon groove" for this phenomenon.) For the next six months or so, the degree of each New and Full Moon decreases one or two degrees each month until another groove ensues. This pattern doesn't conform to a calendar year, so you only can see part of it on the 2012 list.

New Moons occur at about 2° of signs from Nov. 2011 through March 2012. Full Moons occur at about 18° of the signs from Oct. 2011 to March 2012. In the next groove, New Moons occur at 21° from Nov. 2012 until March 2013 and Full Moons are at about 6-7° from Sept. 2012 through April 2013.

If you have a planet in your birth chart at a moon groove degree, it receives extra attention during a groove period. If it's accentuated by New Moons, take new action in the area of your life represented by that planet. If Full Moons spotlight your natal planet, matters culminate in a big way over several months regarding the affairs of that planet. In interpreting effects, consider your birth planet's sign, house and aspects. If a New or Full Moon is on your birthday, that's important! If it falls within the period of a moon groove, the emphasis will likely affect you throughout the entire moon groove time frame.

Read more about Moon cycles in Using This Planner (p. 2), and Lunar Phases (p. 90).

● New Moon   ○ Full Moon   Ⓔ Eclipse   **B** Shadow begins   **R** Retrograde   **D** Direct   **E** Shadow ends

2012 Janet's Plan-its™ On a Page

	MERCURY	VENUS	MARS	CERES	JUPITER	SATURN	CHIRON	URANUS	NEPTUNE	PLUTO	MOON PHASES
	D 12/13/11, 3°51' SG		B 11/18/11, 3°41' VI	D 11/6/11, 16°24' PI	D 12/25/11, 0°22' TA	B 11/4/11, 22°46' LI	D 11/10/11, 0°39' PI	D 12/10/11, 0°39' AR	B 11/9/11, 28°8' AQ	B 12/21/11, 6°57' CP	(E) = ECLIPSE
JANUARY	E 1/1, 20°07' SG		R 1/23, 23°6' VI	E 1/21, 0°40' AR						(next R shadow); E 1/5, 7°30' CP (prior R shadow)	Full 1/9, 18°26' CN; New 1/23, 2°42' AQ
FEBRUARY	B 2/27, 23°50' PI					R 2/7, 29°30' LI	B 2/21, 4°59' PI (next R shadow)		B 2/13, 0°21' PI (next R shadow); E 2/28, 0°56' PI		Full 2/7, 18°32' LE; New 2/21, 2°42' PI
MARCH	R 3/12, 6°49' AR				E 3/17, 10°21' TA		E 2/28, 5°29' PI (prior R shadow)	E 3/25, 4°34' AR; B 3/26, 4°36' AR	(prior R shadow)		Full 3/8, 18°13' VI; New 3/22, 2°22' AR
APRIL	D 4/4, 23°50' PI; E 4/23, 6°49' AR	B 4/12, 7°29' GE	D 4/13, 3°41' VI							R 4/10, 9°34' CP	Full 4/6, 17°23' LI; New 4/21, 1°35' TA
MAY		R 5/15, 23°59' GE									Full 5/5, 16°1' SC; New 5/20, 0°21' GE E
JUNE	B 6/28, 1°25' LE	D 6/27, 7°29' GE	E 6/19, 23°6' VI			D 6/25, 22°46' LI	R 6/12, 9°45' PI		R 6/4, 3°9' PI		Full 6/4, 14°14' SG E; New 6/19, 28°43' GE
JULY	R 7/14, 12°32' LE	E 7/31, 23°59' GE			B 7/10, 6°20' GE			R 7/13, 8°32' AR			Full 7/3, 12°14' CP; New 7/19, 26°55' CN
AUGUST	D 8/8, 1°25' LE; E 8/22, 12°32' LE			B 8/18, 19°45' GE							Full 8/1, 10°15' AQ; New 8/17, 25°8' LE; Full 8/31, 8°34' PI
SEPTEMBER										D 9/18, 6°57' CP	New 9/15, 23°37' VI; Full 9/29, 7°22' AR
OCTOBER	B 10/18, 18°10' SC			R 10/31, 3°43' CN	R 10/4, 16°23' GE	E 10/1, 29°30' LI					New 10/15, 22°32' LI; Full 10/29, 6°48' TA
NOVEMBER	R 11/06, 4°18' SG; D 11/26, 18°10' SC					B 11/14, 4°49' SC	D 11/14, 4°59' PI		D 11/11, 0°21' PI	B 12/22, 8°59' CP	New 11/13, 21°57' SC E; Full 11/28, 6°47' GE E
DECEMBER	E 12/14, 4°18' SG							D 12/13, 4°36' AR		(next R shadow); E 1/7/13, 9°34' CP (prior R shadow)	New 12/13, 21°45' SG; Full 12/28, 7°6' CN
			D 2/4/13, 19°45' GE	D 1/30/13, 6°20' GE		R 2/18/13, 11°32' SC	E 3/5/13, 9°45' PI	E 3/29/13, 8°32' AR	E 3/1/13, 3°9' PI		

NOTE: The shadows of Chiron, Neptune and Pluto can overlap, creating a brief double shadow [darker shading]. Eris begins 2012 Retrograde, turning Direct 1/9 at 21°23' AR. It has an overlapping shadow from 3/1 to 5/26, turning Retrograde 7/18 at 22°43' AR. It next turns Direct 1/8/13 at 21°37' AR. It doesn't make much forward progress in a year!

How to Read an Ephemeris

Components of the Ephemeris

An ephemeris (eh fem' er iss) is a reference book showing precisely when certain celestial phenomena occur. Janet's Plan-its weekly Highlights and Star Pages list a lot of this data so you only need these pages if you want to explore astrology at a deeper level or identify when influences will impact your individual chart. See Making It Personal (p. 4).

Check the Keywords (p. 98) to see the symbols for the planets, signs, aspects and lunar phases. (NOTE: this ephemeris uses a different symbol for Pluto: ♇.) The time listed is calculated for Greenwich Mean Time (GMT), the worldwide standard in England. To convert to your time zone, subtract 4 hours for Atlantic, 5 hours for Eastern, 6 for Central, 7 for Mountain and 8 for Pacific. During Daylight Saving Time, subtract one hour <u>less</u>.

The twelve equal signs of the zodiac are 30 degrees each, measured in celestial "longitude." The longitude table for each month has columns for various celestial factors and a row for each day. (You can ignore the "Sid. Time" column unless you're calculating a chart "from scratch.") A position is listed in this order: degree, space, minute (1/60th of a degree) and in the case of the Sun and Moon, the second (1/60th of a minute). These are measurements in space, not to be confused with clock time. The minutes (other than for the Sun and Moon) use a decimal fraction. The Moon moves so quickly it's listed at both midnight (0 hr) and noon. The other planets' positions are listed at midnight GMT. When planets are Retrograde as a month begins, the second line of the month says R. The column is shaded when the planet is Retrograde and a D shows the day it turns Direct. The position is also listed for the Moon's North Node. (The South Node is always the same degree and minutes of the opposite sign.) The table shows its "true" position, which alternates between Retrograde (normal for it) and Direct. Many astrologers only use the Mean (average) position for the Nodes (see below), which is always Retrograde.

The Star Pages tell you the day a planet enters a sign. The ephemeris shows the exact minute in the "planet ingress" list at the bottom. A space separates the two months that share the page. The "Astro Data" column on the left tells you when planets turn Retrograde (R) or Direct (D) and when two outer planets have an aspect. The degrees of these phenomena are not listed here, but you can "ballpark" them from the row for the applicable date. (You can ignore the items showing when planets rise above (N) or below (S) the "celestial equator," the middle of the zodiac path.)

The "Last Aspect" and "☽ Ingress" columns list the time that the Moon makes its last aspect in a sign, becoming Void of Course (see Using This Planner, p. 2) and when it enters the next sign, ending the Void period. Janet's Plan-its™ daily entries tell the Void and ingress times. Here you can see the Moon's last aspect, an influence that continues throughout the Void period. The "☽ Phases & Eclipses" box lists the main phases of the Moon: New, First Quarter, Full and Last Quarter. First it states the day of the month, then the time, then the phase, and last the zodiac degree, sign and minutes where it occurs. New and Full Moons that aspect anything in your chart within a couple of degrees can have a big influence for you (see 2012 On a Page, p. 60).

A second "Astro Data" box on the right has information you may not need, like the SVP (related to Indian astrology) and the Julian Day (number of days since the century began). It also lists some useful data: the zodiacal longitude on the first of the month for Eris (the new planet out past Pluto) and the asteroids Pallas Athena, Juno, Chiron and Vesta, along with the Mean (average) position of the Moon's North Node.

Relating the Ephemeris to YOUR Chart

Now that you're familiar with the types of information in the ephemeris, how do you figure out when planets affect YOU? Look for aspects to your birth chart. These occur when a moving ("transiting") planet reaches the same degree as one of your natal planets. To figure out the type of aspect, you'll need to look at the order of the signs in the zodiac, from Aries to Pisces. The aspect depends on the sign of the transiting planet relative to the natal planet: same sign = conjunction; the sign immediately before or after = semisextile; 2 signs before or after = sextile; 3 signs before or after = square; 4 signs before or after = trine; 5 signs before or after = quincunx; 6 signs away = opposition. Another type of aspect occurs when the transiting planet is 1-1/2 signs before or after (semisquare) or 4-1/2 signs before or after (sesquiquadrate). These are harder to spot. Allow up to five degrees leeway (the astrological term is "orb"), although the closer to exact, the stronger the influence.

For example, look at your birthday. The degree of the Sun is the same every year on that date (within a degree). Now you can look for other dates in the year when a planet goes through the same degree of the same sign and you'll know that planet is activating your Sun's potentials, strengthening or adding to how you express your purpose and intentions. If any planet is within 5 degrees of a sign three or six signs away, your Sun is receiving a square or an opposition, and that time frame should hold challenges for you personally; you may not get the glory you deserve around then or be able to wield your usual influence. This same process can be applied to any planet in your chart. Aspects from transiting planets amplify what your natal planet signifies by its sign and house positions and its natal aspects. If the transiting aspect is a helpful one, the outcome should be positive with a smooth experience. If the aspect is a difficult one, then your experience is likely to be more stressful or require you to work harder to obtain a happy result.

Find the planetary stations (or see the graph on 2012 On a Page) and check if any of the planets change direction in an aspect to anything in your chart. If so, you're apt to experience a slow-down in the activities associated with your natal planet when the transit stations. The nature of the transiting planet describes the pressures applying to your life and the type of aspect hints as to whether the experience will be pleasant or trying. For instance, if you receive a square from stationing Saturn, obstacles will slow your progress in the area(s) associated with the receiving planet. If you receive a trine from Jupiter, your path should be nearly bump-free for the part(s) of your life that Jupiter affects. Be sure to look for your natal house starting with the sign that your receiving planet rules. Thus if your Mars receives an aspect, look at your house that starts with Aries. The Keyword list includes sign rulers.

You can use these principles to assess your personal impact from the year's astrological phenomena, noted chronologically in the Star Pages (p. 72) and sorted by zodiac degree on the All Star List (p. 70).

Ephemeris pages reproduced by permission of the publisher: Starcrafts, LLC, 334-A Calef Hwy., Epping, NH 03042. astrocom.com & starcraftspublishing.com

LONGITUDE — January 2012

Day	Sid.Time	☉	0 hr ☽	Noon ☽	True ☊	☿	♀	♂	⚳	♃	♄	♅	♆	♇
1 Su	6 40 16	9♑57 30	7♈06 50	13♈04 58	13♐58.7	19♐50.0	13♒49.4	20♍06.8	24♓33.7	0♉25.7	28♎17.4	0♈50.6	28♒53.3	7♑19.4
2 M	6 44 12	10 58 39	19 01 20	24 56 34	13D 59.0	21 10.9	15 03.0	20 21.1	24 49.6	0 27.1	28 21.1	0 51.8	28 55.0	7 21.6
3 Tu	6 48 09	11 59 48	0♉51 17	6♉46 06	14 00.2	22 32.8	16 16.5	20 34.8	25 05.7	0 28.7	28 24.7	0 52.9	28 56.7	7 23.7
4 W	6 52 05	13 00 57	12 41 38	18 38 27	14 02.0	23 55.8	17 30.1	20 48.0	25 21.9	0 30.5	28 28.3	0 54.2	28 58.4	7 25.8
5 Th	6 56 02	14 02 05	24 37 07	0♊38 07	14 03.9	25 19.7	18 43.5	21 00.7	25 38.4	0 32.5	28 31.7	0 55.5	29 00.1	7 28.0
6 F	6 59 58	15 03 14	6♊41 55	12 48 56	14R 05.1	26 44.5	19 57.0	21 12.8	25 55.0	0 34.7	28 35.1	0 56.8	29 01.8	7 30.1
7 Sa	7 03 55	16 04 22	18 59 30	25 13 54	14 05.3	28 10.0	21 10.3	21 24.4	26 11.8	0 37.1	28 38.4	0 58.2	29 03.6	7 32.2
8 Su	7 07 51	17 05 30	1♋32 20	7♋54 57	14 03.9	29 36.3	22 23.7	21 35.4	26 28.7	0 39.7	28 41.6	0 59.6	29 05.4	7 34.4
9 M	7 11 48	18 06 38	14 21 47	20 52 49	14 00.7	1♑03.2	23 36.9	21 45.9	26 45.9	0 42.5	28 44.7	1 01.1	29 07.2	7 36.5
10 Tu	7 15 45	19 07 45	27 27 59	4♌07 06	13 56.0	2 30.8	24 50.1	21 55.8	27 03.1	0 45.4	28 47.7	1 02.6	29 09.1	7 38.6
11 W	7 19 41	20 08 53	10♌49 57	17 36 16	13 50.1	3 59.1	26 03.3	22 05.0	27 20.6	0 48.6	28 50.6	1 04.1	29 10.9	7 40.7
12 Th	7 23 38	21 10 00	24 25 44	1♍18 01	13 43.6	5 27.9	27 16.4	22 13.7	27 38.2	0 52.0	28 53.4	1 05.8	29 12.8	7 42.8
13 F	7 27 34	22 11 06	8♍12 46	15 09 39	13 37.5	6 57.2	28 29.4	22 21.7	27 55.9	0 55.6	28 56.1	1 07.4	29 14.7	7 44.9
14 Sa	7 31 31	23 12 13	22 08 20	29 08 30	13 32.5	8 27.1	29 42.4	22 29.1	28 13.8	0 59.4	28 58.7	1 09.1	29 16.6	7 47.0
15 Su	7 35 27	24 13 20	6♎09 53	13♎12 14	13 29.1	9 57.6	0♓55.3	22 35.9	28 31.8	1 03.3	29 01.2	1 10.9	29 18.5	7 49.1
16 M	7 39 24	25 14 26	20 15 21	27 19 00	13D 27.6	11 28.6	2 08.2	22 42.0	28 50.0	1 07.5	29 03.6	1 12.7	29 20.5	7 51.1
17 Tu	7 43 20	26 15 33	4♏23 03	11♏27 18	13 27.7	13 00.2	3 21.0	22 47.4	29 08.4	1 11.8	29 05.9	1 14.5	29 22.5	7 53.2
18 W	7 47 17	27 16 39	18 31 37	25 35 48	13 28.9	14 32.2	4 33.7	22 52.1	29 26.8	1 16.3	29 08.1	1 16.4	29 24.4	7 55.3
19 Th	7 51 14	28 17 45	2♐39 39	9♐42 56	13R 30.2	16 04.8	5 46.4	22 56.2	29 45.5	1 21.1	29 10.2	1 18.3	29 26.5	7 57.3
20 F	7 55 10	29 18 51	16 45 22	23 46 38	13 30.5	17 38.0	6 59.0	22 59.5	0♈04.2	1 26.0	29 12.2	1 20.3	29 28.5	7 59.3
21 Sa	7 59 07	0♒19 57	0♑46 23	7♑44 13	13 29.1	19 11.7	8 11.5	23 02.1	0 23.1	1 31.0	29 14.1	1 22.3	29 30.5	8 01.4
22 Su	8 03 03	1 21 02	14 39 44	21 32 31	13 25.4	20 46.0	9 24.0	23 04.0	0 42.1	1 36.3	29 15.9	1 24.3	29 32.6	8 03.4
23 M	8 07 00	2 22 06	28 22 08	5♒08 12	13 19.3	22 20.8	10 36.4	23 05.2	1 01.3	1 41.7	29 17.6	1 26.4	29 34.6	8 05.4
24 Tu	8 10 56	3 23 10	11♒50 22	18 28 20	13 11.2	23 56.2	11 48.7	23R 05.6	1 20.6	1 47.4	29 19.2	1 28.6	29 36.7	8 07.4
25 W	8 14 53	4 24 13	25 01 53	1♓30 52	13 01.7	25 32.1	13 01.0	23 05.2	1 40.0	1 53.2	29 20.7	1 30.7	29 38.8	8 09.3
26 Th	8 18 50	5 25 15	7♓55 15	14 15 05	12 51.9	27 08.7	14 13.1	23 04.1	1 59.5	1 59.1	29 22.1	1 32.9	29 40.9	8 11.3
27 F	8 22 46	6 26 16	20 30 29	26 41 41	12 42.8	28 45.9	15 25.2	23 02.2	2 19.2	2 05.3	29 23.4	1 35.2	29 43.1	8 13.2
28 Sa	8 26 43	7 27 16	2♈49 00	8♈52 50	12 35.2	0♒23.7	16 37.2	22 59.6	2 38.9	2 11.6	29 24.5	1 37.5	29 45.2	8 15.2
29 Su	8 30 39	8 28 14	14 53 39	20 51 58	12 29.8	2 02.2	17 49.0	22 56.2	2 58.8	2 18.1	29 25.6	1 39.8	29 47.3	8 17.1
30 M	8 34 36	9 29 12	26 48 21	2♉43 26	12 26.6	3 41.3	19 00.8	22 51.9	3 18.8	2 24.7	29 26.6	1 42.2	29 49.5	8 19.0
31 Tu	8 38 32	10 30 09	8♉37 52	14 32 18	12D 25.6	5 21.1	20 12.5	22 47.0	3 38.9	2 31.5	29 27.4	1 44.6	29 51.7	8 20.9

LONGITUDE — February 2012

Day	Sid.Time	☉	0 hr ☽	Noon ☽	True ☊	☿	♀	♂	⚳	♃	♄	♅	♆	♇
1 W	8 42 29	11♒31 04	20♉27 26	26♉23 56	12♐25.9	7♒01.5	21♓24.1	22♍41.2	3♈59.1	2♉38.5	29♎28.2	1♈47.0	29♒53.9	8♑22.8
2 Th	8 46 25	12 31 58	2♊22 29	8♊23 45	12R 26.8	8 42.7	22 35.6	22R 34.6	4 19.5	2 45.6	29 28.8	1 49.5	29 56.0	8 24.6
3 F	8 50 22	13 32 51	14 28 21	20 36 51	12 27.1	10 24.6	23 47.0	22 27.3	4 39.9	2 52.9	29 29.4	1 52.0	29 58.2	8 26.5
4 Sa	8 54 19	14 33 42	26 49 46	3♋07 34	12 26.0	12 07.2	24 58.3	22 19.1	5 00.4	3 00.3	29 29.8	1 54.6	0♓00.5	8 28.3
5 Su	8 58 15	15 34 32	9♋30 37	15 59 09	12 22.6	13 50.5	26 09.5	22 10.2	5 21.0	3 07.9	29 30.1	1 57.1	0 02.7	8 30.1
6 M	9 02 12	16 35 21	22 33 20	29 13 10	12 16.7	15 34.6	27 20.5	22 00.5	5 41.8	3 15.7	29 30.3	1 59.8	0 04.9	8 31.9
7 Tu	9 06 08	17 36 09	5♌58 33	12♌49 13	12 08.2	17 19.4	28 31.5	21 50.0	6 02.6	3 23.6	29R 30.5	2 02.4	0 07.1	8 33.6
8 W	9 10 05	18 36 55	19 44 48	26 44 48	11 57.8	19 04.9	29 42.3	21 38.7	6 23.5	3 31.6	29 30.5	2 05.1	0 09.4	8 35.4
9 Th	9 14 01	19 37 40	3♍48 36	10♍55 31	11 46.4	20 51.2	0♈53.0	21 26.7	6 44.5	3 39.8	29 30.4	2 07.8	0 11.6	8 37.1
10 F	9 17 58	20 38 24	18 04 48	25 15 43	11 35.4	22 38.1	2 03.5	21 13.9	7 05.6	3 48.1	29 30.2	2 10.5	0 13.9	8 38.8
11 Sa	9 21 54	21 39 06	2♎27 31	9♎39 30	11 26.0	24 25.8	3 14.0	21 00.4	7 26.8	3 56.6	29 29.9	2 13.3	0 16.1	8 40.5
12 Su	9 25 51	22 39 48	16 51 02	24 01 35	11 18.9	26 14.1	4 24.3	20 46.1	7 48.0	4 05.2	29 29.4	2 16.1	0 18.4	8 42.2
13 M	9 29 47	23 40 28	1♏10 41	8♏18 00	11 14.6	28 03.0	5 34.4	20 31.0	8 09.4	4 13.9	29 28.9	2 18.9	0 20.7	8 43.8
14 Tu	9 33 44	24 41 07	15 23 17	22 26 23	11D 12.7	29 52.5	6 44.5	20 15.3	8 30.9	4 22.8	29 28.3	2 21.8	0 22.9	8 45.5
15 W	9 37 41	25 41 46	29 27 11	6♐25 40	11R 12.5	1♓42.5	7 54.4	19 58.9	8 52.4	4 31.8	29 27.6	2 24.7	0 25.2	8 47.1
16 Th	9 41 37	26 42 23	13♐21 50	20 15 43	11 12.6	3 32.9	9 04.1	19 41.7	9 14.0	4 41.0	29 26.7	2 27.6	0 27.5	8 48.6
17 F	9 45 34	27 42 59	27 07 20	3♑56 41	11 11.8	5 23.6	10 13.8	19 24.0	9 35.7	4 50.2	29 25.8	2 30.5	0 29.8	8 50.2
18 Sa	9 49 30	28 43 34	10♑43 46	17 28 32	11 08.8	7 14.4	11 23.2	19 05.5	9 57.5	4 59.7	29 24.8	2 33.5	0 32.0	8 51.8
19 Su	9 53 27	29 44 07	24 10 55	0♒50 48	11 03.0	9 05.2	12 32.6	18 46.5	10 19.3	5 09.2	29 23.6	2 36.5	0 34.3	8 53.3
20 M	9 57 23	0♓44 40	7♒28 03	14 02 31	10 54.0	10 55.7	13 41.8	18 26.9	10 41.2	5 18.8	29 22.4	2 39.5	0 36.6	8 54.8
21 Tu	10 01 20	1 45 10	20 34 02	27 02 27	10 42.4	12 45.8	14 50.8	18 06.7	11 03.2	5 28.6	29 21.1	2 42.5	0 38.9	8 56.2
22 W	10 05 17	2 45 39	3♓27 36	9♓49 22	10 28.9	14 35.2	15 59.6	17 46.1	11 25.3	5 38.5	29 19.6	2 45.6	0 41.2	8 57.7
23 Th	10 09 13	3 46 07	16 07 42	22 22 23	10 14.9	16 23.6	17 08.3	17 24.9	11 47.5	5 48.5	29 18.1	2 48.7	0 43.4	8 59.1
24 F	10 13 10	4 46 33	28 34 00	4♈42 07	10 01.4	18 10.5	18 16.8	17 03.3	12 09.7	5 58.7	29 16.4	2 51.8	0 45.7	9 00.5
25 Sa	10 17 06	5 46 57	10♈47 06	16 49 12	9 49.8	19 55.7	19 25.2	16 41.3	12 31.9	6 08.9	29 14.7	2 54.9	0 48.0	9 01.8
26 Su	10 21 03	6 47 19	22 48 44	28 46 05	9 40.7	21 38.6	20 33.3	16 18.9	12 54.3	6 19.3	29 12.8	2 58.1	0 50.3	9 03.2
27 M	10 24 59	7 47 39	4♉41 43	10♉36 08	9 34.5	23 18.8	21 41.3	15 56.2	13 16.7	6 29.8	29 10.9	3 01.2	0 52.5	9 04.5
28 Tu	10 28 56	8 47 58	16 29 55	22 23 39	9 31.0	24 55.7	22 49.0	15 33.2	13 39.2	6 40.3	29 08.8	3 04.4	0 54.8	9 05.8
29 W	10 32 52	9 48 14	28 18 00	4♊13 39	9D 29.7	26 28.8	23 56.6	15 10.0	14 01.7	6 51.0	29 06.7	3 07.6	0 57.1	9 07.1

Astro Data

	Dy Hr Mn
☽0S	13 16:52
♃⚺♅	18 0:12
♂R	24 0:53
☽0N	26 19:30
♅0N	28 3:36
♄R	7 14:03
♀0N	9 3:27
☽0S	10 0:27
☽0N	23 4:30

Planet Ingress

		Dy Hr Mn
☿	♑	8 6:34
♀	♓	14 5:47
⚳	♈	19 18:37
☉	♒	20 16:10
☿	♒	27 18:12
♆	♓	3 19:03
♀	♈	8 6:01
☿	♓	14 1:38
☉	♓	19 6:18

Last Aspect / ☽ Ingress (January)

Last Aspect Dy Hr Mn			☽ Ingress	Dy Hr Mn
2 20:07	♆	⚹	♉	2 22:16
5 8:46	♆	□	♊	5 10:44
7 19:52	☿	☍	♋	7 21:05
10 2:25	♄	□	♌	10 4:35
12 8:23	♆	☍	♍	12 9:44
14 1:58	☉	△	♎	14 13:28
16 15:28	♆	△	♏	16 16:33
18 18:31	♆	□	♐	18 19:29
20 21:49	♆	⚹	♑	20 22:40
23 1:38	♄	□	♒	23 2:53
25 8:33	♆	☌	♓	25 9:11
27 4:53	♂	☍	♈	27 18:28
30 6:08	♆	⚹	♉	30 6:28

Last Aspect / ☽ Ingress (February)

Last Aspect Dy Hr Mn			☽ Ingress	Dy Hr Mn
1 19:06	♆	□	♊	1 19:14
4 5:06	♄	△	♋	4 6:04
6 12:31	♄	□	♌	6 13:24
8 16:42	♄	⚹	♍	8 17:32
10 5:11	♂	☌	♎	10 19:54
12 21:09	♄	☌	♏	12 22:01
14 17:04	☉	□	♐	15 0:56
17 4:03	♄	⚹	♑	17 5:03
19 9:22	♄	□	♒	19 10:28
21 16:17	♄	△	♓	21 17:31
23 2:24	♂	☍	♈	24 2:48
26 12:52	♄	☍	♉	26 14:29
28 19:46	☿	⚹	♊	29 3:27

☽ Phases & Eclipses

Dy Hr Mn		
1 6:15	☽	10♈13
9 7:30	○	18♋26
16 9:08	☾	25♎38
23 7:39	●	2♒42
31 4:10	☽	10♉41
7 21:54	○	18♌32
14 17:04	☾	25♏24
21 22:35	●	2♓42

Astro Data

1 January 2012
Julian Day # 40908
SVP 5♓05'15"
GC 27♐00.4 ⚴ 16♒21.0
Eris 21♈23.5R ⚵ 22♏26.1
⚷ 1♓54.1 ⚶ 4♓52.9
☽ Mean ☊ 12♐58.7

1 February 2012
Julian Day # 40939
SVP 5♓05'10"
GC 27♐00.5 ⚴ 26♒17.1
Eris 21♈25.9 ⚵ 0♐32.8
⚷ 3♓37.9 ⚶ 18♓35.5
☽ Mean ☊ 11♐20.2

March 2012 — LONGITUDE

Day	Sid.Time	☉	0 hr ☽	Noon ☽	True ☊	☿	♀	♂	⚷	♃	♄	♅	♆	♇
1 Th	10 36 49	10♓48 29	10♊11 16	16♊11 35	9♐29.5	27♓57.5	25♈04.0	14♍46.6	14♈24.3	7♉01.8	29♎04.5	3♈10.8	0♓59.3	9♑08.3
2 F	10 40 45	11 48 41	22 15 17	28 23 03	9R 29.3	29 21.2	26 11.1	14R 23.0	14 46.9	7 12.7	29R 02.2	3 14.1	1 01.6	9 09.5
3 Sa	10 44 42	12 48 52	4♋35 33	10♋53 22	9 28.0	0♈39.4	27 18.1	13 59.4	15 09.6	7 23.7	28 59.8	3 17.3	1 03.8	9 10.7
4 Su	10 48 39	13 49 00	17 17 03	23 47 01	9 24.5	1 51.3	28 24.8	13 35.6	15 32.4	7 34.8	28 57.3	3 20.6	1 06.1	9 11.9
5 M	10 52 35	14 49 07	0♌23 37	7♌07 00	9 18.5	2 56.6	29 31.2	13 11.9	15 55.2	7 46.0	28 54.7	3 23.9	1 08.3	9 13.0
6 Tu	10 56 32	15 49 11	13 57 13	20 54 07	9 09.8	3 54.5	0♉37.5	12 48.2	16 18.1	7 57.3	28 52.1	3 27.2	1 10.5	9 14.1
7 W	11 00 28	16 49 13	27 57 22	5♍06 28	8 59.0	4 44.8	1 43.5	12 24.5	16 41.0	8 08.7	28 49.3	3 30.5	1 12.7	9 15.2
8 Th	11 04 25	17 49 13	12♍20 42	19 39 15	8 47.1	5 26.9	2 49.2	12 01.0	17 04.0	8 20.2	28 46.5	3 33.8	1 14.9	9 16.2
9 F	11 08 21	18 49 11	27 01 07	4♎25 16	8 35.5	6 00.6	3 54.7	11 37.7	17 27.0	8 31.7	28 43.5	3 37.1	1 17.1	9 17.2
10 Sa	11 12 18	19 49 08	11♎50 36	19 16 02	8 25.3	6 25.5	4 59.9	11 14.5	17 50.0	8 43.4	28 40.5	3 40.5	1 19.3	9 18.2
11 Su	11 16 14	20 49 02	26 40 33	4♏03 14	8 17.6	6 41.6	6 04.9	10 51.6	18 13.2	8 55.1	28 37.5	3 43.8	1 21.5	9 19.2
12 M	11 20 11	21 48 55	11♏23 19	18 40 07	8 12.7	6R 48.9	7 09.5	10 28.9	18 36.3	9 06.9	28 34.3	3 47.2	1 23.7	9 20.1
13 Tu	11 24 08	22 48 46	25 53 10	3♐02 08	8D 10.4	6 47.4	8 13.9	10 06.6	18 59.5	9 18.8	28 31.1	3 50.6	1 25.8	9 21.0
14 W	11 28 04	23 48 36	10♐06 48	17 07 06	8 10.0	6 37.3	9 18.0	9 44.6	19 22.8	9 30.8	28 27.8	3 54.0	1 28.0	9 21.9
15 Th	11 32 01	24 48 24	24 03 03	0♑54 45	8R 10.2	6 19.2	10 21.9	9 23.1	19 46.1	9 42.9	28 24.4	3 57.4	1 30.1	9 22.7
16 F	11 35 57	25 48 11	7♑42 20	14 26 00	8 09.7	5 53.3	11 25.4	9 02.0	20 09.4	9 55.0	28 20.9	4 00.8	1 32.3	9 23.5
17 Sa	11 39 54	26 47 55	21 05 57	27 42 22	8 07.4	5 20.5	12 28.6	8 41.3	20 32.8	10 07.2	28 17.4	4 04.2	1 34.4	9 24.3
18 Su	11 43 50	27 47 38	4♒15 27	10♒45 21	8 02.4	4 41.6	13 31.4	8 21.1	20 56.2	10 19.5	28 13.8	4 07.6	1 36.5	9 25.1
19 M	11 47 47	28 47 19	17 12 13	23 36 10	7 54.7	3 57.4	14 34.0	8 01.5	21 19.7	10 31.9	28 10.2	4 11.0	1 38.6	9 25.8
20 Tu	11 51 43	29 46 59	29 57 18	6♓15 39	7 44.6	3 09.0	15 36.2	7 42.5	21 43.1	10 44.4	28 06.5	4 14.4	1 40.6	9 26.5
21 W	11 55 40	0♈46 36	12♓31 18	18 44 18	7 32.7	2 17.5	16 38.1	7 24.0	22 06.7	10 56.9	28 02.7	4 17.8	1 42.7	9 27.1
22 Th	11 59 37	1 46 12	24 54 42	1♈02 33	7 20.2	1 24.2	17 39.6	7 06.2	22 30.2	11 09.5	27 58.8	4 21.3	1 44.7	9 27.8
23 F	12 03 33	2 45 45	7♈07 56	13 10 58	7 08.2	0 30.1	18 40.7	6 49.0	22 53.8	11 22.1	27 54.9	4 24.7	1 46.8	9 28.4
24 Sa	12 07 30	3 45 17	19 11 48	25 10 37	6 57.7	29♓36.3	19 41.4	6 32.5	23 17.5	11 34.8	27 51.0	4 28.1	1 48.8	9 28.9
25 Su	12 11 26	4 44 46	1♉07 39	7♉03 10	6 49.5	28 44.0	20 41.8	6 16.7	23 41.2	11 47.6	27 46.9	4 31.5	1 50.8	9 29.5
26 M	12 15 23	5 44 13	12 57 32	18 51 07	6 44.0	27 54.1	21 41.7	6 01.7	24 04.9	12 00.5	27 42.9	4 35.0	1 52.8	9 30.0
27 Tu	12 19 19	6 43 38	24 44 21	0♊37 44	6 41.0	27 07.5	22 41.2	5 47.3	24 28.6	12 13.4	27 38.8	4 38.4	1 54.7	9 30.4
28 W	12 23 16	7 43 01	6♊31 47	12 27 05	6D 40.2	26 24.8	23 40.3	5 33.7	24 52.3	12 26.3	27 34.6	4 41.8	1 56.7	9 30.9
29 Th	12 27 12	8 42 22	18 24 15	24 23 55	6 40.7	25 46.8	24 38.9	5 20.8	25 16.1	12 39.4	27 30.4	4 45.2	1 58.6	9 31.3
30 F	12 31 09	9 41 40	0♋26 45	6♋33 23	6R 41.6	25 13.7	25 37.0	5 08.7	25 39.9	12 52.4	27 26.2	4 48.7	2 00.5	9 31.7
31 Sa	12 35 05	10 40 56	12 44 30	19 00 45	6 41.9	24 46.0	26 34.7	4 57.4	26 03.8	13 05.6	27 21.9	4 52.1	2 02.4	9 32.0

April 2012 — LONGITUDE

Day	Sid.Time	☉	0 hr ☽	Noon ☽	True ☊	☿	♀	♂	⚷	♃	♄	♅	♆	♇
1 Su	12 39 02	11♈40 10	25♋22 44	1♌50 58	6♐40.9	24♓23.8	27♉31.8	4♍46.9	26♈27.6	13♉18.8	27♎17.5	4♈55.5	2♓04.3	9♑32.3
2 M	12 42 59	12 39 21	8♌25 56	15 07 59	6R 37.8	24R 07.3	28 28.5	4R 37.2	26 51.5	13 32.0	27R 13.2	4 58.9	2 06.1	9 32.6
3 Tu	12 46 55	13 38 30	21 57 19	28 54 00	6 32.7	23 56.5	29 24.6	4 28.2	27 15.4	13 45.3	27 08.8	5 02.3	2 07.9	9 32.9
4 W	12 50 52	14 37 37	5♍57 54	13♍08 42	6 25.9	23D 51.4	0♊20.1	4 20.0	27 39.4	13 58.6	27 04.4	5 05.7	2 09.7	9 33.1
5 Th	12 54 48	15 36 41	20 25 50	27 48 36	6 18.0	23 51.8	1 15.0	4 12.6	28 03.3	14 12.0	26 59.9	5 09.1	2 11.5	9 33.3
6 F	12 58 45	16 35 44	5♎16 03	12♎47 08	6 10.1	23 57.6	2 09.3	4 06.0	28 27.3	14 25.4	26 55.4	5 12.5	2 13.3	9 33.4
7 Sa	13 02 41	17 34 44	20 20 37	27 55 16	6 03.2	24 08.7	3 03.0	4 00.2	28 51.3	14 38.9	26 50.9	5 15.8	2 15.0	9 33.6
8 Su	13 06 38	18 33 42	5♏29 50	13♏03 04	5 58.1	24 24.8	3 56.1	3 55.2	29 15.3	14 52.4	26 46.4	5 19.2	2 16.8	9 33.7
9 M	13 10 34	19 32 38	20 33 53	28 01 16	5 55.1	24 45.8	4 48.5	3 50.9	29 39.3	15 06.0	26 41.9	5 22.6	2 18.5	9 33.7
10 Tu	13 14 31	20 31 33	5♐24 24	12♐42 39	5D 54.2	25 11.3	5 40.2	3 47.4	0♉03.4	15 19.6	26 37.3	5 25.9	2 20.1	9R 33.8
11 W	13 18 28	21 30 26	19 55 32	27 02 46	5 54.7	25 41.4	6 31.2	3 44.6	0 27.4	15 33.2	26 32.7	5 29.2	2 21.8	9 33.8
12 Th	13 22 24	22 29 17	4♑04 10	10♑59 45	5 56.0	26 15.6	7 21.5	3 42.7	0 51.5	15 46.9	26 28.1	5 32.6	2 23.4	9 33.7
13 F	13 26 21	23 28 06	17 49 37	24 33 56	5R 57.0	26 53.8	8 11.0	3 41.4	1 15.6	16 00.6	26 23.5	5 35.9	2 25.0	9 33.7
14 Sa	13 30 17	24 26 54	1♒12 58	7♒47 01	5 56.9	27 35.8	8 59.8	3D 40.9	1 39.7	16 14.4	26 18.9	5 39.2	2 26.6	9 33.6
15 Su	13 34 14	25 25 40	14 16 24	20 41 27	5 55.2	28 21.5	9 47.7	3 41.2	2 03.8	16 28.1	26 14.3	5 42.4	2 28.2	9 33.5
16 M	13 38 10	26 24 24	27 02 32	3♓19 57	5 51.7	29 10.6	10 34.8	3 42.2	2 28.0	16 42.0	26 09.7	5 45.7	2 29.7	9 33.3
17 Tu	13 42 07	27 23 06	9♓34 03	15 45 06	5 46.6	0♈02.9	11 21.0	3 43.9	2 52.1	16 55.8	26 05.1	5 49.0	2 31.2	9 33.1
18 W	13 46 03	28 21 47	21 53 24	27 59 12	5 40.3	0 58.4	12 06.2	3 46.3	3 16.3	17 09.7	26 00.5	5 52.2	2 32.7	9 32.9
19 Th	13 50 00	29 20 26	4♈02 45	10♈04 16	5 33.6	1 56.8	12 50.6	3 49.4	3 40.5	17 23.6	25 55.9	5 55.4	2 34.1	9 32.7
20 F	13 53 57	0♉19 03	16 03 59	22 02 06	5 27.1	2 58.1	13 34.0	3 53.2	4 04.6	17 37.5	25 51.3	5 58.6	2 35.6	9 32.4
21 Sa	13 57 53	1 17 38	27 58 50	3♉54 25	5 21.5	4 02.2	14 16.3	3 57.7	4 28.8	17 51.5	25 46.7	6 01.8	2 37.0	9 32.1
22 Su	14 01 50	2 16 11	9♉49 05	15 43 04	5 17.3	5 08.8	14 57.6	4 02.9	4 53.0	18 05.5	25 42.1	6 05.0	2 38.4	9 31.8
23 M	14 05 46	3 14 43	21 36 39	27 30 08	5 14.7	6 18.0	15 37.8	4 08.8	5 17.2	18 19.5	25 37.6	6 08.1	2 39.7	9 31.4
24 Tu	14 09 43	4 13 12	3♊23 52	9♊18 11	5D 13.8	7 29.5	16 16.9	4 15.3	5 41.5	18 33.5	25 33.0	6 11.3	2 41.0	9 31.0
25 W	14 13 39	5 11 40	15 13 29	21 10 13	5 14.2	8 43.4	16 54.8	4 22.5	6 05.7	18 47.6	25 28.5	6 14.4	2 42.3	9 30.6
26 Th	14 17 36	6 10 05	27 08 50	3♋09 49	5 15.5	9 59.6	17 31.4	4 30.3	6 29.9	19 01.7	25 24.0	6 17.4	2 43.6	9 30.1
27 F	14 21 32	7 08 29	9♋13 42	15 21 01	5 17.3	11 18.0	18 06.7	4 38.7	6 54.1	19 15.8	25 19.5	6 20.5	2 44.8	9 29.7
28 Sa	14 25 29	8 06 50	21 32 19	27 48 09	5 18.8	12 38.6	18 40.7	4 47.8	7 18.4	19 29.9	25 15.1	6 23.6	2 46.0	9 29.2
29 Su	14 29 26	9 05 09	4♌09 03	10♌35 32	5R 19.7	14 01.2	19 13.4	4 57.4	7 42.6	19 44.0	25 10.7	6 26.6	2 47.2	9 28.6
30 M	14 33 22	10 03 27	17 08 04	23 47 02	5 19.6	15 25.9	19 44.5	5 07.6	8 06.8	19 58.1	25 06.3	6 29.6	2 48.4	9 28.1

Astro Data

	Dy Hr Mn
☿0N	1 3:45
⚷0N	4 20:20
☽0S	8 10:06
☿ R	12 7:48
♃△♇	13 4:43
☉0N	20 5:14
☽0N	21 11:30
☿0S	28 21:18
☿ D	4 10:11
☽0S	4 20:34
♇ R	10 16:24
♂ D	14 3:53
☽0N	17 16:51
☿0N	22 22:51

Planet Ingress

		Dy Hr Mn
☿	♈	2 11:41
♀	♉	5 10:25
☉	♈	20 5:14
☿	♓R	23 13:22
♀	♊	3 15:18
⚷	♉	9 20:39
☿	♈	16 22:42
☉	♉	19 16:12

Last Aspect / ☽ Ingress

Last Aspect Dy Hr Mn		☽ Ingress	Dy Hr Mn
2 13:14	♄ △	♋	2 15:08
4 22:17	♀ □	♌	4 23:17
7 1:27	♄ ⚹	♍	7 3:27
8 9:39	☉ ☍	♎	9 4:50
11 3:09	♄ ☌	♏	11 5:24
12 18:30	☉ △	♐	13 6:53
15 7:34	♄ ⚹	♑	15 10:24
17 13:00	♄ □	♒	17 16:11
19 20:31	♄ △	♓	20 0:05
21 8:39	♀ ⚹	♈	22 9:57
24 17:17	♄ ☍	♉	24 21:43
27 4:35	☿ ⚹	♊	27 10:43
29 18:05	♄ △	♋	29 23:07

Last Aspect / ☽ Ingress

Last Aspect Dy Hr Mn		☽ Ingress	Dy Hr Mn
1 4:20	♀ ⚹	♌	1 8:35
3 13:47	♀ □	♍	3 13:53
5 5:37	☿ ☍	♎	5 15:32
7 10:15	♄ ☌	♏	7 15:17
9 6:56	☿ △	♐	9 15:12
11 11:06	♄ ⚹	♑	11 17:02
13 17:05	☿ ⚹	♒	13 21:48
15 22:42	☉ ⚹	♓	16 5:38
17 14:34	♃ ⚹	♈	18 15:59
20 19:35	♄ ☍	♉	21 4:05
22 17:10	♃ ☌	♊	23 17:05
25 20:31	♄ △	♋	26 5:42
28 7:05	♄ □	♌	28 16:10
30 14:17	♄ ⚹	♍	30 23:02

☽ Phases & Eclipses

Dy Hr Mn	
1 1:21	☽ 10♊52
8 9:39	○ 18♍13
15 1:25	☾ 24♐52
22 14:37	● 2♈22
30 19:41	☽ 10♋30
6 19:19	○ 17♎23
13 10:50	☾ 23♑55
21 7:18	● 1♉35
29 9:57	☽ 9♌29

Astro Data

1 March 2012
Julian Day # 40968
SVP 5♓05'06"
GC 27♐00.6 ⚳ 5♓55.5
Eris 21♈37.0 ⚵ 5♐37.5
⚷ 5♓31.8 ⚶ 1♈57.2
☽ Mean ☊ 9♐48.0

1 April 2012
Julian Day # 40999
SVP 5♓05'03"
GC 27♐00.6 ⚳ 16♓04.5
Eris 21♈55.3 ⚵ 6♐58.4R
⚷ 7♓28.4 ⚶ 16♈22.0
☽ Mean ☊ 8♐09.5

LONGITUDE — May 2012

Day	Sid.Time	☉	0 hr ☽	Noon ☽	True ☊	☿	♀	♂	⚳	♃	♄	♅	♆	♇
1 Tu	14 37 19	11♉01 42	0♍32 46	7♍25 27	5♐18.4	16♈52.7	20♊14.2	5♍18.5	8♉31.1	20♉12.3	25♎01.9	6♈32.6	2♓49.5	9♑27.5
2 W	14 41 15	11 59 55	14 25 08	21 31 43	5R 16.3	18 21.4	20 42.3	5 29.8	8 55.3	20 26.5	24R 57.6	6 35.5	2 50.6	9R 26.8
3 Th	14 45 12	12 58 06	28 44 55	6♎04 17	5 13.5	19 52.1	21 08.8	5 41.8	9 19.5	20 40.6	24 53.4	6 38.4	2 51.6	9 26.2
4 F	14 49 08	13 56 15	13♎29 08	20 58 39	5 10.6	21 24.8	21 33.6	5 54.2	9 43.7	20 54.8	24 49.1	6 41.3	2 52.7	9 25.5
5 Sa	14 53 05	14 54 22	28 31 50	6♏07 32	5 08.1	22 59.4	21 56.7	6 07.2	10 08.0	21 09.0	24 44.9	6 44.2	2 53.7	9 24.8
6 Su	14 57 01	15 52 27	13♏44 33	21 21 38	5 06.3	24 36.0	22 17.9	6 20.7	10 32.2	21 23.2	24 40.8	6 47.0	2 54.7	9 24.1
7 M	15 00 58	16 50 31	28 57 31	6♐31 02	5D 05.5	26 14.5	22 37.4	6 34.7	10 56.4	21 37.4	24 36.7	6 49.9	2 55.6	9 23.3
8 Tu	15 04 55	17 48 34	14♐01 05	21 26 43	5 05.5	27 55.0	22 54.9	6 49.3	11 20.6	21 51.6	24 32.6	6 52.6	2 56.5	9 22.6
9 W	15 08 51	18 46 34	28 47 11	6♑01 50	5 06.3	29 37.4	23 10.4	7 04.3	11 44.8	22 05.8	24 28.6	6 55.4	2 57.4	9 21.8
10 Th	15 12 48	19 44 34	13♑10 14	20 12 09	5 07.4	1♉21.7	23 23.9	7 19.7	12 09.0	22 20.1	24 24.7	6 58.2	2 58.2	9 20.9
11 F	15 16 44	20 42 32	27 07 26	3♒56 09	5 08.5	3 08.0	23 35.3	7 35.7	12 33.2	22 34.3	24 20.8	7 00.9	2 59.1	9 20.1
12 Sa	15 20 41	21 40 29	10♒38 27	17 14 35	5R 09.3	4 56.2	23 44.6	7 52.1	12 57.4	22 48.5	24 17.0	7 03.5	2 59.9	9 19.2
13 Su	15 24 37	22 38 24	23 44 52	0♓09 43	5 09.5	6 46.4	23 51.7	8 08.9	13 21.6	23 02.8	24 13.2	7 06.2	3 00.6	9 18.3
14 M	15 28 34	23 36 18	6♓29 32	12 44 47	5 09.2	8 38.6	23 56.5	8 26.2	13 45.8	23 17.0	24 09.5	7 08.8	3 01.3	9 17.4
15 Tu	15 32 30	24 34 11	18 55 57	25 03 30	5 08.4	10 32.6	23R 59.1	8 43.9	14 10.0	23 31.2	24 05.8	7 11.4	3 02.0	9 16.4
16 W	15 36 27	25 32 03	1♈07 53	7♈09 33	5 07.3	12 28.6	23 59.3	9 02.1	14 34.2	23 45.4	24 02.2	7 13.9	3 02.7	9 15.5
17 Th	15 40 24	26 29 53	13 08 56	19 06 28	5 06.0	14 26.5	23 57.2	9 20.7	14 58.3	23 59.6	23 58.7	7 16.4	3 03.3	9 14.5
18 F	15 44 20	27 27 42	25 02 31	0♉57 27	5 04.9	16 26.2	23 52.7	9 39.7	15 22.5	24 13.8	23 55.2	7 18.9	3 03.9	9 13.4
19 Sa	15 48 17	28 25 30	6♉51 37	12 45 21	5 04.0	18 27.8	23 45.8	9 59.0	15 46.6	24 28.0	23 51.8	7 21.4	3 04.5	9 12.4
20 Su	15 52 13	29 23 17	18 38 57	24 32 42	5 03.5	20 31.1	23 36.5	10 18.8	16 10.7	24 42.2	23 48.5	7 23.8	3 05.0	9 11.3
21 M	15 56 10	0♊21 02	0♊26 55	6♊21 51	5D 03.2	22 36.0	23 24.8	10 39.0	16 34.8	24 56.4	23 45.2	7 26.2	3 05.5	9 10.3
22 Tu	16 00 06	1 18 46	12 17 47	18 15 01	5 03.2	24 42.5	23 10.6	10 59.6	16 58.9	25 10.6	23 42.1	7 28.5	3 06.0	9 09.2
23 W	16 04 03	2 16 29	24 13 48	0♋14 27	5 03.4	26 50.3	22 54.1	11 20.5	17 23.0	25 24.8	23 39.0	7 30.8	3 06.4	9 08.0
24 Th	16 07 59	3 14 10	6♋17 17	12 22 35	5 03.6	28 59.4	22 35.2	11 41.8	17 47.1	25 38.9	23 35.9	7 33.1	3 06.8	9 06.9
25 F	16 11 56	4 11 50	18 30 43	24 42 00	5R 03.8	1♊09.6	22 14.1	12 03.4	18 11.1	25 53.1	23 33.0	7 35.3	3 07.2	9 05.7
26 Sa	16 15 53	5 09 29	0♌56 48	7♌15 30	5 03.8	3 20.5	21 50.7	12 25.4	18 35.1	26 07.2	23 30.1	7 37.5	3 07.5	9 04.5
27 Su	16 19 49	6 07 06	13 38 26	20 05 58	5 03.8	5 32.1	21 25.2	12 47.8	18 59.2	26 21.3	23 27.3	7 39.7	3 07.8	9 03.3
28 M	16 23 46	7 04 41	26 38 26	3♍16 08	5D 03.7	7 44.0	20 57.7	13 10.5	19 23.1	26 35.4	23 24.6	7 41.8	3 08.1	9 02.1
29 Tu	16 27 42	8 02 15	9♍59 21	16 48 17	5 03.7	9 55.9	20 28.3	13 33.5	19 47.1	26 49.4	23 22.0	7 43.9	3 08.3	9 00.9
30 W	16 31 39	8 59 48	23 43 02	0♎43 39	5 03.8	12 07.7	19 57.2	13 56.8	20 11.1	27 03.5	23 19.5	7 45.9	3 08.5	8 59.6
31 Th	16 35 35	9 57 19	7♎50 02	15 01 57	5 04.1	14 19.0	19 24.4	14 20.4	20 35.0	27 17.5	23 17.0	7 47.9	3 08.7	8 58.4

LONGITUDE — June 2012

Day	Sid.Time	☉	0 hr ☽	Noon ☽	True ☊	☿	♀	♂	⚳	♃	♄	♅	♆	♇
1 F	16 39 32	10♊54 49	22♎19 04	29♎40 51	5♐04.5	16♊29.5	18♊50.3	14♍44.4	20♉58.9	27♉31.5	23♎14.7	7♈49.9	3♓08.8	8♑57.1
2 Sa	16 43 28	11 52 17	7♏06 40	14♏35 42	5 05.1	18 39.0	18R 15.0	15 08.6	21 22.8	27 45.5	23R 12.4	7 51.8	3 09.0	8R 55.8
3 Su	16 47 25	12 49 45	22 07 02	29 39 39	5R 05.5	20 47.3	17 38.8	15 33.2	21 46.6	27 59.4	23 10.2	7 53.7	3 09.0	8 54.5
4 M	16 51 22	13 47 11	7♐12 27	14♐44 20	5 05.7	22 54.1	17 01.8	15 58.0	22 10.5	28 13.4	23 08.1	7 55.6	3R 09.1	8 53.1
5 Tu	16 55 18	14 44 37	22 14 11	29 40 57	5 05.4	24 59.2	16 24.3	16 23.1	22 34.3	28 27.3	23 06.1	7 57.4	3 09.1	8 51.8
6 W	16 59 15	15 42 01	7♑03 40	14♑21 30	5 04.6	27 02.5	15 46.6	16 48.5	22 58.1	28 41.2	23 04.2	7 59.1	3 09.1	8 50.4
7 Th	17 03 11	16 39 25	21 33 45	28 39 53	5 03.3	29 03.8	15 08.8	17 14.2	23 21.8	28 55.0	23 02.4	8 00.9	3 09.0	8 49.1
8 F	17 07 08	17 36 48	5♒39 31	12♒32 27	5 01.9	1♋03.0	14 31.4	17 40.1	23 45.6	29 08.8	23 00.6	8 02.5	3 08.9	8 47.7
9 Sa	17 11 04	18 34 11	19 18 37	25 58 08	5 00.4	3 00.0	13 54.4	18 06.2	24 09.3	29 22.6	22 59.0	8 04.2	3 08.8	8 46.3
10 Su	17 15 01	19 31 32	2♓31 12	8♓58 08	4 59.2	4 54.7	13 18.1	18 32.7	24 33.0	29 36.4	22 57.4	8 05.8	3 08.7	8 44.9
11 M	17 18 57	20 28 54	15 19 20	21 35 16	4D 58.6	6 47.1	12 42.8	18 59.4	24 56.6	29 50.1	22 56.0	8 07.3	3 08.5	8 43.5
12 Tu	17 22 54	21 26 14	27 46 28	3♈53 28	4 58.6	8 37.1	12 08.7	19 26.3	25 20.2	0♊03.8	22 54.6	8 08.8	3 08.3	8 42.1
13 W	17 26 51	22 23 35	9♈56 51	15 57 11	4 59.3	10 24.7	11 35.9	19 53.5	25 43.8	0 17.4	22 53.3	8 10.3	3 08.0	8 40.6
14 Th	17 30 47	23 20 55	21 55 03	27 51 01	5 00.6	12 09.8	11 04.7	20 20.9	26 07.4	0 31.0	22 52.2	8 11.7	3 07.7	8 39.2
15 F	17 34 44	24 18 14	3♉45 37	9♉39 23	5 02.1	13 52.5	10 35.2	20 48.6	26 30.9	0 44.6	22 51.1	8 13.1	3 07.4	8 37.7
16 Sa	17 38 40	25 15 33	15 32 48	21 26 20	5 03.6	15 32.6	10 07.6	21 16.5	26 54.4	0 58.2	22 50.1	8 14.4	3 07.1	8 36.2
17 Su	17 42 37	26 12 52	27 20 24	3♊15 25	5R 04.5	17 10.3	9 41.9	21 44.7	27 17.9	1 11.7	22 49.3	8 15.7	3 06.7	8 34.8
18 M	17 46 33	27 10 10	9♊11 43	15 09 38	5 04.7	18 45.4	9 18.3	22 13.0	27 41.3	1 25.1	22 48.5	8 16.9	3 06.3	8 33.3
19 Tu	17 50 30	28 07 28	21 09 27	27 11 26	5 03.7	20 18.0	8 57.0	22 41.6	28 04.7	1 38.5	22 47.8	8 18.1	3 05.9	8 31.8
20 W	17 54 26	29 04 45	3♋15 49	9♋22 46	5 01.7	21 48.0	8 37.8	23 10.5	28 28.1	1 51.9	22 47.2	8 19.3	3 05.4	8 30.3
21 Th	17 58 23	0♋02 02	15 32 29	21 45 07	4 58.5	23 15.4	8 21.0	23 39.5	28 51.4	2 05.2	22 46.7	8 20.4	3 04.9	8 28.8
22 F	18 02 20	0 59 19	28 00 49	4♌19 43	4 54.6	24 40.3	8 06.5	24 08.7	29 14.7	2 18.5	22 46.4	8 21.4	3 04.4	8 27.3
23 Sa	18 06 16	1 56 34	10♌41 56	17 07 34	4 50.4	26 02.5	7 54.4	24 38.2	29 37.9	2 31.8	22 46.1	8 22.4	3 03.8	8 25.8
24 Su	18 10 13	2 53 50	23 36 46	0♍09 38	4 46.3	27 22.0	7 44.7	25 07.9	0♊01.1	2 44.9	22 45.9	8 23.4	3 03.2	8 24.3
25 M	18 14 09	3 51 04	6♍46 16	13 26 47	4 43.1	28 38.7	7 37.3	25 37.7	0 24.3	2 58.1	22D 45.8	8 24.3	3 02.6	8 22.8
26 Tu	18 18 06	4 48 18	20 11 17	26 59 51	4 40.9	29 52.8	7 32.3	26 07.8	0 47.4	3 11.1	22 45.8	8 25.1	3 02.0	8 21.3
27 W	18 22 02	5 45 32	3♎52 32	10♎49 21	4D 40.1	1♌03.9	7D 29.7	26 38.1	1 10.4	3 24.2	22 45.9	8 26.0	3 01.3	8 19.8
28 Th	18 25 59	6 42 44	17 50 17	24 55 15	4 40.5	2 12.2	7 29.4	27 08.5	1 33.4	3 37.1	22 46.2	8 26.7	3 00.6	8 18.2
29 F	18 29 55	7 39 57	2♏04 04	9♏16 29	4 41.7	3 17.5	7 31.4	27 39.2	1 56.4	3 50.0	22 46.5	8 27.4	2 59.8	8 16.7
30 Sa	18 33 52	8 37 09	16 32 11	23 50 41	4 43.1	4 19.8	7 35.7	28 10.0	2 19.3	4 02.9	22 46.9	8 28.1	2 59.1	8 15.2

Astro Data

	Dy Hr Mn
☽0S	2 6:11
♃∠♅	8 2:09
☽0N	14 22:10
♀R	15 14:33
♃⚻♄	16 22:42
♃⚼♇	17 23:22
☽0S	29 14:01
♆R	4 21:04
☽0N	11 5:08
♅□♇	24 9:12
♃□♆	25 7:56
♄D	25 8:00
☽0S	25 20:25
♀D	27 15:07

Planet Ingress

		Dy Hr Mn
☿	♉	9 5:14
☉	♊	20 15:15
☿	♊	24 11:12
☿	♋	7 11:16
♃	♊	11 17:22
☉	♋	20 23:09
⚳	♊	23 22:52
☿	♌	26 2:24

Last Aspect / ☽ Ingress (May)

Last Aspect Dy Hr Mn		☽ Ingress	Dy Hr Mn
2 10:58	♀□	♎	3 2:04
4 18:02	♄☌	♏	5 2:20
6 12:14	♃☍	♐	7 1:39
9 1:34	☿△	♑	9 2:00
10 19:11	♄□	♒	11 5:03
13 0:52	♄△	♓	13 11:42
15 11:59	☉✶	♈	15 21:45
17 21:44	♄☍	♉	18 10:03
20 12:35	♃☌	♊	20 23:05
22 22:51	♄△	♋	23 11:31
25 14:34	♃✶	♌	25 22:11
27 23:54	♃□	♍	28 6:06
30 5:50	♃△	♎	30 10:46

Last Aspect / ☽ Ingress (June)

Last Aspect Dy Hr Mn		☽ Ingress	Dy Hr Mn
1 1:31	♄☌	♏	1 12:31
3 9:29	♃☍	♐	3 12:32
5 5:08	☿☍	♑	5 12:31
7 12:38	♃△	♒	7 14:17
9 18:33	♃□	♓	9 19:22
11 10:41	☉□	♈	12 4:21
14 3:08	☉✶	♉	14 16:22
16 12:09	♂△	♊	17 5:24
19 15:02	☉☌	♋	19 17:34
21 16:48	♀☌	♌	22 3:47
23 22:26	♄✶	♍	24 11:42
26 10:53	♂☌	♎	26 17:15
28 8:22	♄☌	♏	28 20:32
30 19:46	♂✶	♐	30 22:04

☽ Phases & Eclipses

Dy Hr Mn	
6 3:35	○ 16♏01
12 21:47	☾ 22♒33
20 23:47	● 0♊21
20 23:52:45	● A 05'36"
28 20:16	☽ 7♍53
4 11:12	○ 14♐14
4 11:03	● P 0.370
11 10:41	☾ 20♓54
19 15:02	● 28♊43
27 3:30	☽ 5♎54

Astro Data

1 May 2012
Julian Day # 41029
SVP 5♓05'00"
GC 27♐00.7 ⚴ 25♓15.1
Eris 22♈14.8 ⚵ 3♐25.3R
⚷ 8♓55.5 ⚶ 0♉08.2
☽ Mean ☊ 6♐34.2

1 June 2012
Julian Day # 41060
SVP 5♓04'56"
GC 27♐00.8 ⚴ 3♈26.1
Eris 22♈32.0 ⚵ 26♏43.8R
⚷ 9♓41.6 ⚶ 13♉53.9
☽ Mean ☊ 4♐55.7

July 2012 — LONGITUDE

Day	Sid.Time	☉	0 hr ☽	Noon ☽	True ☊	☿	♀	♂	⚳	♃	♄	♅	♆	♇
1 Su	18 37 49	9♋34 20	1♐11 26	8♐33 46	4♐43.9	5♌18.9	7♊42.1	28♍41.0	2♊42.2	4♊15.7	22♎47.4	8♈28.7	2♓58.3	8♑13.7
2 M	18 41 45	10 31 32	15 56 56	23 20 06	4R 43.5	6 14.8	7 50.7	29 12.2	3 05.0	4 28.4	22 48.0	8 29.3	2R 57.5	8R 12.2
3 Tu	18 45 42	11 28 43	0♑42 22	8♑02 51	4 41.5	7 07.3	8 01.5	29 43.6	3 27.8	4 41.1	22 48.7	8 29.8	2 56.6	8 10.6
4 W	18 49 38	12 25 54	15 20 38	22 34 51	4 37.7	7 56.4	8 14.3	0♎15.1	3 50.6	4 53.7	22 49.6	8 30.3	2 55.8	8 09.1
5 Th	18 53 35	13 23 05	29 44 45	6♒49 38	4 32.5	8 41.9	8 29.1	0 46.8	4 13.2	5 06.3	22 50.5	8 30.8	2 54.9	8 07.6
6 F	18 57 31	14 20 16	13♒48 58	20 42 21	4 26.5	9 23.7	8 45.8	1 18.7	4 35.9	5 18.8	22 51.5	8 31.1	2 53.9	8 06.1
7 Sa	19 01 28	15 17 27	27 29 30	4♓10 19	4 20.3	10 01.7	9 04.5	1 50.7	4 58.4	5 31.2	22 52.6	8 31.5	2 53.0	8 04.6
8 Su	19 05 25	16 14 38	10♓44 51	17 13 15	4 14.9	10 35.8	9 24.9	2 22.9	5 21.0	5 43.5	22 53.8	8 31.8	2 52.0	8 03.1
9 M	19 09 21	17 11 50	23 35 48	29 52 53	4 10.7	11 05.7	9 47.2	2 55.3	5 43.4	5 55.8	22 55.1	8 32.0	2 51.0	8 01.6
10 Tu	19 13 18	18 09 02	6♈04 59	12♈12 36	4 08.1	11 31.5	10 11.1	3 27.8	6 05.8	6 08.0	22 56.5	8 32.2	2 50.0	8 00.1
11 W	19 17 14	19 06 14	18 16 20	24 16 49	4D 07.3	11 52.8	10 36.7	4 00.5	6 28.2	6 20.2	22 58.0	8 32.3	2 48.9	7 58.6
12 Th	19 21 11	20 03 27	0♉14 39	6♉10 31	4 07.8	12 09.7	11 03.8	4 33.3	6 50.5	6 32.3	22 59.6	8 32.4	2 47.8	7 57.1
13 F	19 25 07	21 00 41	12 05 04	17 58 54	4 09.0	12 22.1	11 32.5	5 06.3	7 12.7	6 44.3	23 01.3	8R 32.5	2 46.8	7 55.7
14 Sa	19 29 04	21 57 55	23 52 41	29 46 58	4R 10.3	12 29.7	12 02.7	5 39.5	7 34.9	6 56.2	23 03.0	8 32.5	2 45.6	7 54.2
15 Su	19 33 00	22 55 09	5♊42 20	11♊39 18	4 10.7	12R 32.5	12 34.3	6 12.8	7 57.0	7 08.0	23 04.9	8 32.4	2 44.5	7 52.7
16 M	19 36 57	23 52 25	17 38 19	23 39 50	4 09.7	12 30.6	13 07.2	6 46.3	8 19.0	7 19.8	23 06.9	8 32.3	2 43.3	7 51.3
17 Tu	19 40 54	24 49 40	29 44 11	5♋51 41	4 06.6	12 23.8	13 41.4	7 19.9	8 41.0	7 31.5	23 09.0	8 32.2	2 42.1	7 49.8
18 W	19 44 50	25 46 56	12♋02 34	18 17 01	4 01.4	12 12.2	14 16.9	7 53.6	9 02.9	7 43.1	23 11.1	8 32.0	2 40.9	7 48.4
19 Th	19 48 47	26 44 13	24 35 08	0♌56 59	3 54.1	11 55.9	14 53.6	8 27.6	9 24.8	7 54.6	23 13.4	8 31.7	2 39.7	7 47.0
20 F	19 52 43	27 41 30	7♌22 32	13 51 44	3 45.3	11 35.0	15 31.5	9 01.6	9 46.5	8 06.1	23 15.7	8 31.4	2 38.4	7 45.6
21 Sa	19 56 40	28 38 48	20 24 29	27 00 39	3 35.9	11 09.8	16 10.5	9 35.8	10 08.2	8 17.4	23 18.2	8 31.1	2 37.2	7 44.2
22 Su	20 00 36	29 36 05	3♍40 04	10♍22 34	3 26.8	10 40.4	16 50.5	10 10.2	10 29.8	8 28.7	23 20.7	8 30.7	2 35.9	7 42.8
23 M	20 04 33	0♌33 24	17 07 57	23 56 05	3 19.0	10 07.3	17 31.6	10 44.7	10 51.4	8 39.9	23 23.3	8 30.2	2 34.5	7 41.4
24 Tu	20 08 29	1 30 42	0♎46 46	7♎39 54	3 13.1	9 31.0	18 13.7	11 19.3	11 12.9	8 51.0	23 26.1	8 29.8	2 33.2	7 40.0
25 W	20 12 26	2 28 01	14 35 21	21 33 00	3 09.6	8 51.8	18 56.7	11 54.0	11 34.2	9 02.0	23 28.9	8 29.2	2 31.9	7 38.7
26 Th	20 16 23	3 25 20	28 32 46	5♏34 34	3D 08.2	8 10.5	19 40.7	12 28.9	11 55.6	9 12.9	23 31.8	8 28.6	2 30.5	7 37.4
27 F	20 20 19	4 22 40	12♏38 18	19 43 50	3 08.4	7 27.7	20 25.5	13 04.0	12 16.8	9 23.7	23 34.8	8 28.0	2 29.1	7 36.0
28 Sa	20 24 16	5 20 00	26 51 00	3♐59 37	3R 08.9	6 44.0	21 11.2	13 39.1	12 37.9	9 34.4	23 37.8	8 27.3	2 27.7	7 34.7
29 Su	20 28 12	6 17 21	11♐09 23	18 19 59	3 08.8	6 00.4	21 57.7	14 14.4	12 59.0	9 45.0	23 41.0	8 26.6	2 26.3	7 33.4
30 M	20 32 09	7 14 42	25 31 00	2♑41 56	3 07.0	5 17.4	22 45.1	14 49.8	13 20.0	9 55.5	23 44.2	8 25.9	2 24.8	7 32.2
31 Tu	20 36 05	8 12 04	9♑52 14	17 01 16	3 02.7	4 36.1	23 33.2	15 25.4	13 40.9	10 05.9	23 47.6	8 25.1	2 23.4	7 30.9

August 2012 — LONGITUDE

Day	Sid.Time	☉	0 hr ☽	Noon ☽	True ☊	☿	♀	♂	⚳	♃	♄	♅	♆	♇
1 W	20 40 02	9♌09 26	24♑08 25	1♒13 00	2♐55.9	3♌57.1	24♊22.0	16♎01.0	14♊01.7	10♊16.2	23♎51.0	8♈24.2	2♓21.9	7♑29.7
2 Th	20 43 58	10 06 49	8♒14 22	15 11 56	2R 46.8	3R 21.2	25 11.6	16 36.8	14 22.4	10 26.4	23 54.5	8R 23.3	2R 20.5	7R 28.4
3 F	20 47 55	11 04 13	22 05 09	28 53 34	2 36.2	2 49.1	26 01.9	17 12.7	14 43.0	10 36.5	23 58.1	8 22.4	2 19.0	7 27.2
4 Sa	20 51 52	12 01 38	5♓36 50	12♓14 44	2 25.3	2 21.4	26 52.8	17 48.7	15 03.5	10 46.5	24 01.7	8 21.4	2 17.5	7 26.0
5 Su	20 55 48	12 59 04	18 47 08	25 14 06	2 15.2	1 58.8	27 44.4	18 24.9	15 24.0	10 56.3	24 05.5	8 20.3	2 15.9	7 24.9
6 M	20 59 45	13 56 31	1♈35 44	7♈52 17	2 06.7	1 41.7	28 36.7	19 01.1	15 44.3	11 06.1	24 09.3	8 19.3	2 14.4	7 23.7
7 Tu	21 03 41	14 53 59	14 04 06	20 11 38	2 00.6	1 30.6	29 29.5	19 37.5	16 04.5	11 15.8	24 13.2	8 18.2	2 12.9	7 22.6
8 W	21 07 38	15 51 29	26 15 23	2♉15 55	1 56.8	1D 25.8	0♋23.0	20 14.0	16 24.7	11 25.3	24 17.2	8 17.0	2 11.3	7 21.5
9 Th	21 11 34	16 49 00	8♉13 50	14 09 48	1D 55.2	1 27.6	1 17.0	20 50.6	16 44.7	11 34.7	24 21.3	8 15.8	2 09.8	7 20.4
10 F	21 15 31	17 46 32	20 04 30	25 58 35	1 54.9	1 36.1	2 11.5	21 27.4	17 04.6	11 44.0	24 25.4	8 14.5	2 08.2	7 19.3
11 Sa	21 19 27	18 44 06	1♊52 46	7♊47 43	1R 55.0	1 51.6	3 06.6	22 04.2	17 24.5	11 53.2	24 29.7	8 13.3	2 06.6	7 18.3
12 Su	21 23 24	19 41 41	13 44 06	19 42 32	1 54.5	2 14.0	4 02.2	22 41.2	17 44.2	12 02.3	24 34.0	8 11.9	2 05.0	7 17.2
13 M	21 27 21	20 39 17	25 43 37	1♋47 53	1 52.4	2 43.5	4 58.3	23 18.3	18 03.8	12 11.2	24 38.3	8 10.6	2 03.4	7 16.2
14 Tu	21 31 17	21 36 55	7♋55 48	14 07 49	1 48.0	3 20.0	5 54.9	23 55.5	18 23.3	12 20.0	24 42.8	8 09.2	2 01.8	7 15.2
15 W	21 35 14	22 34 35	20 24 13	26 45 15	1 40.9	4 03.4	6 52.0	24 32.8	18 42.7	12 28.7	24 47.3	8 07.7	2 00.2	7 14.3
16 Th	21 39 10	23 32 15	3♌11 04	9♌41 42	1 31.3	4 53.6	7 49.5	25 10.3	19 01.9	12 37.3	24 51.9	8 06.2	1 58.6	7 13.3
17 F	21 43 07	24 29 57	16 17 05	22 57 03	1 19.9	5 50.4	8 47.4	25 47.8	19 21.1	12 45.7	24 56.6	8 04.7	1 57.0	7 12.4
18 Sa	21 47 03	25 27 41	29 41 19	6♍29 35	1 07.5	6 53.7	9 45.7	26 25.5	19 40.1	12 54.0	25 01.3	8 03.2	1 55.3	7 11.5
19 Su	21 51 00	26 25 25	13♍21 25	20 16 21	0 55.5	8 03.2	10 44.5	27 03.2	19 59.0	13 02.2	25 06.1	8 01.6	1 53.7	7 10.7
20 M	21 54 56	27 23 11	27 13 55	4♎13 38	0 44.9	9 18.6	11 43.6	27 41.1	20 17.7	13 10.2	25 11.0	7 59.9	1 52.1	7 09.8
21 Tu	21 58 53	28 20 58	11♎15 01	18 17 38	0 36.9	10 39.7	12 43.1	28 19.1	20 36.4	13 18.1	25 16.0	7 58.3	1 50.4	7 09.0
22 W	22 02 49	29 18 46	25 21 05	2♏25 03	0 31.6	12 06.0	13 43.0	28 57.2	20 54.9	13 25.8	25 21.0	7 56.6	1 48.8	7 08.2
23 Th	22 06 46	0♍16 36	9♏29 14	16 33 25	0 29.0	13 37.3	14 43.3	29 35.4	21 13.2	13 33.4	25 26.1	7 54.8	1 47.1	7 07.4
24 F	22 10 43	1 14 26	23 37 26	0♐41 09	0 28.2	15 13.0	15 43.9	0♏13.7	21 31.4	13 40.9	25 31.2	7 53.1	1 45.5	7 06.7
25 Sa	22 14 39	2 12 18	7♐44 27	14 47 13	0 28.2	16 52.8	16 44.8	0 52.2	21 49.5	13 48.2	25 36.4	7 51.3	1 43.9	7 06.0
26 Su	22 18 36	3 10 11	21 49 23	28 50 47	0 27.5	18 36.3	17 46.1	1 30.7	22 07.5	13 55.4	25 41.7	7 49.4	1 42.2	7 05.3
27 M	22 22 32	4 08 06	5♑51 16	12♑50 38	0 25.0	20 22.9	18 47.7	2 09.3	22 25.3	14 02.4	25 47.1	7 47.6	1 40.6	7 04.6
28 Tu	22 26 29	5 06 01	19 48 38	26 45 00	0 20.0	22 12.1	19 49.6	2 48.0	22 42.9	14 09.3	25 52.5	7 45.7	1 38.9	7 04.0
29 W	22 30 25	6 03 58	3♒39 22	10♒31 23	0 12.1	24 03.7	20 51.9	3 26.8	23 00.4	14 16.0	25 57.9	7 43.7	1 37.3	7 03.4
30 Th	22 34 22	7 01 56	17 20 41	24 06 54	0 01.8	25 57.1	21 54.4	4 05.7	23 17.8	14 22.5	26 03.5	7 41.8	1 35.7	7 02.8
31 F	22 38 18	7 59 56	0♓49 39	7♓28 38	29♏49.8	27 51.9	22 57.2	4 44.8	23 34.9	14 29.0	26 09.1	7 39.8	1 34.0	7 02.3

Astro Data	Dy Hr Mn	Planet Ingress	Dy Hr Mn
♂0S	5 0:42	♂ ♎	3 12:31
☽0N	8 14:04	☉ ♌	22 10:01
♅R	13 9:49		
☿R	15 2:15	♀ ♋	7 13:43
♃⚻♇	18 9:46	☉ ♍	22 17:07
♃⚼♄	21 2:00	♂ ♏	23 15:24
♃⚹♅	22 4:04	☊ ♏R	30 3:40
☽0S	23 2:32		
☽0N	4 23:54		
☿D	8 5:39		
☽0S	19 9:38		

Last Aspect Dy Hr Mn		☽ Ingress Dy Hr Mn	Last Aspect Dy Hr Mn		☽ Ingress Dy Hr Mn
2 22:21	♂ □	♑ 2 22:51	31 23:30	♄ □	♒ 1 9:56
4 12:25	♄ □	♒ 5 0:26	3 7:24	♀ △	♓ 3 13:58
6 15:49	♄ △	♓ 7 4:29	5 17:56	♀ □	♈ 5 20:58
8 11:00	☉ △	♈ 9 12:14	7 20:04	♄ ☍	♉ 8 7:28
11 9:23	♄ ☍	♉ 11 23:30	9 18:55	☉ □	♊ 10 20:11
13 19:46	☉ ⚹	♊ 14 12:26	12 21:49	♄ △	♋ 13 8:27
16 10:56	♄ △	♋ 17 0:31	15 8:21	♄ □	♌ 15 18:05
19 4:24	☉ ☌	♌ 19 10:13	17 17:55	♂ ⚹	♍ 18 0:33
21 5:17	♄ ⚹	♍ 21 17:24	18 23:26	♃ □	♎ 20 4:45
23 0:44	♀ □	♎ 23 22:38	22 7:13	☉ ⚹	♏ 22 7:54
25 15:22	♄ ☌	♏ 26 2:29	23 9:34	♀ △	♐ 24 10:50
26 15:38	☿ □	♐ 28 5:18	26 6:39	♄ ⚹	♑ 26 13:58
29 21:01	♄ ⚹	♑ 30 7:29	28 10:33	♄ □	♒ 28 17:38
			30 17:48	☿ ☍	♓ 30 22:31

☽ Phases & Eclipses Dy Hr Mn		Astro Data
3 18:52	○ 12♑14	1 July 2012
11 1:48	☾ 19♈11	Julian Day # 41090
19 4:24	● 26♋55	SVP 5♓04'51"
26 8:56	☽ 3♏47	GC 27♐00.8 ⚴ 9♈12.0
		Eris 22♈41.8 ⚵ 22♏03.8R
2 3:27	○ 10♒15	⚷ 9♓35.3R ⚶ 26♉28.3
9 18:55	☾ 17♉34	☽ Mean ☊ 3♐20.4
17 15:54	● 25♌08	
24 13:54	☽ 1♐48	1 August 2012
31 13:58	○ 8♓34	Julian Day # 41121
		SVP 5♓04'46"
		GC 27♐00.9 ⚴ 11♈29.0R
		Eris 22♈42.5R ⚵ 22♏02.4
		⚷ 8♓40.0R ⚶ 8♊14.5
		☽ Mean ☊ 1♐41.9

Ephemeris pages reproduced by permission of the publisher: Starcrafts, LLC, 334-A Calef Hwy., Epping, NH 03042. astrocom.com & starcraftspublishing.com

LONGITUDE — September 2012

Day	Sid.Time	☉	0 hr ☽	Noon ☽	True ☊	☿	♀	♂	⚳	♃	♄	♅	♆	♇
1 Sa	22 42 15	8♍57 57	14♓03 34	20♓34 16	29♏37.3	29♌47.7	24♋00.4	5♏23.9	23♊52.0	14♊35.2	26♎14.7	7♈37.8	1♓32.4	7♑01.7
2 Su	22 46 12	9 56 00	27 00 36	3♈22 31	29R 25.5	1♍44.3	25 03.8	6 03.1	24 08.8	14 41.3	26 20.4	7R 35.8	1R 30.8	7R 01.2
3 M	22 50 08	10 54 04	9♈40 04	15 53 24	29 15.5	3 41.2	26 07.4	6 42.4	24 25.6	14 47.2	26 26.1	7 33.7	1 29.2	7 00.8
4 Tu	22 54 05	11 52 11	22 02 45	28 08 24	29 08.0	5 38.3	27 11.4	7 21.8	24 42.1	14 53.0	26 31.9	7 31.6	1 27.5	7 00.3
5 W	22 58 01	12 50 19	4♉10 46	10♉10 18	29 03.1	7 35.2	28 15.6	8 01.3	24 58.5	14 58.6	26 37.8	7 29.5	1 25.9	6 59.9
6 Th	23 01 58	13 48 30	16 07 31	22 02 59	29 00.6	9 31.9	29 20.1	8 40.9	25 14.7	15 04.1	26 43.7	7 27.4	1 24.3	6 59.5
7 F	23 05 54	14 46 42	27 57 19	3♊51 09	28D 59.9	11 28.0	0♌24.9	9 20.6	25 30.7	15 09.4	26 49.7	7 25.2	1 22.7	6 59.2
8 Sa	23 09 51	15 44 56	9♊45 10	15 40 03	29R 00.1	13 23.6	1 29.8	10 00.4	25 46.5	15 14.5	26 55.7	7 23.0	1 21.2	6 58.8
9 Su	23 13 47	16 43 13	21 36 30	27 35 11	29 00.1	15 18.4	2 35.1	10 40.2	26 02.2	15 19.4	27 01.8	7 20.8	1 19.6	6 58.6
10 M	23 17 44	17 41 31	3♋36 46	9♋41 54	28 58.9	17 12.4	3 40.5	11 20.2	26 17.7	15 24.2	27 07.9	7 18.6	1 18.0	6 58.3
11 Tu	23 21 41	18 39 52	15 51 09	22 05 05	28 55.7	19 05.4	4 46.2	12 00.3	26 33.0	15 28.8	27 14.1	7 16.4	1 16.5	6 58.1
12 W	23 25 37	19 38 14	28 24 08	4♌48 41	28 50.2	20 57.6	5 52.2	12 40.5	26 48.0	15 33.2	27 20.3	7 14.1	1 14.9	6 57.9
13 Th	23 29 34	20 36 39	11♌18 59	17 55 11	28 42.2	22 48.7	6 58.3	13 20.8	27 02.9	15 37.4	27 26.6	7 11.8	1 13.4	6 57.7
14 F	23 33 30	21 35 05	24 37 18	1♍25 11	28 32.4	24 38.8	8 04.6	14 01.1	27 17.6	15 41.5	27 32.9	7 09.5	1 11.9	6 57.5
15 Sa	23 37 27	22 33 34	8♍18 35	15 17 06	28 21.7	26 27.9	9 11.2	14 41.6	27 32.1	15 45.4	27 39.2	7 07.2	1 10.4	6 57.4
16 Su	23 41 23	23 32 04	22 20 11	29 27 12	28 11.1	28 15.9	10 17.9	15 22.2	27 46.4	15 49.0	27 45.6	7 04.9	1 08.9	6 57.3
17 M	23 45 20	24 30 37	6♎37 27	13♎50 08	28 01.9	0♎02.8	11 24.9	16 02.8	28 00.4	15 52.6	27 52.1	7 02.6	1 07.4	6 57.3
18 Tu	23 49 16	25 29 11	21 04 29	28 19 44	27 54.9	1 48.7	12 32.0	16 43.5	28 14.2	15 55.9	27 58.5	7 00.2	1 05.9	6D 57.3
19 W	23 53 13	26 27 47	5♏35 08	12♏50 01	27 50.5	3 33.6	13 39.3	17 24.4	28 27.8	15 59.0	28 05.1	6 57.9	1 04.5	6 57.3
20 Th	23 57 10	27 26 25	20 03 49	27 16 02	27D 48.6	5 17.4	14 46.9	18 05.3	28 41.2	16 01.9	28 11.6	6 55.5	1 03.0	6 57.3
21 F	0 01 06	28 25 04	4♐26 18	11♐34 17	27 48.5	7 00.2	15 54.5	18 46.3	28 54.4	16 04.7	28 18.2	6 53.1	1 01.6	6 57.4
22 Sa	0 05 03	29 23 45	18 39 48	25 42 41	27R 49.2	8 41.9	17 02.4	19 27.4	29 07.3	16 07.3	28 24.8	6 50.7	1 00.2	6 57.5
23 Su	0 08 59	0♎22 28	2♑42 51	9♑40 14	27 49.5	10 22.7	18 10.4	20 08.6	29 20.0	16 09.6	28 31.5	6 48.3	0 58.8	6 57.6
24 M	0 12 56	1 21 13	16 34 51	23 26 38	27 48.4	12 02.5	19 18.6	20 49.9	29 32.4	16 11.8	28 38.2	6 45.9	0 57.5	6 57.8
25 Tu	0 16 52	2 19 59	0♒15 36	7♒01 43	27 45.2	13 41.4	20 27.0	21 31.3	29 44.6	16 13.8	28 45.0	6 43.5	0 56.1	6 58.0
26 W	0 20 49	3 18 47	13 44 57	20 25 14	27 39.7	15 19.3	21 35.6	22 12.7	29 56.6	16 15.6	28 51.7	6 41.1	0 54.8	6 58.2
27 Th	0 24 45	4 17 36	27 02 31	3♓36 42	27 32.2	16 56.3	22 44.2	22 54.2	0♋08.3	16 17.2	28 58.5	6 38.7	0 53.5	6 58.5
28 F	0 28 42	5 16 28	10♓07 44	16 35 30	27 23.3	18 32.4	23 53.1	23 35.8	0 19.7	16 18.6	29 05.4	6 36.3	0 52.2	6 58.8
29 Sa	0 32 38	6 15 21	22 59 58	29 21 04	27 13.9	20 07.6	25 02.1	24 17.5	0 30.9	16 19.8	29 12.2	6 33.9	0 50.9	6 59.1
30 Su	0 36 35	7 14 16	5♈38 48	11♈53 11	27 05.1	21 41.9	26 11.3	24 59.3	0 41.8	16 20.8	29 19.1	6 31.5	0 49.6	6 59.4

LONGITUDE — October 2012

Day	Sid.Time	☉	0 hr ☽	Noon ☽	True ☊	☿	♀	♂	⚳	♃	♄	♅	♆	♇
1 M	0 40 32	8♎13 13	18♈04 16	24♈12 11	26♏57.6	23♎15.3	27♌20.6	25♏41.2	0♋52.4	16♊21.6	29♎26.0	6♈29.0	0♓48.4	6♑59.8
2 Tu	0 44 28	9 12 13	0♉17 07	6♉19 16	26R 52.1	24 47.9	28 30.1	26 23.1	1 02.8	16 22.2	29 33.0	6R 26.6	0R 47.2	7 00.2
3 W	0 48 25	10 11 14	12 18 56	18 16 26	26 48.8	26 19.6	29 39.7	27 05.2	1 12.9	16 22.6	29 40.0	6 24.2	0 46.0	7 00.7
4 Th	0 52 21	11 10 18	24 12 11	0♊06 37	26D 47.6	27 50.5	0♍49.5	27 47.3	1 22.7	16R 22.9	29 46.9	6 21.8	0 44.9	7 01.1
5 F	0 56 18	12 09 24	6♊00 13	11 53 32	26 47.9	29 20.5	1 59.4	28 29.5	1 32.2	16 22.9	29 54.0	6 19.4	0 43.7	7 01.6
6 Sa	1 00 14	13 08 32	17 47 07	23 41 36	26 49.3	0♏49.8	3 09.5	29 11.7	1 41.5	16 22.7	0♏01.0	6 17.0	0 42.6	7 02.2
7 Su	1 04 11	14 07 43	29 37 34	5♋35 42	26 50.8	2 18.1	4 19.7	29 54.1	1 50.4	16 22.3	0 08.1	6 14.6	0 41.5	7 02.7
8 M	1 08 07	15 06 55	11♋36 37	17 41 00	26R 51.8	3 45.7	5 30.0	0♐36.5	1 59.0	16 21.7	0 15.2	6 12.2	0 40.5	7 03.3
9 Tu	1 12 04	16 06 10	23 49 28	0♌02 38	26 51.5	5 12.3	6 40.5	1 19.0	2 07.4	16 20.9	0 22.3	6 09.9	0 39.4	7 04.0
10 W	1 16 01	17 05 28	6♌21 03	12 45 12	26 49.6	6 38.1	7 51.1	2 01.7	2 15.4	16 19.9	0 29.4	6 07.5	0 38.4	7 04.6
11 Th	1 19 57	18 04 48	19 15 31	25 52 19	26 46.1	8 03.0	9 01.8	2 44.3	2 23.1	16 18.7	0 36.5	6 05.1	0 37.4	7 05.3
12 F	1 23 54	19 04 09	2♍35 47	9♍25 58	26 41.2	9 27.0	10 12.6	3 27.1	2 30.4	16 17.3	0 43.7	6 02.8	0 36.4	7 06.0
13 Sa	1 27 50	20 03 34	16 22 45	23 25 53	26 35.5	10 50.1	11 23.6	4 09.9	2 37.5	16 15.7	0 50.8	6 00.5	0 35.5	7 06.8
14 Su	1 31 47	21 03 00	0♎34 56	7♎49 17	26 29.7	12 12.1	12 34.7	4 52.9	2 44.2	16 13.9	0 58.0	5 58.1	0 34.6	7 07.6
15 M	1 35 43	22 02 29	15 08 12	22 30 47	26 24.6	13 33.2	13 45.8	5 35.9	2 50.5	16 11.9	1 05.2	5 55.8	0 33.7	7 08.4
16 Tu	1 39 40	23 01 59	29 56 06	7♏23 06	26 20.9	14 53.1	14 57.1	6 19.0	2 56.6	16 09.6	1 12.4	5 53.5	0 32.9	7 09.2
17 W	1 43 36	24 01 32	14♏50 46	22 18 05	26D 18.9	16 11.9	16 08.6	7 02.1	3 02.3	16 07.2	1 19.7	5 51.3	0 32.0	7 10.1
18 Th	1 47 33	25 01 06	29 44 05	7♐07 55	26 18.5	17 29.5	17 20.1	7 45.4	3 07.6	16 04.6	1 26.9	5 49.0	0 31.2	7 11.0
19 F	1 51 30	26 00 43	14♐28 50	21 46 13	26 19.3	18 45.8	18 31.7	8 28.7	3 12.6	16 01.8	1 34.1	5 46.8	0 30.5	7 11.9
20 Sa	1 55 26	27 00 21	28 59 35	6♑08 33	26 20.8	20 00.7	19 43.4	9 12.1	3 17.2	15 58.8	1 41.4	5 44.6	0 29.7	7 12.9
21 Su	1 59 23	28 00 01	13♑12 54	20 12 30	26 22.2	21 14.1	20 55.2	9 55.6	3 21.4	15 55.6	1 48.6	5 42.4	0 29.0	7 13.9
22 M	2 03 19	28 59 43	27 07 18	3♒57 21	26R 22.9	22 25.8	22 07.1	10 39.1	3 25.3	15 52.2	1 55.9	5 40.2	0 28.4	7 14.9
23 Tu	2 07 16	29 59 26	10♒42 45	17 23 38	26 22.4	23 35.7	23 19.1	11 22.7	3 28.9	15 48.7	2 03.1	5 38.1	0 27.7	7 15.9
24 W	2 11 12	0♏59 11	24 00 11	0♓32 35	26 20.8	24 43.7	24 31.2	12 06.4	3 32.0	15 44.9	2 10.4	5 36.0	0 27.1	7 17.0
25 Th	2 15 09	1 58 58	7♓01 04	13 25 48	26 18.0	25 49.5	25 43.4	12 50.2	3 34.8	15 40.9	2 17.6	5 33.9	0 26.5	7 18.1
26 F	2 19 05	2 58 46	19 47 02	26 04 55	26 14.5	26 52.9	26 55.7	13 34.0	3 37.2	15 36.8	2 24.9	5 31.8	0 26.0	7 19.2
27 Sa	2 23 02	3 58 36	2♈19 41	8♈31 30	26 10.8	27 53.7	28 08.1	14 17.9	3 39.2	15 32.5	2 32.2	5 29.8	0 25.4	7 20.3
28 Su	2 26 59	4 58 28	14 40 33	20 47 02	26 07.3	28 51.6	29 20.5	15 01.8	3 40.8	15 28.0	2 39.4	5 27.7	0 24.9	7 21.5
29 M	2 30 55	5 58 22	26 51 07	2♉53 00	26 04.4	29 46.2	0♎33.1	15 45.9	3 42.1	15 23.3	2 46.7	5 25.8	0 24.5	7 22.7
30 Tu	2 34 52	6 58 18	8♉52 54	14 51 01	26 02.5	0♐37.3	1 45.7	16 30.0	3 42.9	15 18.5	2 53.9	5 23.8	0 24.1	7 24.0
31 W	2 38 48	7 58 15	20 47 36	26 42 55	26D 01.5	1 24.3	2 58.4	17 14.1	3R 43.4	15 13.5	3 01.2	5 21.9	0 23.7	7 25.2

Astro Data

	Dy Hr Mn
☽0N	1 9:05
☽0S	15 18:19
♇D	18 5:06
☿0S	18 8:03
♅□♇	19 5:57
☉0S	22 14:49
☽0N	28 16:24
♃R	4 13:18
♄△♆	11 2:38
☽0S	13 4:09
♃⚻♄	15 16:56
☽0N	25 21:59
♀0S	31 13:36
⚳R	31 15:46

Planet Ingress

		Dy Hr Mn
☿	♍	1 2:32
♀	♌	6 14:48
☿	♎	16 23:22
☉	♎	22 14:49
⚳	♋	26 7:00
♀	♍	3 6:59
☿	♏	5 10:35
♄	♏	5 20:34
♂	♐	7 3:21
☉	♏	23 0:14
♀	♎	28 13:04
☿	♐	29 6:18

Last Aspect / ☽ Ingress (September)

Last Aspect Dy Hr Mn			☽ Ingress	Dy Hr Mn
1 20:02	♀	△	♈	2 5:37
4 11:06	♀	□	♉	4 15:41
5 18:54	☉	△	♊	7 4:10
9 10:59	♄	△	♋	9 16:49
11 21:58	♄	□	♌	12 3:00
14 5:14	♄	⚹	♍	14 9:30
16 11:26	☿	☌	♎	16 12:55
18 11:30	♄	☌	♏	18 14:46
20 13:11	☉	⚹	♐	20 16:34
22 16:45	♄	⚹	♑	22 19:20
24 21:19	♄	□	♒	24 23:32
27 3:33	♄	△	♓	27 5:23
29 2:34	♂	△	♈	29 13:14

Last Aspect / ☽ Ingress (October)

Last Aspect Dy Hr Mn			☽ Ingress	Dy Hr Mn
1 22:32	♄	☍	♉	1 23:26
4 7:44	♂	☍	♊	4 11:47
5 21:08	♃	☌	♋	7 0:45
8 7:33	☉	□	♌	9 11:55
10 21:40	☉	⚹	♍	11 19:23
12 23:48	♃	□	♎	13 23:02
15 12:02	☉	☌	♏	16 0:06
17 2:23	☿	☌	♐	18 0:26
19 20:27	☉	⚹	♑	20 1:41
22 3:32	☉	□	♒	22 5:02
24 1:27	☿	□	♓	24 11:00
26 15:04	♀	☍	♈	26 19:31
28 1:32	♃	⚹	♉	29 6:15
29 21:01	♇	△	♊	31 18:40

☽ Phases & Eclipses

Dy Hr Mn		
8 13:15	☾	16♊17
16 2:11	●	23♍37
22 19:41	☽	0♑12
30 3:19	○	7♈22
8 7:33	☾	15♋26
15 12:02	●	22♎32
22 3:32	☽	29♑09
29 19:49	○	6♉48

Astro Data

1 September 2012
Julian Day # 41152
SVP 5♓04'42"
GC 27♐01.0 ⚴ 8♈21.9R
Eris 22♈33.7R ⚵ 26♏29.0
⚷ 7♓14.9R ⚶ 17♊59.3
☽ Mean ☊ 0♐03.4

1 October 2012
Julian Day # 41182
SVP 5♓04'40"
GC 27♐01.0 ⚴ 0♈48.3R
Eris 22♈18.4R ⚵ 3♐44.1
⚷ 5♓54.4R ⚶ 24♊10.5
☽ Mean ☊ 28♏28.1

© 2011 Janet Booth | 1-877-293-1607 | JanetsPlan-its.com

November 2012 LONGITUDE

Day	Sid.Time	☉	0 hr ☽	Noon ☽	True ☊	☿	♀	♂	⚳	♃	♄	♅	♆	♇
1 Th	2 42 45	8♏58 15	2♊37 16	8♊30 58	26♏01.6	2♐06.9	4♎11.2	17♐58.4	3♋43.5	15♊08.3	3♏08.4	5♈20.0	0♓23.3	7♑26.5
2 F	2 46 41	9 58 16	14 24 21	20 17 50	26 02.4	2 44.6	5 24.1	18 42.7	3R 43.1	15R 02.9	3 15.6	5R 18.1	0R 23.0	7 27.8
3 Sa	2 50 38	10 58 20	26 11 49	2♋06 46	26 03.7	3 16.8	6 37.0	19 27.0	3 42.4	14 57.4	3 22.9	5 16.3	0 22.7	7 29.1
4 Su	2 54 34	11 58 26	8♋03 10	14 01 30	26 05.1	3 42.8	7 50.1	20 11.5	3 41.2	14 51.8	3 30.1	5 14.5	0 22.4	7 30.5
5 M	2 58 31	12 58 33	20 02 20	26 06 12	26 06.3	4 02.2	9 03.2	20 56.0	3 39.7	14 45.9	3 37.3	5 12.7	0 22.2	7 31.9
6 Tu	3 02 28	13 58 43	2♌13 40	8♌25 18	26 07.1	4R 14.1	10 16.4	21 40.5	3 37.7	14 40.0	3 44.5	5 11.0	0 22.0	7 33.3
7 W	3 06 24	14 58 55	14 41 39	21 03 14	26R 07.4	4 18.0	11 29.7	22 25.2	3 35.4	14 33.8	3 51.7	5 09.3	0 21.8	7 34.7
8 Th	3 10 21	15 59 09	27 30 34	4♍04 05	26 07.2	4 13.2	12 43.0	23 09.9	3 32.6	14 27.6	3 58.8	5 07.6	0 21.7	7 36.2
9 F	3 14 17	16 59 25	10♍44 06	17 30 55	26 06.5	3 59.2	13 56.4	23 54.6	3 29.4	14 21.1	4 06.0	5 06.0	0 21.6	7 37.7
10 Sa	3 18 14	17 59 42	24 24 38	1♎25 16	26 05.6	3 35.4	15 09.9	24 39.5	3 25.8	14 14.6	4 13.1	5 04.4	0 21.5	7 39.2
11 Su	3 22 10	19 00 02	8♎32 39	15 46 26	26 04.7	3 01.6	16 23.4	25 24.4	3 21.7	14 07.9	4 20.2	5 02.8	0D 21.5	7 40.7
12 M	3 26 07	20 00 24	23 06 06	0♏30 57	26 03.9	2 17.7	17 37.0	26 09.3	3 17.3	14 01.1	4 27.3	5 01.3	0 21.5	7 42.3
13 Tu	3 30 03	21 00 48	8♏00 08	15 32 39	26 03.5	1 24.2	18 50.6	26 54.4	3 12.5	13 54.2	4 34.4	4 59.8	0 21.6	7 43.8
14 W	3 34 00	22 01 13	23 07 21	0♐43 05	26D 03.3	0 21.8	20 04.4	27 39.4	3 07.2	13 47.1	4 41.5	4 58.4	0 21.6	7 45.4
15 Th	3 37 57	23 01 40	8♐18 37	15 52 45	26 03.4	29♏11.6	21 18.1	28 24.6	3 01.6	13 40.0	4 48.5	4 57.0	0 21.8	7 47.0
16 F	3 41 53	24 02 09	23 24 23	0♑52 27	26 03.5	27 55.6	22 32.0	29 09.8	2 55.5	13 32.7	4 55.5	4 55.7	0 21.9	7 48.7
17 Sa	3 45 50	25 02 39	8♑16 06	15 34 36	26 03.7	26 35.8	23 45.8	29 55.1	2 49.1	13 25.3	5 02.5	4 54.4	0 22.1	7 50.3
18 Su	3 49 46	26 03 10	22 47 22	29 54 02	26R 03.7	25 14.7	24 59.8	0♑40.4	2 42.2	13 17.9	5 09.5	4 53.1	0 22.3	7 52.0
19 M	3 53 43	27 03 43	6♒54 22	13♒48 18	26 03.7	23 55.0	26 13.7	1 25.8	2 35.0	13 10.3	5 16.4	4 51.9	0 22.6	7 53.7
20 Tu	3 57 39	28 04 17	20 35 53	27 17 17	26D 03.6	22 39.3	27 27.7	2 11.2	2 27.4	13 02.7	5 23.3	4 50.7	0 22.8	7 55.4
21 W	4 01 36	29 04 52	3♓52 47	10♓22 41	26 03.6	21 30.2	28 41.8	2 56.7	2 19.4	12 55.0	5 30.2	4 49.6	0 23.2	7 57.2
22 Th	4 05 32	0♐05 28	16 47 24	23 07 20	26 03.8	20 29.5	29 55.9	3 42.3	2 11.0	12 47.2	5 37.0	4 48.5	0 23.5	7 58.9
23 F	4 09 29	1 06 05	29 22 55	5♈34 35	26 04.2	19 38.9	1♏10.0	4 27.9	2 02.3	12 39.3	5 43.9	4 47.5	0 23.9	8 00.7
24 Sa	4 13 26	2 06 44	11♈42 49	17 48 00	26 04.8	18 59.4	2 24.2	5 13.5	1 53.2	12 31.4	5 50.6	4 46.5	0 24.3	8 02.5
25 Su	4 17 22	3 07 23	23 50 34	29 50 54	26 05.5	18 31.5	3 38.5	5 59.2	1 43.8	12 23.4	5 57.4	4 45.5	0 24.8	8 04.3
26 M	4 21 19	4 08 04	5♉49 23	11♉46 21	26 06.3	18D 15.2	4 52.7	6 45.0	1 34.0	12 15.4	6 04.1	4 44.6	0 25.3	8 06.1
27 Tu	4 25 15	5 08 46	17 42 08	23 37 02	26R 06.8	18 10.2	6 07.0	7 30.8	1 23.9	12 07.4	6 10.8	4 43.8	0 25.8	8 08.0
28 W	4 29 12	6 09 30	29 31 20	5♊25 19	26 06.9	18 16.1	7 21.4	8 16.6	1 13.5	11 59.3	6 17.4	4 43.0	0 26.3	8 09.8
29 Th	4 33 08	7 10 14	11♊19 14	17 13 22	26 06.4	18 31.9	8 35.8	9 02.6	1 02.7	11 51.1	6 24.0	4 42.2	0 26.9	8 11.7
30 F	4 37 05	8 11 00	23 07 57	29 03 15	26 05.3	18 56.9	9 50.2	9 48.5	0 51.7	11 43.0	6 30.6	4 41.5	0 27.6	8 13.6

December 2012 LONGITUDE

Day	Sid.Time	☉	0 hr ☽	Noon ☽	True ☊	☿	♀	♂	⚳	♃	♄	♅	♆	♇
1 Sa	4 41 01	9♐11 48	4♋59 34	10♋57 09	26♏03.6	19♏30.3	11♏04.7	10♑34.5	0♋40.3	11♊34.8	6♏37.1	4♈40.9	0♓28.2	8♑15.5
2 Su	4 44 58	10 12 36	16 56 20	22 57 24	26R 01.5	20 11.0	12 19.2	11 20.6	0R 28.7	11R 26.7	6 43.6	4R 40.3	0 28.9	8 17.4
3 M	4 48 55	11 13 26	29 00 44	5♌06 41	25 59.1	20 58.4	13 33.7	12 06.6	0 16.8	11 18.5	6 50.0	4 39.7	0 29.6	8 19.3
4 Tu	4 52 51	12 14 17	11♌15 38	17 27 59	25 56.9	21 51.6	14 48.3	12 52.8	0 04.7	11 10.3	6 56.4	4 39.2	0 30.4	8 21.3
5 W	4 56 48	13 15 09	23 44 09	0♍04 35	25 55.1	22 49.8	16 02.9	13 39.0	29♊52.3	11 02.1	7 02.7	4 38.7	0 31.2	8 23.2
6 Th	5 00 44	14 16 03	6♍29 40	12 59 51	25D 54.1	23 52.5	17 17.6	14 25.2	29 39.6	10 53.9	7 09.0	4 38.3	0 32.0	8 25.2
7 F	5 04 41	15 16 58	19 35 31	26 16 59	25 53.9	24 59.1	18 32.3	15 11.5	29 26.8	10 45.8	7 15.3	4 37.9	0 32.9	8 27.2
8 Sa	5 08 37	16 17 54	3♎04 34	9♎58 27	25 54.6	26 09.0	19 47.0	15 57.8	29 13.7	10 37.7	7 21.5	4 37.6	0 33.7	8 29.2
9 Su	5 12 34	17 18 52	16 58 44	24 05 23	25 56.0	27 21.8	21 01.7	16 44.2	29 00.4	10 29.6	7 27.6	4 37.4	0 34.7	8 31.2
10 M	5 16 30	18 19 51	1♏18 13	8♏36 55	25 57.4	28 37.1	22 16.5	17 30.6	28 47.0	10 21.5	7 33.7	4 37.2	0 35.6	8 33.2
11 Tu	5 20 27	19 20 51	16 00 57	23 29 37	25R 58.5	29 54.6	23 31.2	18 17.1	28 33.4	10 13.5	7 39.8	4 37.0	0 36.6	8 35.2
12 W	5 24 24	20 21 52	1♐02 02	8♐37 10	25 58.7	1♐13.9	24 46.1	19 03.6	28 19.7	10 05.6	7 45.8	4 36.9	0 37.6	8 37.3
13 Th	5 28 20	21 22 54	16 13 53	23 50 54	25 57.6	2 34.9	26 00.9	19 50.1	28 05.8	9 57.7	7 51.7	4D 36.8	0 38.7	8 39.3
14 F	5 32 17	22 23 57	1♑26 58	9♑00 48	25 55.1	3 57.3	27 15.8	20 36.7	27 51.9	9 49.9	7 57.6	4 36.8	0 39.8	8 41.4
15 Sa	5 36 13	23 25 00	16 31 11	23 57 03	25 51.5	5 20.9	28 30.6	21 23.3	27 37.8	9 42.1	8 03.5	4 36.9	0 40.9	8 43.5
16 Su	5 40 10	24 26 04	1♒17 27	8♒31 39	25 47.2	6 45.5	29 45.5	22 10.0	27 23.7	9 34.4	8 09.2	4 37.0	0 42.0	8 45.5
17 M	5 44 06	25 27 09	15 39 05	22 39 26	25 43.0	8 11.1	1♐00.4	22 56.7	27 09.5	9 26.8	8 14.9	4 37.1	0 43.2	8 47.6
18 Tu	5 48 03	26 28 14	29 32 31	6♓18 22	25 39.3	9 37.5	2 15.4	23 43.4	26 55.3	9 19.3	8 20.6	4 37.4	0 44.4	8 49.7
19 W	5 51 59	27 29 19	12♓57 10	19 29 12	25 36.9	11 04.6	3 30.3	24 30.2	26 41.1	9 11.9	8 26.2	4 37.6	0 45.6	8 51.8
20 Th	5 55 56	28 30 25	25 54 55	2♈14 48	25D 35.9	12 32.3	4 45.3	25 17.0	26 26.9	9 04.6	8 31.7	4 37.9	0 46.9	8 53.9
21 F	5 59 53	29 31 30	8♈29 24	14 39 18	25 36.2	14 00.6	6 00.2	26 03.8	26 12.7	8 57.4	8 37.1	4 38.3	0 48.2	8 56.0
22 Sa	6 03 49	0♑32 36	20 45 07	26 47 27	25 37.6	15 29.4	7 15.2	26 50.7	25 58.5	8 50.3	8 42.5	4 38.7	0 49.5	8 58.1
23 Su	6 07 46	1 33 42	2♉46 55	8♉44 06	25 39.4	16 58.6	8 30.2	27 37.6	25 44.4	8 43.3	8 47.9	4 39.2	0 50.9	9 00.2
24 M	6 11 42	2 34 49	14 39 33	20 33 49	25R 41.0	18 28.3	9 45.2	28 24.5	25 30.4	8 36.4	8 53.1	4 39.7	0 52.2	9 02.3
25 Tu	6 15 39	3 35 56	26 27 22	2♊20 39	25 41.6	19 58.3	11 00.2	29 11.4	25 16.5	8 29.7	8 58.3	4 40.2	0 53.7	9 04.4
26 W	6 19 35	4 37 02	8♊14 06	14 08 03	25 40.6	21 28.8	12 15.3	29 58.4	25 02.6	8 23.1	9 03.4	4 40.9	0 55.1	9 06.6
27 Th	6 23 32	5 38 09	20 02 52	25 58 48	25 37.7	22 59.5	13 30.3	0♒45.4	24 48.9	8 16.6	9 08.5	4 41.5	0 56.6	9 08.7
28 F	6 27 28	6 39 17	1♋56 06	7♋55 01	25 32.7	24 30.6	14 45.4	1 32.4	24 35.4	8 10.3	9 13.5	4 42.3	0 58.0	9 10.8
29 Sa	6 31 25	7 40 24	13 55 43	19 58 21	25 25.9	26 02.1	16 00.4	2 19.5	24 22.0	8 04.1	9 18.4	4 43.0	0 59.6	9 12.9
30 Su	6 35 22	8 41 32	26 03 07	2♌10 07	25 17.8	27 33.9	17 15.5	3 06.6	24 08.7	7 58.0	9 23.2	4 43.9	1 01.1	9 15.1
31 M	6 39 18	9 42 40	8♌19 30	14 31 25	25 09.0	29 06.0	18 30.6	3 53.7	23 55.7	7 52.1	9 28.0	4 44.7	1 02.7	9 17.2

Astro Data

	Dy Hr Mn
☿ R	6 23:04
☽ 0S	9 13:54
♆ D	11 7:52
♄ ⚻ ♅	16 0:27
☽ 0N	22 3:24
☿ D	26 22:50
☽ 0S	6 22:21
♅ D	13 12:02
☽ 0N	19 10:46
♃ ⚻ ♇	21 3:35
♃ ⚻ ♄	22 15:02
♄ ⚹ ♇	27 1:41

Planet Ingress

		Dy Hr Mn
☿	♏R	14 7:42
♂	♑	17 2:36
☉	♐	21 21:50
♀	♏	22 1:20
⚳	♊R	4 9:05
☿	♐	11 1:40
♀	♐	16 4:38
☉	♑	21 11:12
♂	♒	26 0:49
☿	♑	31 14:03

Last Aspect / ☽ Ingress

Last Aspect Dy Hr Mn			☽ Ingress	Dy Hr Mn
2 9:21	♂	☍	♋	3 7:43
4 8:37	☉	△	♌	5 19:39
7 15:27	♂	△	♍	8 4:35
10 0:27	♂	□	♎	10 9:35
12 5:13	♂	⚹	♏	12 11:10
14 10:39	☿	☌	♐	14 10:52
16 9:44	♂	☌	♑	16 10:35
18 5:54	☉	⚹	♒	18 12:10
20 14:31	☉	□	♓	20 16:55
22 6:32	☿	△	♈	23 1:12
24 1:34	♃	⚹	♉	25 12:18
27 0:57	☿	☍	♊	28 0:58
29 1:04	♃	☌	♋	30 13:55

Last Aspect / ☽ Ingress

Last Aspect Dy Hr Mn			☽ Ingress	Dy Hr Mn
2 6:55	☿	△	♌	3 1:57
4 22:07	☿	□	♍	5 11:51
7 10:35	☿	⚹	♎	7 18:35
9 0:37	☉	⚹	♏	9 21:51
11 13:08	♀	☌	♐	11 22:22
13 8:42	☉	☌	♑	13 21:42
15 21:15	♀	⚹	♒	15 21:53
17 18:12	☉	⚹	♓	18 0:48
20 5:19	☉	□	♈	20 7:43
22 12:57	♂	□	♉	22 18:25
25 5:58	♂	△	♊	25 7:13
27 6:50	☿	☍	♋	27 20:06
28 14:43	♄	△	♌	30 7:45

☽ Phases & Eclipses

Dy Hr Mn		
7 0:36	☾	15♌00
13 22:08	●	21♏57
13 22:11:47	●	T 04'02"
20 14:31	☽	28♒41
28 14:46	○	6♊47
28 14:33	●	A 0.915
6 15:31	☾	14♍55
13 8:42	●	21♐45
20 5:19	☽	28♓44
28 10:21	○	7♋06

Astro Data

1 November 2012
Julian Day # 41213
SVP 5♓04'37"
GC 27♐01.1 ⚴ 23♓51.3R
Eris 22♈00.0R ⚵ 13♐10.7
⚷ 5♓04.5R ⚶ 25♊09.1R
☽ Mean ☊ 26♏49.6

1 December 2012
Julian Day # 41243
SVP 5♓04'32"
GC 27♐01.2 ⚴ 22♓46.2
Eris 21♈45.1R ⚵ 23♐27.9
⚷ 5♓06.5 ⚶ 19♊49.1R
☽ Mean ☊ 25♏14.2

Ephemeris pages reproduced by permission of the publisher: Starcrafts, LLC, 334-A Calef Hwy., Epping, NH 03042. astrocom.com & starcraftspublishing.com

© 2011 Janet Booth | 1-877-293-1607 | JanetsPlan-its.com

Moon Family Table

by Dietrech Pessin

Take the guess work out of forecasting for yourself, clients, business matters and more.
The unique patterns of this powerful predictive tool unlock the mystery of the timing of events.

New Moon			First Quarter Moon			Full Moon			Third Quarter Moon		
18/Oct/2009	24° ♎	58	18/Jul/2010	25° ♎	41	18/Apr/2011	27° ♎	44	16/Jan/2012	25° ♎	37
16/Nov/2009	24° ♏	34	16/Aug/2010	23° ♏	46	17/May/2011	26° ♏	13	14/Feb/2012	25° ♏	24
16/Dec/2009	24° ♐	39	15/Sep/2010	22° ♐	17	**15/Jun/2011**	**24° ♐**	**23**	15/Mar/2012	24° ♐	51
15/Jan/2010	**25° ♑**	**1**	14/Oct/2010	21° ♑	25	15/Jul/2011	22° ♑	27	13/Apr/2012	23° ♑	54
14/Feb/2010	25° ♒	17	13/Nov/2010	21° ♒	11	13/Aug/2011	20° ♒	41	12/May/2012	22° ♒	33
15/Mar/2010	25° ♓	10	13/Dec/2010	21° ♓	27	12/Sep/2011	19° ♓	17	11/Jun/2012	20° ♓	54
14/Apr/2010	24° ♈	27	12/Jan/2011	21° ♈	54	12/Oct/2011	18° ♈	24	11/Jul/2012	19° ♈	10
14/May/2010	23° ♉	9	11/Feb/2011	22° ♉	12	10/Nov/2011	18° ♉	4	9/Aug/2012	17° ♉	34
12/Jun/2010	21° ♊	23	12/Mar/2011	22° ♊	3	**10/Dec/2011**	**18° ♊**	**10**	8/Sep/2012	16° ♊	17
11/Jul/2010	**19° ♋**	**23**	11/Apr/2011	21° ♋	15	9/Jan/2012	18° ♋	25	8/Oct/2012	15° ♋	25
10/Aug/2010	17° ♌	24	10/May/2011	19° ♌	50	7/Feb/2012	18° ♌	31	7/Nov/2012	15° ♌	0
8/Sep/2010	15° ♍	40	9/Jun/2011	17° ♍	56	8/Mar/2012	18° ♍	13	6/Dec/2012	14° ♍	55
7/Oct/2010	14° ♎	23	8/Jul/2011	15° ♎	47	6/Apr/2012	17° ♎	23	5/Jan/2013	14° ♎	58
6/Nov/2010	13° ♏	40	6/Aug/2011	13° ♏	39	6/May/2012	16° ♏	1	3/Feb/2013	14° ♏	54
5/Dec/2010	13° ♐	28	4/Sep/2011	11° ♐	51	**4/Jun/2012**	**14° ♐**	**13**	4/Mar/2013	14° ♐	29
4/Jan/2011	**13° ♑**	**38**	4/Oct/2011	10° ♑	33	3/Jul/2012	12° ♑	13	3/Apr/2013	13° ♑	35
3/Feb/2011	13° ♒	53	2/Nov/2011	09° ♒	54	2/Aug/2012	10° ♒	15	2/May/2013	12° ♒	12
4/Mar/2011	13° ♓	55	2/Dec/2011	09° ♓	51	31/Aug/2012	08° ♓	33	31/May/2013	10° ♓	28
3/Apr/2011	13° ♈	29	1/Jan/2012	10° ♈	13	30/Sep/2012	07° ♈	22	30/Jun/2013	08° ♈	34
3/May/2011	12° ♉	30	31/Jan/2012	10° ♉	40	29/Oct/2012	06° ♉	47	29/Jul/2013	06° ♉	45
1/Jun/2011	**11° ♊**	**1**	1/Mar/2012	10° ♊	51	**28/Nov/2012**	**06° ♊**	**46**	28/Aug/2013	05° ♊	14
1/Jul/2011	**09° ♋**	**12**	30/Mar/2012	10° ♋	30	28/Dec/2012	07° ♋	5	27/Sep/2013	04° ♋	12
30/Jul/2011	07° ♌	15	29/Apr/2012	09° ♌	29	27/Jan/2013	07° ♌	24	26/Oct/2013	03° ♌	43
29/Aug/2011	05° ♍	27	28/May/2012	07° ♍	53	25/Feb/2013	07° ♍	24	25/Nov/2013	03° ♍	41
27/Sep/2011	04° ♎	0	27/Jun/2012	05° ♎	53	27/Mar/2013	06° ♎	52	25/Dec/2013	03° ♎	55
26/Oct/2011	03° ♏	2	26/Jul/2012	03° ♏	46	**25/Apr/2013**	**05° ♏**	**45**	24/Jan/2014	04° ♏	7
25/Nov/2011	**02° ♐**	**36**	24/Aug/2012	01° ♐	47	**25/May/2013**	**04° ♐**	**8**	22/Feb/2014	03° ♐	59
24/Dec/2011	02° ♑	34	22/Sep/2012	00° ♑	11	23/Jun/2013	02° ♑	9	24/Mar/2014	03° ♑	20
23/Jan/2012	02° ♒	41	22/Oct/2012	29° ♑	8	22/Jul/2013	00° ♒	5	22/Apr/2014	02° ♒	6
21/Feb/2012	02° ♓	42	20/Nov/2012	28° ♒	40	21/Aug/2013	28° ♒	10	21/May/2014	00° ♓	24
22/Mar/2012	02° ♈	22	20/Dec/2012	28° ♓	43	19/Sep/2013	26° ♓	40	19/Jun/2014	28° ♓	24
21/Apr/2012	01° ♉	35	18/Jan/2013	29° ♈	3	**18/Oct/2013**	**25° ♈**	**45**	19/Jul/2014	26° ♈	21
20/May/2012	**00° ♊**	**20**	17/Feb/2013	29° ♉	20	17/Nov/2013	25° ♉	26	17/Aug/2014	24° ♉	31
19/Jun/2012	28° ♊	43	19/Mar/2013	29° ♊	16	17/Dec/2013	25° ♊	36	16/Sep/2014	23° ♊	8
19/Jul/2012	26° ♋	54	18/Apr/2013	28° ♋	38	16/Jan/2014	25° ♋	58	15/Oct/2014	22° ♋	21
17/Aug/2012	25° ♌	8	18/May/2013	27° ♌	24	14/Feb/2014	26° ♌	12	14/Nov/2014	22° ♌	9
16/Sep/2012	23° ♍	37	16/Jun/2013	25° ♍	43	16/Mar/2014	26° ♍	1	14/Dec/2014	22° ♍	26
15/Oct/2012	22° ♎	32	16/Jul/2013	23° ♎	46	**15/Apr/2014**	**25° ♎**	**15**	13/Jan/2015	22° ♎	52
13/Nov/2012	**21° ♏**	**56**	14/Aug/2013	21° ♏	49	14/May/2014	23° ♏	54	12/Feb/2015	23° ♏	5
13/Dec/2012	21° ♐	45	12/Sep/2013	20° ♐	5	13/Jun/2014	22° ♐	5	13/Mar/2015	22° ♐	49

How to Use: Read Moon Family table left to right. Notice how each phase occurs nine months beyond the one before it. The symbolism of a New Moon relates to new developments, the budding growth of an issue is apparent at the First Quarter, the complete awareness is openly charged at the Full Moon, and the pay-off is gained at the Third Quarter phase. The Moon Families with solar or lunar eclipses (in bold print) are bursting with even more activity. Compare the zodiacal degrees of Moon Families to a natal chart to note what's impacted. See if you can make a connection to current events and developments. **Eclipses are shown in bold print.**

2012 begins with the Jan. 16 Third Quarter phase. The New Moon of its family was in Oct. 2009, followed by a related First Quarter and Full Moon. In the New Moon column, find the first New Moon of 2012 on Jan. 23. Its family lasts into 2015.

★ALL STAR LIST★

This list organizes the major astrological phenomena for 2012 according to zodiac position. Degrees of signs in the same Mode (see Keywords, p. 98) will be either conjunct, square or opposition. These are the aspects that bring action into our lives. The degree is listed, followed by the minutes of arc (1/60 of a degree). Find which parts of your chart are being contacted by this year's planetary phenomena. Locate the sign and degree of any part of your chart. Look down the list for that degree (+/− 2 degrees) in signs which aspect that sign (explained on p. 62).

Sign	Degree	Date	Phenomenon	Sign	Degree	Date	Phenomenon
AR	0°40'	01/21/12	Ceres ends shadow	GE	0°00'	06/11/12	Jupiter enters Gemini
AR	1°16'	01/17/12	Uranus semisextile Jupiter	GE	0°21'	05/20/12	Solar Eclipse New Moon
AR	2°22'	03/22/12	New Moon	GE	2°49'	07/10/12	South Node square Neptune
AR	4°34'	03/25/12	Uranus ends prior R shadow	GE	3°20'	06/25/12	Jupiter square Neptune
AR	4°36'	03/26/12	Uranus begins next R shadow	GE	3°31'	06/27/12	South Node conjunct Jupiter
AR	4°36'	12/13/12	Uranus turns Direct	GE	6°10'	07/10/12	Ceres conjunct Jupiter
AR	4°56'	11/15/12	Uranus quincunx Saturn	GE	6°20'	07/10/12	Jupiter begins shadow
AR	4°59'	11/13/12	Uranus semisextile Chiron	GE	6°20'	01/30/13	Jupiter turns Direct
AR	6°49'	03/12/12	Mercury turns Retrograde	GE	6°47'	11/28/12	Lunar Eclipse Full Moon
AR	6°49'	04/23/12	Mercury exits shadow	GE	7°29'	04/12/12	Venus begins shadow
AR	6°52'	05/07/12	Uranus semisquare Jupiter	GE	7°29'	06/27/12	Venus turns Direct
AR	6°57'	09/19/12	Uranus square Pluto	GE	7°43'	07/17/12	Jupiter semisquare Eris
AR	7°22'	09/29/12	Full Moon	GE	7°47'	07/18/12	Jupiter quincunx Pluto
AR	8°12'	08/11/12	Uranus semisextile Chiron	GE	7°49'	04/07/12	South Node square Chiron
AR	8°23'	06/24/12	Uranus square Pluto	GE	8°18'	07/20/12	Jupiter sesquiquadrate Saturn
AR	8°30'	07/22/12	Uranus sextile Jupiter	GE	8°30'	07/22/12	Jupiter sextile Uranus
AR	8°32'	07/13/12	Uranus turns Retrograde	GE	8°45'	12/22/12	Jupiter quincunx Saturn
AR	21°23'	01/09/12	Eris turns Direct	GE	8°56'	07/24/12	Jupiter square Chiron
AR	21°37'	03/01/12	Eris begins next R shadow	GE	8°56'	12/20/12	Jupiter quincunx Pluto
AR	21°37'	01/08/13	Eris turns Direct	GE	12°04'	8/12/12	Vesta conjunct Jupiter
AR	21°48'	03/20/12	Eris semisquare Chiron	GE	16°10'	10/15/12	Jupiter sesquiquadrate Saturn
AR	22°30'	05/26/12	Eris ends prior R shadow	GE	16°23'	10/04/12	Jupiter turns Retrograde
AR	22°36'	08/24/12	Eris semisquare Chiron	GE	19°45'	08/18/12	Ceres enters shadow
AR	22°42'	07/17/12	Eris semisquare Jupiter	GE	19°45'	02/02/13	Ceres turns Direct
AR	22°43'	07/18/12	Eris turns Retrograde	GE	23°59'	05/15/12	Venus turns Retrograde
				GE	23°59'	07/31/12	Venus ends shadow
TA	0°22'	12/25/11	Jupiter turns Direct	GE	28°43'	06/19/12	New Moon
TA	1°16'	01/17/12	Jupiter semisextile Uranus				
TA	1°35'	04/21/12	New Moon	CN	3°43'	10/31/12	Ceres turns Retrograde
TA	4°32'	02/14/12	Jupiter sextile Chiron	CN	7°06'	12/28/12	Full Moon
TA	6°48'	10/29/12	Full Moon	CN	18°26'	01/09/12	Full Moon
TA	9°21'	03/13/12	Jupiter trine Pluto	CN	26°55'	07/19/12	New Moon
TA	10°21'	03/17/12	Jupiter ends shadow				
TA	21°52'	05/07/12	Jupiter semisquare Uranus	LE	1°25'	06/28/12	Mercury begins shadow
TA	23°58'	05/16/12	Jupiter quincunx Saturn	LE	1°25'	08/08/12	Mercury turns Direct
TA	24°13'	05/17/12	Jupiter sesquiquadrate Pluto	LE	12°32'	07/14/12	Mercury turns Retrograde
TA	29°59'	09/01/12	South Node enters Taurus	LE	12°32'	08/22/12	Mercury exits shadow
				LE	18°32'	02/07/12	Full Moon
				LE	25°08'	08/17/12	New Moon

Sign	Degree	Date	Phenomenon	Sign	Degree	Date	Phenomenon
VI	3°41'	11/18/11	Mars begins shadow	CP	6°57'	12/21/11	Pluto begins next R shadow
VI	3°41'	04/13/12	Mars turns Direct	CP	6°57'	09/18/12	Pluto turns Direct
VI	18°13'	03/08/12	Full Moon	CP	6°57'	09/19/12	Pluto square Uranus
VI	23°06'	01/23/12	Mars turns Retrograde	CP	6°59'	09/06/12	Pluto sextile Chiron
VI	23°06'	06/19/12	Mars ends shadow	CP	7°09'	08/19/12	Pluto quintile Saturn
VI	23°37'	09/15/12	New Moon	CP	7°30'	01/05/12	Pluto ends prior R shadow
				CP	7°47'	07/18/12	Pluto quincunx Jupiter
LI	17°23'	04/06/12	Full Moon	CP	8°23'	06/24/12	Pluto square Uranus
LI	22°32'	10/15/12	New Moon	CP	8°56'	12/20/12	Pluto quincunx Jupiter
LI	22°46'	11/04/11	Saturn begins shadow	CP	8°59'	12/22/12	Pluto enters next R shadow
LI	22°46'	06/25/12	Saturn turns Direct	CP	9°08'	12/26/12	Pluto sextile Saturn
LI	23°18'	07/20/12	Saturn sesquiquadrate Jupiter	CP	9°13'	05/17/12	Pluto sesquiquadrate Jupiter
LI	23°44'	07/29/12	Saturn sesquiquadrate Chiron	CP	9°18'	05/12/12	Pluto sextile Chiron
LI	23°58'	05/16/12	Saturn quincunx Jupiter	CP	9°21'	03/13/12	Pluto trine Jupiter
LI	24°17'	05/11/12	Saturn sesquiquadrate Chiron	CP	9°34'	04/10/12	Pluto turns Retrograde
LI	24°49'	08/15/12	Mars conjunct Saturn	CP	9°34'	01/07/13	Pluto ends prior R shadow
LI	25°09'	08/19/12	Saturn quintile Pluto	CP	12°14'	07/03/12	Full Moon
LI	29°30'	02/07/12	Saturn turns Retrograde				
LI	29°30'	10/01/12	Saturn ends shadow	AQ	2°42'	01/23/12	New Moon (Chinese New Year)
				AQ	10°15'	08/01/12	Full Moon
SC	0°00'	10/05/12	Saturn enters Scorpio				
SC	0°37'	10/10/12	Saturn trine Neptune	PI	0°00'	02/03/12	Neptune enters Pisces
SC	1°10'	10/15/12	Saturn sesquiquadrate Jupiter	PI	0°21'	02/13/12	Neptune begins next R shadow
SC	4°49'	11/14/12	Saturn begins shadow	PI	0°21'	11/11/12	Neptune turns Direct
SC	4°56'	11/15/12	Saturn quincunx Uranus	PI	0°37'	10/10/12	Neptune trine Saturn
SC	4°58'	11/16/12	Saturn trine Chiron	PI	0°56'	02/28/12	Neptune ends prior R shadow
SC	8°45'	12/22/12	Saturn quincunx Jupiter	PI	2°42'	02/21/12	New Moon
SC	9°08'	12/26/12	Saturn sextile Pluto	PI	2°49'	07/10/12	Neptune square Nodes
SC	16°01'	05/05/12	Full Moon	PI	3°09'	06/04/12	Neptune turns Retrograde
SC	18°10'	10/18/12	Mercury begins shadow	PI	3°20'	06/25/12	Neptune square Jupiter
SC	18°10'	11/26/12	Mercury turns Direct	PI	4°32'	02/14/12	Chiron sextile Jupiter
SC	21°57'	11/13/12	Solar Eclipse New Moon	PI	4°58'	11/16/12	Chiron trine Saturn
SC	29°59'	09/01/12	North Node enters Scorpio	PI	4°59'	02/21/12	Chiron begins next R shadow
				PI	4°59'	11/13/12	Chiron semisextile Uranus
SG	2°49'	07/10/12	North Node square Neptune	PI	4°59'	11/14/12	Chiron turns Direct
SG	4°18'	11/06/12	Mercury turns Retrograde	PI	5°29'	02/28/12	Chiron ends prior R shadow
SG	4°18'	12/14/12	Mercury exits shadow	PI	6°43'	03/20/12	Chiron semisquare Eris
SG	7°49'	04/07/12	North Node square Chiron	PI	6°59'	09/06/12	Chiron sextile Pluto
SG	14°14'	06/04/12	Lunar Eclipse Full Moon	PI	7°36'	08/24/12	Chiron semisquare Eris
SG	20°70'	01/01/12	Mercury ends shadow	PI	7°49'	04/07/12	Chiron square Nodes
SG	21°45'	12/13/12	New Moon	PI	8°12'	08/11/12	Chiron semisextile Uranus
				PI	8°34'	08/31/12	Full Moon
				PI	8°44'	07/29/12	Chiron sesquiquadrate Saturn
				PI	8°56'	07/24/12	Chiron square Jupiter
				PI	9°17'	05/11/12	Chiron sesquiquadrate Saturn
				PI	9°18'	05/12/12	Chiron sextile Pluto
				PI	9°45'	06/12/12	Chiron turns Retrograde
				PI	23°50'	02/27/12	Mercury begins shadow
				PI	23°50'	04/04/12	Mercury turns Direct

AR = Aries/Cardinal   LI = Libra/Cardinal
TA = Taurus/Fixed   SC = Scorpio/Fixed
GE = Gemini/Mutable   SG = Sagittarius/Mutable
CN = Cancer/Cardinal   CP = Capricorn/Cardinal
LE = Leo/Fixed   AQ = Aquarius/Fixed
VI = Virgo/Mutable   PI = Pisces/Mutable

Janet's Plan-its™ STAR PAGES

The Star Pages will fill you in on some important astrological details, month by month.

NOTE: The abbreviations for signs used here are the same as for 2012 On a Page (p. 60).

Check the Keywords (p. 98) for more about planets, signs and aspects.

★ ★ ★ ★ ★ TYPES OF DATA LISTED IN STAR PAGES ★ ★ ★ ★ ★

1) Time frames when a planet (other than the Moon) is traveling through a sign and its influence there.

2) Beginning and end of Retrograde and Direct motion – see **2012 On a Page** for further explanation.

3) Dates of important aspects. Aspects show links between planets' influences. They occur when the planets are separated by certain fractions of the circle of the sky, measured by degrees - see Keywords or How to Read an Ephemeris (p. 62). The date listed is when an aspect is exact - that's when its strength peaks, although it's strong for a while before and after it's exact, sometimes mentioned here or in the weekly Highlights. Dates are noted when aspects occurred before or will occur again (repeating due to Retrogrades).

After each star is the number of the day of the month. Times are listed in both Pacific (P) and Eastern (E) zones. Sometimes the same moment is on adjacent calendar days, late night Pacific and after midnight Eastern.

While anyone can utilize these recommendations to advantage, the impact from a particular planetary influence is felt most personally when a part of your chart is touched by a degree discussed (within 2° of the same sign or any sign of the same Mode – see Keywords). Read Making It Personal (p. 4), see the 2012 All Star List (p. 70), and you may want to learn how to use the ephemeris (p. 62).

Things are always on the move in astrology, so keep abreast of the planets' zodiac positions. The slow-moving outer planets (from Saturn out to Eris) don't change signs often. In 2012, Neptune settles into Pisces, after entering it briefly in 2011. Jupiter passes through parts of two signs this year and Ceres visits five. The quicker planets – Mercury, Venus and Mars – shift signs frequently (except when Retrograde). The Sun's sign changes once a month, like clockwork.

The Moon speeds around the zodiac in 27 days, changing signs every 2-3 days (see the weekly pages). Just as the Moon reflects the light of the Sun, people's emotions reflect the Moon's sign position.

SIGN	When the Moon travels through this sign, people tend to be . . .
Aries	quick to react, sometimes in an angry way but this passes quickly, focused on oneself, need personal attention
Taurus	security-oriented, calm (slow to enrage), self-indulgent (like sweets), need affection
Gemini	distrustful of emotions (more thought-oriented), talkative especially about feelings, flexible, changeable
Cancer	more attuned to a 6th sense, moody, attached to family, safety conscious and security-oriented, interested in food
Leo	brave, dramatic, creative, stubborn, strong-willed, need attention
Virgo	nervous, health conscious, practical, helpful, communicative, critical, analytical
Libra	diplomatic, just, conflict-averse, rational, indecisive, need companionship
Scorpio	extreme, over-reactionary, determined, harsh, need an emotional outlet, interested in intimacy and sex, act on survival instincts
Sagittarius	easy-going, restless, drifting, inconsistent, optimistic, philosophical, bookish or adventurous
Capricorn	rather unemotional, thick-skinned, play things safe, matter-of-fact, need recognition
Aquarius	unpredictable, humanitarian, usually friendly but possibly cool and aloof, filter feelings through intellect, need space
Pisces	easily moved, empathetic, charitable, escapist, need to believe in something/someone

AS WE BEGIN 2012...

Here are the positions of the planets (and the Moon's Nodes), noted from the farthest out to the innermost.

Eris in Aries [1926 - 2044-45] With an orbit three times farther out than Pluto, taking 556.7 years to circle the Sun and the zodiac, chances are almost everyone you know has Eris (named for Mars' bitchy sister) in Aries. This is the period of history of the rise of women's power. We could speculate a culture-wide affect for generations in which the Aries traits of aggression, self-centeredness and haste add to Eris' attributes of disorder and discord We might all try slowing down and becoming more conscious of others. The positive side of Eris in Aries is strength, confidence and independence. In 2012, Eris is at 21-22°of Aries. If it connects to something in your chart, perhaps you'll have an especially stressful year in which you must learn to accept and adapt to some level of chaos in your life.

Pluto in Capricorn [11/26/08-2024; before 1/25/08-6/13/08] It's likely entire systems will be discarded and slowly rebuilt on new ground. Pluto's extremes impact Capricorn's arena of conformity and may lead to authoritarianism. Personally, we'll feel the weight of responsibilities and obligations more than ever. Pluto can help us let go of a need to be in control or act maturely. Using keywords, you could translate this as death (Pluto) of the boss/father/old man (Saturn, ruler of Capricorn). Expect a big transition in how the elderly are treated.

Neptune in Aquarius [8/4/11-2/3/12; before 1998-4/4/11] We are realizing the importance of being our own source of what to believe rather than relying on tradition, doctrine and authorities. The interconnectedness of all humanity becomes more and more evident. This last hurrah of Neptune in Aquarius is likely to produce some strange music and art.

Uranus in Aries [3/11/11-2018-19; before 5/27/10-8/13/10] The planet of unpredictability and technology in the sign of conflict and armaments may bring surprise attacks and inventions of high-tech weaponry. Aries is also the sign for sports and competition, so expect new types of exercise equipment or computer games. Unrest or anxiety is likely on a group or individual level. You might reinvent yourself or become more your true self. Spontaneous outbursts are possible, especially if you have chronic anger issues or a strong temper.

Chiron in Pisces [2/8/11-2018-19; before 4/20/10-7/20/10] This indicator of repair or healing is powerful in the sign of health, spirituality and charity. All these arenas are slated for attention and improvement now. The down side: sometimes difficulties have to be painfully experienced before solutions are sought. Look for significant medical discoveries and increased sympathy for people on the lowest rungs of society's ladder. More focus will be on water quality and availability as well as the condition of the world's oceans, especially since Neptune (ruler of the seas) will be in Pisces even longer than Chiron.

Saturn in Libra [7/21/10-10/5/12; before 10/29/09-4/7/10] Some people may experience indecision about goals. Others will work to achieve better balance between their professional obligations and personal concerns, including their relationships. Many partners will face tests around commitment, responsibility, respect and equality in their union. Advancement in career is aided by networking and contacts. This is a time to build bridges on solid foundations.

Jupiter in Taurus [6/4/11-6/11/12] We strive for financial stability, asset accumulation and retiring debt that's piled up the past few years. Like the tortoise in Aesop's Fables, slow and steady wins the race. It's a beautiful sight each month when the Moon in Taurus passes Jupiter. This is your cue to watch out for an increase in appetite. The Moon rules eating, Jupiter amplifies whatever is nearby, and Taurus is the most indulgent sign – especially for sweets and dairy products. (See the "Musings on Moon Signs" article in the Information Booth at JanetsPlan-its.com.)

Ceres in Pisces [8/10/11-1/19/2012; before 3/21/11-7/11/11] People feel "we're all in this boat together" and tune into their milieu and environment. Empathy levels increase and kindness pays off. The ocean as a source of food comes under discussion.

Mars in Virgo [11/10/11-7/3/12, going Retrograde in this sign] We're more fastidious and precise in our actions and prefer not to do dirty work, unless it's cleaning. Arguments are laced with judgments. The pen is mightier than the sword. Time to work out and shape up!

North Node in Sagittarius, South Node in Gemini [2/13/11-9/1/12] The Moon's Nodes are always in the same degree of opposite signs. They spend about 18 months in a pair of signs, traveling in reverse (compared to the planets). Their signs show where eclipses occur and the arenas for increased activity and major changes. In Sagittarius and Gemini, they reshape education, travel, transportation and all manner of information exchange (including publishing and the internet). We'll probably need new forms of identification for foreign travel and nations may require additional documentation for immigrants. Communication between countries will be an important issue.

Sun in Capricorn [12/21/11 (P), 12/22/11 (E)-1/20/12] The bottom line is at the top of our list and we value efficient means to our intended ends. We're willing to do our duty, whatever form it takes, especially if it helps us up the ladder toward success. Gaining respect may take some work but it's worth the effort.

Venus in Aquarius [12/20/11-1/13/12 (P), 1/14/12 (E)] Tastes in art and people tend toward the unusual; the mainstream seems boring to us now. We treat others with a friendly demeanor and enjoy socializing in groups. Spending might be a bit impulsive.

Mercury in Sagittarius [11/2/11-1/7/12 (P), 1/8/12 (E)] A thirst for learning sparks new adventures, whether acted upon or just in our heads. A bright outlook makes us think we can do anything and everything. However, that could be over-optimistic and it would be smart to add a dose of realism.

NOTE: *When you come to the Star Pages from a daily message with a star, please be aware there may be more than one entry for a particular day.*

LONG-TERM INFLUENCES:

Uranus square Pluto These two very slow planets, both strongly related to change and evolution, have been roughly 90° apart for a couple years now, already wreaking havoc on financial markets and prompting many uprisings. This year, they begin a series of seven exact squares lasting into 2015 (see June 24). The rollercoaster ride continues as people buck the system. The status quo has got to go! Quick-moving planets frequently connect to this square, amplifying its effects. The toughest links are by square and opposition, forming a T-square. For several years, like a saving grace, Chiron bolsters both Uranus and Pluto (see below), interceding to ensure that even the most turbulent clouds have silver linings.

Chiron semisextile Uranus Traveling approximately one sign apart for two decades, Chiron (the asteroid nicknamed the "wounded healer") is in a mildly positive relationship with Uranus, which can't sit by on the sidelines when change is needed. Chiron in Pisces wants to gently nudge us toward gradual modifications whereas Uranus in Aries would rather give us a kick or shock us into awareness. They'll work together to bring improvements (Chiron's forte) for the populace as a whole (Uranus's purview). They are in an exact semisextile 23 times between 2010 and 2021. By the time this link is over, each planet will have changed its sign. (See Aug. 11, below.)

Chiron sextile Pluto Chiron is about two signs ahead of Pluto from 2011 to 2015, often within one degree of a sextile, though many times not forming the aspect exactly (see April 21). Pluto's job is to bring about transformation, while Chiron specializes in repairs. Frequently Pluto perpetrates destruction preceding reconstruction and Chiron often indicates a hurt that we have to get over. Operating in concert, they build anew on what's outworn or injurious. This sextile serves as a base for Finger of God triangles (see Keywords) whenever another planet is in the same degree of Leo where Chiron is in Pisces and Pluto is in Capricorn. If planets occupy the Chiron and Pluto degrees in both Cancer and Virgo, a Mystic Rectangle pattern results. There are ample opportunities for this benign restorative force to wield its influence.

Saturn opposite Eris The planet of order in the sign of peace dukes it out with the planet of chaos in the sign of war. Sound like trouble? We don't know whether to compromise or fight, but we'll have to figure it out. This aspect was exact last fall (10/27/11) and does not repeat but comes very close to an exact opposition (within 1°) midyear. (See May 26, below.)

Saturn trine Neptune and Chiron Beginning this fall and lasting into 2013, these connections direct our attention and resources to what needs to be repaired or healed. (See Oct. 10 and Nov. 16, below.)

"OUT OF BOUNDS" PLANETS:

The circle of signs forms the circumference of the zodiac belt, which also has a width defined by the earth's 23°27' tilt on its axis in relation to the Sun. Planets sometimes ride higher or lower in the sky than the swath in which the Sun appears to travel. In such an instance, the "out of bounds" planet doesn't play by the rules, going too far in whatever it represents.

Mercury [1/7-1/20, 5/30-6/19, 11/1-11/6, 12/26/12-1/14/13] We over-think situations or speak too little or too much. Instruments and communication devices may not work correctly.

Venus [4/2-6/3] There's too much love or not enough, or it stems from the wrong reasons. Fiscal matters may be grossly out of balance, such as a decrease in income or increase in expenses.

Mars [10/26-12/9] People are more rash, impatient, selfish or angry than usual. Skirmishes escalate. Energy levels are off the scale.

Ceres [11/20/12-7/19/13] The maternal instinct is applied inappropriately or absent altogether. We try to reap what is not ours or lose out on getting what we deserve.

MUTUAL RECEPTIONS:

This condition blends the effects of two planets that are in the signs ruled by each other.

Sun and Mercury [8/22-8/31] When the Sun goes through Virgo (ruled by Mercury) in late summer, in many years Mercury visits Leo (ruled by the Sun) at the same time. This mixture instills a witty mental creativity and assists us in merging work and fun.

Sun and Venus [9/22-10/2 (P), 10/3 (E)] In autumn if Venus trails behind the Sun as a Morning Star, the Sun can be in Libra (ruled by Venus) as Venus moves through Leo (ruled by the Sun). It's easier to love oneself and others when your heart is sunny and in a good space. Creativity increases with this combination and is especially enjoyable when projects are shared with a partner or in a team setting.

Mercury and Venus [5/8 (P), 5/9 (E)-5/24] As Mercury moves through Taurus (ruled by Venus) in the spring, in some years Venus simultaneously traverses Gemini (ruled by Mercury). People are attracted to each other's minds and find ideas appealing, wanting to implement the best and profit from them. A variation on this theme can arise in the late summer or early fall, when Mercury is in Libra (a second sign ruled by Venus) while Venus is in Virgo (Mercury's other sign of rulership). This happens in 2012 for less than 48 hours: 10/3-10/5. In this case, the importance of communication in relationships is emphasized, taking care not to judge one's partner.

Mercury and Mars [3/2-3/23; again 4/16-5/8 (P), 5/9 (E)] Mars spends a long time in Virgo (ruled by Mercury), during which time Mercury travels in Aries (ruled by Mars) twice, split in two due to Mercury's Retrograde back into Pisces. We tend to be more critical and combative than usual and may blurt harsh comments. This is a good time to begin a health regimen or workout program and to initiate activities in service to others.

Mercury and Jupiter [10/28 (P), 10/29 (E)-11/13 (P), 11/14 (E); again 12/10-12/31] Jupiter visits Mercury-ruled Gemini for about a year, during which time Mercury passes through Sagittarius, ruled by Jupiter, in the winter. The accent is on learning, teaching and communicating with those at a distance, such as sharing information via the internet. Dialogue between nations may improve or at least be more important than usual.

To get Janet's free e-newsletters, click the sign-up box on the homepage at JanetsPlan-its.com.

Mars and Uranus [12/25/12-2/1/13] This is the first of four periods that Mars travels through Uranus-ruled Aquarius during the seven years Uranus is in Mars-ruled Aries. The masses are rebellious and agitated, impatient for change. New technologies and humanitarian organizations emerge. Individuals have a stronger need for freedom.

Saturn and Pluto [10/5/12-12/23/14; again 6/14/15-9/17/15] Pluto visits a long time in Saturn-ruled Capricorn while Saturn passes through Pluto-ruled Scorpio for a few years. It forms a positive sextile with Pluto from late this year into 2013 (see Dec. 26). When it's further into Scorpio, it will be semisquare Pluto from late 2014 into 2015. Saturn and Capricorn are associated with structure and systems, including government and industry. Pluto and Scorpio relate to transition and getting rid of what no longer works, as well as indicating shared resources and means of exchange. The interplay of these energies promotes regulation and revision of financial systems and creating methods to bring about change. This is a time to get serious or disciplined about paring down to simplicity.

SEASONAL SYNOPSES *Also see the weekly Highlights when seasons begin.*

During winter and spring it may be difficult to make progress. Both seasons commence in the final phase of the lunar cycle, which doesn't promote newness but rather the finishing of ventures. Mercury is in the exiting shadow of a Retrograde at the winter solstice and in the middle of a Retrograde at the spring equinox. Spring has the further handicap of its ruling planet, Mars, also being Retrograde. Summer begins in a New Moon phase, and autumn and the next winter start near First Quarter Moons, all of which accelerate forward momentum.

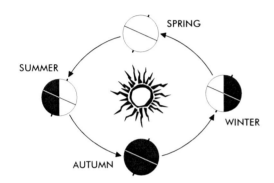

Seasons Change as the Earth Travels Around the Sun

The earth tilts on its axis. This causes a variation in the way the Sun's rays reach us, resulting in the seasons.

WINTER 2011-2012 [12/21/11 (P), 12/22/11 (E)-3/19/12 (P), 3/20/12 (E)] We sense a new day around the corner but something must be finalized before we can move forward. It's important to separate what's true from what's imagined and learn how to envision what we want to be real and trust that it can become so. Too many people have been operating on the basis of fear for too long. We give our power away when we let ourselves be manipulated by people who prey on our worries or sense of lack. If we can take stock of what we do have instead of what's missing, then we can initiate smart action to preserve and increase assets. It will take a lot of work to achieve this goal, though.

SPRING [3/19 (P), 3/20 (E)-6/20] Spring usually brings "get up and go" but with Aries' ruler, Mars, Retrograde in Virgo, we scrutinize plans to the Nth degree before even taking a step. "Analysis leads to paralysis." We can find lots of reasons not to do something or we're crippled by lack of confidence (related to being too self-critical). Not knowing what to do, where to go, or with whom to align can lead to pain or problems. We worry that if we aren't affiliated with the right associates and heading in a good direction, all manner of chaos could result. However, there are people willing to share their knowledge and resources to make a meaningful difference in some way.

SUMMER [6/20-9/22] Coming only a day after a New Moon (see Highlights), many indications are similar, with the important exception that the Sun and Moon are in Cancer rather than Gemini. This is the first season since Autumn 2009 to begin with a New Moon, helping us get the ball rolling on new endeavors. The biggest tensions come from the natural conflicts between order versus chaos and consensus versus disagreement (see May 26). Fairness is also an issue. Caring communication (perhaps parental in style) can span the gap between opposing parties but knowing what to say is hard. Negative words or thoughts throw up blockades. Anyone could experience heartache or financial difficulties this summer, but particularly people with planets in the first 10° of the mutable signs (Gemini, Virgo, Sagittarius, Pisces).

AUTUMN [9/22-12/21] Fun, creativity and joyous socializing beckon to us. We're optimistic and communication flows pretty well. However, secrets or private matters may cause a problem, especially when there's a reluctance to reveal them. For those who are comfortable with openness, it's possible to overcome fears in sharing. Trust builds when a relationship is stable and the interchange is nurturing and supportive. A dose of philosophy and a dash of humor make sensitive conversations easier to swallow. Try to view any strange changes as part of a transition process that will have a healing effect in the long run.

WINTER 2012-2013 [12/21/12-3/20/13] As ruler of Capricorn, the first sign of winter, Saturn is the boss of the season. As winter begins, Saturn is involved in a Finger of God pattern (see Dec. 20) pointing to the importance of understanding a situation thoroughly before implementing any changes. In addition, this is the first of three Winter Solstices when Saturn and Pluto are in a mutual reception (see above), signaling periods of slow but significant transition. For ideas to pay off, they need to be backed up by solid planning and collective resources or efforts. Solo activities are not as apt to succeed. Yet cooperation will not come about without honest and forthright communication and trust, which don't just happen with a snap of the fingers.

★ The planets (and the Moon's Nodes) each represent a set of conditions, modified by their zodiac positions. As they move through the signs, they set the stage for the areas of life with which they are associated. Certain angular connections between planets (called aspects) indicate times when their energies interact. When these form between slow-moving heavenly bodies (Jupiter, Saturn, Chiron, Uranus, Neptune, Pluto and Eris), the link strongly colors the atmosphere for many days (sometimes weeks) before and after the date when the aspect is exact. Interactions between quicker planets (Sun, Mercury, Venus and Mars – more often noted in the weekly Highlights than in the Star Pages) have a shorter-lived impact, for just a few days centered on the date of occurrence. When you see three (and sometimes more) dates listed for an influence, this is due to the planet retracing its steps while Retrograde (see 2012 On a Page, p. 60). It can be helpful to check the weekly Highlights for the applicable time frame of the phenomena noted in the Star Pages. Also, see the Overview of 2012 (p. 1), 2012 On a Page and the Keywords (p. 98).

JANUARY 2012

★ **1** See "As We Begin 2012," p. 73.

★ **2** *Jupiter (0-1°TA) and Saturn (28-29° LI) two degrees from exact opposition* [in effect strongly for first 2 weeks of January and still somewhat strong the rest of the month; emphasized by the Moon on 1/2 and 1/16 and by both the Moon and Sun on 1/19 and at the New Moon Jan. 22-23, when they're less than 3° from an exact opposition as the Moon and Sun make a T-square with them] The exact opposition occurred three times from 2010-2011 but following Jupiter's recent Retrograde and preceding Saturn's upcoming backward jaunt, they come pretty close to an opposition again. We'll feel their tug at least until the next New Moon on Feb. 7. Their opposition marked the halfway point of their 20-year cycle that began in May 2000 in the sign of Taurus (where Jupiter is again now), a long period impacting the rules of the game in business, including financial regulations. During the first half of the cycle, wealth rose upward like cream, leaving the rich richer and the middle class and poor poorer. It remains to be seen if that trend will continue or reverse. Saturn in Libra lobbies for fairness. Jupiter in Aries at the exact opposition tilted toward selfishness. Now that Jupiter is in Taurus, perhaps common sense will prevail.

★ **7** *(P)*, **8** *(E) Mercury enters Capricorn* [until 1/27/12] Mental acuity results from concentrating on one item at a time. Focus is easy to achieve, but at the cost of tenderness. Some turn a cold shoulder toward weakness, in themselves or others. Get organized in your communications and say things simply, without frills.

★ **8** *(P)*, **9** *(E) Eris (21°23' AR) turns Direct* Retrograde since 7/18/12 (E), 7/19/12 (P); Direct until 7/18/12] Eris spends about half of each year traveling backward. No wonder it doesn't make much progress around the zodiac circle! When it's Direct, we have tests concerning discord and rivalry. When it's Retrograde, we are our own enemy.

★ **13** *Friday the 13th* (We also have a Friday the 13th in April and July of this year.) Friday is named for Freya, the Norse goddess of sex and fertility (somewhat like Venus, whose name you hear in the French name for Friday, Vendredi). Thirteen is a number sacred to goddess worshippers, the number of moon cycles in a year. On Friday the 13th, instead of working, you were supposed to stay home and make love to honor the goddess. You can see how a patriarchal, repressive religion would regard this as bad and cast a pall on the day by vilifying it.

★ **13** *(P)*, **14** *(E) Venus enters Pisces* [until 2/7 (P), 2/8 (E)] Compassion and artistic sensibilities increase. Fantasies abound and are natural now, but delusions in romance or finances take vigilance to avoid. Some people will be self-indulgent in their addictions, such as gambling, shopping, eating, smoking, drinking or self-medicating.

★ **17** *Jupiter (1°16' TA) semisextile Uranus (1°16' AR)* [before 6/28/11 and 12/13/11] These planets were conjunct in 2010. Jupiter moves about a sign per year and is presently one sign past Uranus. This mildly positive connection may not produce dramatically visible results but you can use its energy to help solidify or promote the advancement of undertakings begun in 2010, especially in the technological arena or for individual development. We march more steadily to the beat of our own drummers. Past innovation could pay off now.

★ **19** *Ceres enters Aries* [until 4/9] Ceres is a planet of bounty and growth. In the sign of spring, it prompts us to set wheels in motion for new projects and bravely try things we haven't done before. Taking risks should work out better this time around (Ceres goes through Aries every 3-4 years) because it kicks off its visit by joining forces with Uranus on 1/24. (See Highlights for the week of January 23.)

★ **20** *Sun enters Aquarius* [until 2/18 (P), 2/19 (E)] "Do Your Own Thing," as the saying went back in the '60s and '70s. The Hippies' philosophy was very Aquarian, including its humanitarian bent. Find your creative expression and your place in the "family of man."

★ **22** *(P)*, **23** *(E) Chinese New Year, Year of the Dragon* [until 2/10/13] The Chinese celebrate their new year at the second new moon after the winter solstice (sometimes in January, sometimes in February). This always turns out to be the Aquarius New Moon. They wear clothing that is red (to ward away evil spirits and bad fortune) and new (for a fresh start to the new year). They also clean house thoroughly for this holiday. 2012 is the Year of the Dragon (Year 4709). Though western cultures consider dragons to be monsters, in China they bring good fortune. In Dragon years, we want to be free from restrictions and do things on a grand scale. The element for this Dragon year is water, contributing sensitivity to others and patience (which are not always present in Dragon years of other elements). The Chinese favor this sign so much that many will try to marry or have their children this year.

★ **23** *Mars (23°6' VI) turns Retrograde* [Direct since 3/10/10; Retrograde until 4/13/12] Mars is not Retrograde every year, more like in alternating years. Since it's the planet of action, we find it harder to take bold steps when Mars is backwards and confidence may waver. Anger is under Mars' purview and Retrogrades tend to turn a planet's influence inward. Thus many people will give themselves a hard time now, especially since the sign of its backtrack is Virgo, the most critical and self-critical of all. Examine your inner desires and drives. Do you expect things to come to you or do you go after them proactively? See if the effort you put in yields the results you want. You may have lessons to learn or re-learn about your way of doing things or about haste. Mars's Virgo placement suggests you could get lost in details and not accomplish what you want to, or you may find you need assistance from others in areas where you're used to being independent.

★ **27** *Mercury enters Aquarius* [until 2/13] We want to study or apply knowledge in unique ways. Expect conversations to be animated, though some people may be close-minded, holding fast to their opinions. Technology is appealing and it's easy now to learn how to use new programs or equipment.

FEBRUARY

★ **3** *Neptune enters Pisces* [before 4/4/11-8/4/11; until 2025-26] Neptune's visit to its home waters from 1847-48 to 1861 (shortly after it was discovered in 1846) saw Darwin's theory of evolution; the Gold Rush; Pasteur's germ theory and vaccines; popularity of séances, spiritualism and hypnotism; introduction of a model of electromagnetism; the heyday of whaling; oil-drilling began; abolitionism, the Underground Railroad and the Temperance movement. This time around, medical imaging equipment will improve by leaps and bounds. Many people will have a greater sixth sense and more respect for psychics, including medical intuitives. Art, music and dance will develop in extremely imaginative ways. What we glamorize as a culture will shift to being more emotion-based rather than intelligence-based, as has been the case during Neptune's visit to Aquarius now concluding. The techno geek was in; the next hero may be the psychic or healer. We'll pay more attention to our oceans and sea-life, as well as the seafood supply. (See Overview of 2012 (p. 1) and Highlights for the week of Jan. 30 - Feb. 5.)

★ **7** *Saturn (29°30' LI) turns Retrograde* [Direct since 6/12/11; Retrograde until 6/25/12] Over the coming four months, we backtrack to address obligations we've overlooked or avoided. We look to ourselves for the standards to apply to our lives, rather than accepting other people's notions of right and wrong.

★ **7** *(P),* **8** *(E) Venus enters Aries* [until 3/5] Go after your heart's desires, whether that's in the form of a relationship or a material acquisition. Be proactive in social matters and fight for fairness, equality and individual rights.

★ **8** *Finger of God: Mercury and the Sun are traveling together (around 21° AQ), both sextile Eris (21° AR) and all three are quincunx Mars (21° VI)* [through 2/10] Be confident as you tap your unique skills to become better at your work. Don't let competition trigger comparison or self-criticism. Striving to do your best will make you stronger, as will having a mission to help people.

★ **11** *Sun (22° AQ) quintile Jupiter (4° TA) and North Node (11° SG)* [North Node biquintile Jupiter is exact 2/15] Creativity spurs luck and we get a little help from our friends, too. This is a good day for science, studies, travel or legal matters.

★ **13** *Mercury enters Pisces* [until 3/2; again 3/23 - 4/16] Mercury's visit to Pisces this year is split in two due to its Retrogradation (see Star Pages for March 2). This is not so much a time for clear thinking as it is for understanding with your heart or receiving messages expressed in symbols or signs. Fantasy and feelings, impressions and instincts overshadow facts and logic. People may prey upon your sympathies easily, though you may be happy to help.

★ **14** *Jupiter (4°32' TA) sextile Chiron (4°32' PI)* [before 7/2/11 & 12/6/11] Patience, practicality and determination are needed to solve problems or complete repairs. Compassion brings healing, benefiting those who give it as well as the receivers.

★ **18** *(P),* **19** *(E) Sun enters Pisces* [until 3/19 (P), 3/20 (E)] You're inspired to delve more deeply into your spirituality or the arts. Identify with people in need or who've been mistreated and take the lead in helping them.

MARCH

★ **2** *Mercury enters Aries* [until 3/23; again 4/16 - 5/8 (P), 5/9 (E)] This is a two-part visit due to retreating back into Pisces while Retrograde (see Highlights for March 12-18). This is a time to be forward and forceful in communications, though be aware that you could come on too strong for some people's tastes. In the Pisces repeat period (3/23 - 4/16), you'll have a chance to backpedal or soften your statements. Then in the second Aries time frame, ensure you take care of your own needs and don't weaken your case. In both Aries periods, Mercury is in a mutual reception with Mars (see beginning of the Star Pages), emphasizing the importance of blending thought and action. Careful consideration should precede initiating anything new but over-analysis could slow you down too much. Strive for a balance.

★ **5** *Venus enters Taurus* [until 4/3] Venus's love of beauty and desire for material security are strongest when she sashays through this sign that she rules. Attend to accounts, add to possessions, spruce up your home or garden, and enjoy all the good things in life, especially physical expressions of love.

★ **5** *Mercury (3°25' AR) conjunct Uranus (3°25' AR)* [again 3/18 & 4/22] This pairing stimulates our synapses to produce brilliant or quirky ideas and often slips a foot into a mouth. You might find topics that arise this week need to be addressed again near the next two dates. You can use these related times for three steps in a project involving communications. (For example, a first draft, then revisions and final proofing of a document.) Uranus relates to metaphysical matters as well as anything impacting large groups of people. There may be news related to these arenas around the three dates. (Mercury rules news and what's on people's lips.)

★ **11-12** *Quintile Triangle: Sun (22° PI) quintile Pluto (9° CP) and biquintile Saturn (28° LI)* [Saturn quintile Pluto is exact 3/28] Combine imagination and creativity with a desire to bring about positive change. Add a little teamwork and the results will be impressive.

★ **12** *Mercury (6°49' AR) turns Retrograde* [until 4/4] As the "Messenger of the Gods" retraces its steps, we review recent conversations, documents or decisions. Matters in which you've charged ahead may need revision. You can voluntarily slow down for a second look or circumstances will likely force you to. Be careful in your current communications that you aren't creating problems that will necessitate re-doing or that later make you say, "What was I thinking?" Watch your speed on the road and be especially careful in transit if you're angry. You might need vehicular maintenance or repair.

★ **12** (P), **13** (E) *Jupiter (9°21' TA) trine Pluto (9°21' CP)* [before 7/7/11 & 10/20/11] Progress comes easily when you stay on course at an even, unhurried pace and focus on goals. Practicality and working within conventional parameters assure success. Appreciating the simple things in life creates a feeling of abundance, even if your funds are meager. Get rid of what's extraneous or doesn't have lasting worth. Growth and positive improvements are likely around now, especially in business or financial affairs.

★ **19** (P), **20** (E) *Spring Equinox* See Seasonal Synopses, p. 75. Mars' tough Grand Cross with the Moon's Nodes and Chiron is also tangled in a knot with Ceres and Eris. We reap discord if we can't communicate kindly. Mars is also in a beautiful Grand Trine in earth signs (aiding abundance) with Pluto and beneficial Venus and Jupiter.

★ **19** (P), **20** (E) *Sun enters Aries* [until 4/19] As nature awakens from winter hibernation, people are motivated to be more physically active and to initiate new projects. The drive to distinguish oneself from the pack heightens. This is a natural time to exhibit leadership tendencies. Impatience also increases and many are in a rush.

★ **20** *Chiron (6°48' PI) semisquare Eris (21°48' AR)* [again 8/24 & 1/13/13] Compassion moves us to come to the rescue of victims. We find it necessary but difficult to repair damage resulting from haste, battles, selfishness or even cruelty. A sense of superiority is an Achilles heel.

★ **23** *Mercury re-enters Pisces* [before 2/13-3/2; until 4/16] See Feb. 13, above.

★ **27** *Venus (22°58' TA) at maximum eastern elongation* (farthest ahead of the Sun) See Highlights for week of Feb. 27-March 4. Enjoy beautiful Venus's visage in the western sky for more than two-and-a-half hours after sunset.

★ **28** *Saturn (27°31' LI) quintile Pluto (9°31' CP)* The Sun turns this longlasting link into a Quintile Triangle on March 11-12; Venus does likewise on April 6-7. In both cases, we can make joyful, loving choices to employ better boundaries in relationships. We benefit from responsibility and maturity in our interactions.

APRIL

★ **3** *Venus enters Gemini* [until 8/7, a very long visit for Venus since it goes Retrograde here – see May 15] People are youthful, playful and flirtatious, possibly leading on more than one partner. Some may even find both genders attractive. Concepts and words are appealing and tact in conversations should come easily although this might be a lesson that needs re-emphasis during Venus Retrograde.

★ **4** *Mercury (23°50' PI) turns Direct* [Retrograde since 3/12; Direct until 7/14] We may feel like we're waking up from a dream as Mercury starts crawling forward again. Thinking and communicating aren't likely to become very clear or forceful until Mercury reaches Aries again on April 16. In the mean time, immerse yourself in the arts or charitable activities.

★ **6-7** *Quintile Triangle: Venus (3° GE) biquintile Saturn (27° LI) and Pluto (9° CP)* [Saturn quintile Pluto was exact 3/28] Relationships improve by being well defined and operating within agreed-upon guidelines. Respectful communication smoothes all interactions. Creative cooperation results in solid accomplishments.

★ **7** *North Node (7°49' SG) and South Node (7°49' GE) square Chiron (7°49' PI)* As we strive for higher knowledge and wisdom, we have to leave behind petty small-minded thinking. To do so, we need to process hurts and address what we perceive as being an issue.

★ **7** *Venus (3°55' GE) square Mars (3°55' VI)* [again 6/4] Men and women may not see eye-to-eye. Some people will let faults slide but others can't help pointing out problems, spoiling otherwise pleasant conversations. Offering assistance helps achieve peace. (See Highlights for the week of May 14.)

★ **9** *Ceres enters Taurus* [until 6/23] The planet of fertility in the sign of earthly delights is perfect for the flowering season. Creative (and procreative) urges are strong. Get your hands in the dirt, on some art materials or even on someone else's body.

★ **10** *Pluto (9°34' CP) turns Retrograde* [Direct since 9/16/11; Retrograde until 9/17 (P), 9/18 (E)] This influence can be subtle and go unnoticed, showing its effects more in retrospect. It signals a turning point, perhaps on a deep inner level, when we begin to re-assess values and resources, our own and other people's, to determine what's most important. The backward journey of Pluto is a time to be our own force for change in our lives, rather than expecting outside influences to turn our lives in a new direction. Financial matters may be strained around the time of the directional changes. With Pluto Retrograde in Capricorn, we re-examine the power structure of organizations and corporations to see what internal changes are needed. In our personal lives, we re-visit what we need to eliminate or move past, or what we can invest to further our careers.

★ **13** *Third Quarter Moon (23°54' CP) semisquare North Node (7°30' GE) and Chiron (8°08' PI), square the Sun-Eris conjunction (22°-24° AR), and sesquiquadrate Venus (8°31' GE) and South Node (7°30' GE), which semisquare Sun and Eris* A tangled jumble of difficult aspects that has no official term in astrology! The Moon stimulates the other planets' connections very early in the morning in North America. This produces confusion about goals and the direction in which to head involving disagreements about principles and values, confounded by some people's feeling of being wounded or mistreated. Bossiness and a disproportionate sense of entitlement make matters worse.

★ **13** *Mars (3°41' VI) turns Direct* [Retrograde since 1/23; Direct until 3/1/14] Mars is action-oriented and its energy is all about forward motion, going places and doing things. We feel like we're grinding gears when it's Retrograde. When it's Direct, we find it easier to be assertive and go after what we want. Confidence increases.

★ **16** *Mercury re-enters Aries* [before 3/2-3/23; until 5/8 (P), 5/9 (E)] See March 2, above.

★ **19** *Sun enters Taurus* [until 5/20] Our delight in nature and beauty is at its height, and we're creative in the material realm (arts and crafts, gardening). Our practical side takes priority, with a focus on finances and possessions. Seek and give physical expressions of affection.

★ **21** *Chiron (8°32' PI) sextile Pluto (9°32' CP) within one degree* [until 6/9 (exact 5/12); before 6/17/11-7/23/11; again 8/8/12-9/29/12 (exact 9/6), 3/15/13-4/23/13, 10/4/13-11/30/13, 1/23/14-3/20/14 and 11/29/14-2/2/15] See Long-term Influences near the beginning of the Star Pages. The first and last of these seven one-degree range periods have no exact sextile. The five periods in between do have exact sextiles. This aspect represents the need and ability for healing to come through regeneration, casting off the outworn and starting anew. Chiron's position in Pisces shows that our belief systems are undergoing a renovation and Pluto's transit through Capricorn is expected to transform all kinds of systems, organizations, rules, corporations and governments. For individuals, it's a time to re-write the rules you live by in order to be healthier and more successful.

MAY

★ **7** *Jupiter (21°52' TA) semisquare Uranus (6°52' AR)* Rash impulsiveness threatens to undermine the benefits of steady progress and sound judgment. Think twice before you take any big risks, yet don't let reluctance to try something new stop you from a good opportunity that arises out of the blue.

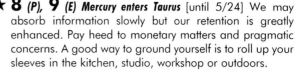

★ **8** *(P),* **9** *(E) Mercury enters Taurus* [until 5/24] We may absorb information slowly but our retention is greatly enhanced. Pay heed to monetary matters and pragmatic concerns. A good way to ground yourself is to roll up your sleeves in the kitchen, studio, workshop or outdoors.

★ **11** *Saturn (24°17' LI) sesquiquadrate Chiron (9°17' PI)* [before 10/28/10, 2/27/11, 9/17/11; again 7/29/12 - Chiron sometimes makes five occurrences of an aspect.] In trying to be fair to one side of an altercation, the other party may get short shrift. Listen sympathetically to everyone, endeavor to be non-judgmental, and chuck any notion of "being cruel to be kind."

★ **12** *Chiron (9°18' PI) sextile Pluto (9°18' CP)* [again 9/6/12, 4/4/13, 10/28/13 & 2/25/14] See April 21, above.

★ **13** *Sun (23°10' TA) conjunct Jupiter (23°10' TA)* The Sun passes Jupiter once a year, bringing a powerful blend of creative and expansive energies and fostering a bright and sunny mood. This year, they join within one degree of an important union between Jupiter with Saturn back in May, 2000. These planetary heavyweights congregate every twenty years, setting the pace for cultural developments. Their meet-up in Taurus signaled a period for awareness of earth's resources and how they're shared (or not). Perhaps there will be news around this date comparing current financial circumstances to those at the start of the new millennium.

★ **15** *Venus (23°59' GE) turns Retrograde* [Direct since 11/18/10; Retrograde until 6/27] Venus goes Retrograde five times in eight earth years, like clockwork. If you plot the degrees of the Retrograde stations on the zodiac circle, they create a five-pointed star (related to using pentagrams in magic). Much of the Mayan calendar is based on the relationship between the orbits of earth and Venus around the Sun. (Learn more at LunarPlanner.com, Ancient-World-Mysteries.com and CropCircleConnector. com.) During a Venus retrograde, some people may re-connect with a former lover or person of significance in their lives, or a current relationship may repeat a pattern of a prior one. This is a time to re-affirm your love for yourself or work on issues of self-acceptance.

★ **16** *Jupiter (23°58' TA) quincunx Saturn (23°58 LI)* [again 12/22, 3/23/13] Both planets are in signs ruled by Venus, so this influence is likely to impact monetary matters and relationships (business or personal). In our quest for expansion and progress, we have to make adjustments or strike compromises, even though that slows the process down. Pragmatic concerns have to be balanced against obligations to the people important to us.

★ **17** *Jupiter (24°13' TA) sesquiquadrate Pluto (9°13' CP)* Tensions build to a breaking point and something's got to give. Disagreements about priorities or expenditures as well as power struggles arise.

★ **20** *Sun enters Gemini* [until 6/20] Like social butterflies, everyone's flitting from one event or gathering to another, hearing stories and telling their own. Speech is dramatic and mental or verbal originality is widely evident.

Thank you for using Janet's Plan-it's Celestial Planner!

★ **20** *Solar Eclipse New Moon (0°21′ GE)* Centered in the Pacific Ocean, the shadow is detectable in most of North America except for the East, where darkness descends before the Moon's shadow arrives from the west. (Wikipedia has a cool animation showing the Eclipse path.) The Sun and Moon are close to the Moon's South Node, marking this as a lunar cycle for releasing outworn patterns. In Gemini, old ways of thinking and communicating are what have to go. A square to Neptune, in a T-square with the Nodes, indicates our shift must be away from malaise, worry, futility, projection and all forms of imagination used negatively, and toward compassion, positive visualization, artistic expression and helping those in need. But Neptune is nearly motionless (turning Retrograde June 4), enshrouding us in a mental fog. Mercury and Venus in friendly cooperation open hearts and minds for smoother relations. A Mercury-Uranus semisquare adds a potential for interruptions and an element of surprise.

★ **24** *Mercury enters Gemini* [until 6/7] Curiosity drives us to learn something in every activity. There's a lot more talk than usual, and more traveling in the local area. Increased contact with neighbors or siblings is likely.

★ **26** *Saturn (23°29′ LI) within 1° opposite Eris (22°29′ AR)* [the only exact opposition was 10/27/11; they are within one degree of exact until 7/29, coming closest to an exact opposition (5′ off) June 25-29, around the time of Saturn's Direct station on June 25.] We try to put a cultured, reserved face on basic, even primitive, emotions like competition and domination but it's not easy to squelch strong disagreements or to buck the pecking order. (See Highlights for weeks of May 28 - June 3 and July 16-22.)

JUNE

★ **1** *Mercury (18°20′ GE) conjunct Venus (18°20′ GE)* These planets between earth and Sun move around the zodiac more quickly than the earth does. From our perspective, they're never far from the Sun, always within a sign or two. It's not all that rare for them to join together; they do it at least once a year, some years more often. In 2011 and again in 2013, trios of conjunctions occurred in a two-month period. This year, they meet just this once, very close to Venus's conjunction with the Sun June 5. This combination infuses all communications with loving gentility or a creative flair. Conversations may center on values, finances, romance or relationships.

★ **4** *Lunar Eclipse Full Moon (14°14′ SG)* There is always an opposition at a Full Moon, by definition. This makes it easy for a T-square to occur and we have one from Mars. Venus joins the Sun in an exact square to Mars, putting a lot of pressure on male-female relationships. There is also the clash between self (Mars) and other (Venus), as well as war and peace. This eclipse is close to the North Node in Sagittarius, pulling us toward higher principles and open-mindedness. A Lunar Eclipse is visible only if it occurs at night in your location. (In North America, only the western region can witness this one.) You don't have to see it to be affected by its influence, though. The biggest impact is on any planets you have in 12-18° of mutable signs. Chiron at

nearly 10° of Pisces plays into the T-square, loosely forming a Grand Cross, so you could stretch that range down to 9°. It adds an element of healing, whether personal or interpersonal wounds, though you need to be careful not to cause any new hurts, especially through careless words.

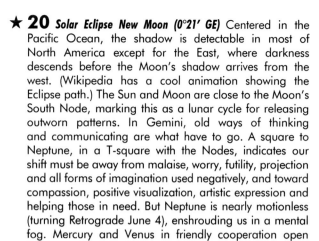

Eclipse of the Moon

★ **4** *Neptune (3°09′ PI) turns Retrograde* [Direct since 11/9/11; Retrograde until 11/10 (P), 11/11 (E)] Our personal connection to the Divine is more important to us than what others believe. Some may question their faith (or even their belief in themselves) but this is part of the process of re-affirming it. Now is a time when our busy lives remind us of the need for downtime.

★ **4** *Venus (16°23 GE) square Mars (16°23 VI)* [before 4/7] See Star Pages for April 7, above.

★ **5** *Venus (15°44′ GE) conjunct Sun (15°44′ GE) "Transit of Venus"* (also called a "passage" of Venus) Over the course of about six hours, Venus passes directly between the earth and the Sun, like the Moon does during an eclipse. This last occurred in 2004 but don't let that fool you as to its frequency. The other most "recent" occurrences were in 1631 & 1639, 1761 & 1769 and 1874 & 1882, pairs eight years apart repeating after a gap of 113 years. It's an awesome sight BUT remember you can't look directly at the Sun without special gear. Every Retrograde Venus marks a time to focus on your love of yourself, not in a vain way but rather through self-approval and acceptance. This is most evident when it joins the Sun at the halfway point of its Retrograde. Because this is the extraordinary "transit of Venus," the need to boost self-esteem is much stronger than usual. Occurring in Gemini, how one talks to oneself is the crux of the matter. This is a good opportunity to review your life and forgive yourself for mistakes, praise your successes and commit to being your own best friend. (See Overview of 2012, p. 1.)

★ **7** *Mercury enters Cancer* [until 6/25] Thoughts are colored by feelings and logic may elude us at times. Discussing or journaling about emotions brings insights. Our minds are on home or family issues and there could be news on this front. ESP is enhanced.

★ **11** *Jupiter enters Gemini* [until 6/25/13] Expect a lot of progress in the field of communications, similar to the mid-90s into the new millennium when transformative Pluto traveled through Jupiter-ruled Sagittarius. We went from rich people paying through the nose for car phones to every kid at the mall having a cell phone. More attention will be paid to schools and education. In general, people will be more open-minded and curious, finding it easier to learn new languages. You can experience a boost in the areas of your life associated with the house(s) where Gemini is in your chart.

★ **11** *(P)*, **12** *(E) Chiron (9°45' PI) turns Retrograde* Direct since 11/10/11; Retrograde until 11/14/12] It's time to address old hurts and put them in a current context to see the lessons learned. Look inward for healing and wisdom rather than receiving these from external sources.

★ **20** *Summer Solstice* See Seasonal Synopses, p. 75.

★ **20** *Sun enters Cancer* [until 7/22] People are more sensitive and emotional when the Sun is in Cancer. It's natural to put feelings into action, showing lots of care. Our attention is on nutrition and enjoying culinary ingenuity. People get into being homebodies and may have a greater interest in heritage and nationality.

★ **23** *Ceres enters Gemini* [until 9/26; again 12/4/12 - 4/4/13 when it retrogrades back into this sign] We communicate in a nurturing, caring way, mothering those around us. Minds are fertile. Being informed and educated pays off.

★ **24** *Uranus (8°23' AR) square Pluto (8°23' CP)* [again 9/18 (P), 9/19 (E); 5/20/13; 11/1/13, 4/21/14, 12/15/14 & 3/16/15 – 7 times!] This clash between the two planets most associated with disruptive changes is behind many of the difficulties we face in the current period. Because they're so slow, we have to deal for many years with their push to throw out the old to prepare for what comes next. The economy (under Pluto's purview) has been shaken by Uranus's turbulence. Energy production (primarily linked to Uranus) is undergoing an evolution. Individuals need to learn to be more self-reliant (a feature of both Uranus and Aries) and work in groups (another Uranian association) instead of counting on support from collective coffers (Pluto's arena). Whatever is entrenched in our lives (our Capricorn foundation) is subject to a shake-up, forcing us to embody the Aries qualities of courage and forging a new path. If you used keywords for these two daunting planets, you might say people (Uranus) versus Plutocrats (Pluto) or a revolution (Uranus) in how resources are distributed (Pluto). On the downside, it can even equate to mass (Uranus) murder (Pluto) or widespread death. We could see destruction of power-generating capabilities or a radically new energy delivery system. The square is cushioned to an extent by Chiron sextile Pluto (see 5/12 & 9/6) and semisextile Uranus (see 8/11 & 11/13). (See Overview of 2012 (p. 1) and Long-term Influences at the beginning of the Star Pages.)

★ **25** *Jupiter (3°2' GE) square Neptune (3°2' PI)* Anxiety is fed by overactive minds or conversations that stretch the truth. Not enough sleep interferes with clear thinking. Escapist tendencies are strong. More attention is paid to problems of air and water quality as well as students' use of drugs and prescriptions. Turn to humor to combat apprehension. (See Highlights for the week of June 25.)

★ **25** *Saturn (22°46' LI) turns Direct* [Retrograde since 2/7; Direct until 2/18/13] Putting things into clear form and understanding the rules of the game are easier when Saturn is Direct. People are better at responding to external authority and conforming to the objective standards, relying less on personal judgments.

★ **25** *Mercury enters Leo* [until 8/31 – a relatively long visit to a sign for Mercury because it goes Retrograde here]

Our playful side emerges, along with lots of creativity. It's easy to communicate with children and to express joy. People speak dramatically and might be stubborn or self-concerned in their thinking. Artistic or communication projects begun now may be interrupted, then completed later because of Mercury's Retrograde.

★ **27** *South Node (3°31' GE) conjunct Jupiter (3°31' GE)* "Thinking" you know something could be problematic; check the facts to be sure. You might miss important information by taking too narrow a view. Zoom out to see the big picture. And yet it may be easy to be too open or say more than you intended to.

★ **27** *Venus (7°29' GE) turns Direct* [Retrograde since 5/15; Direct until 12/21/13] When Venus is Direct, we feel more in balance. People are better able to relate and to take care of personal money matters. Values are more easily understood and expressed.

★ **29** *Mercury begins repeated aspects of Retrograde cycle* (see July 14, below).

★ **29** *Sun (8° CA) opposite Pluto (8° CP) and square Uranus (8° AR) in a T-square.* If you were not successful implementing certain changes six months ago, now forces outside yourself push you to do so.

JULY

★ **3** *Mars enters Libra* [until 8/23] Libra is opposite Aries, the sign Mars rules, and Mars doesn't get to be its usual independent and assertive self now. We offer cooperation instead of being defensive. Physical vitality might be low and we accept aid more readily.

★ **3** *Mercury (8° LE) forms two Fingers of God this week, one with the ongoing Chiron (8° PI) sextile Pluto (8° CP) on 7/3 (P)/7/4 (E) to 7/5, another on 7/4 with Venus (8° GE) and Pluto.* Mercury is in the shadow of its upcoming Retrograde and repeats its quincunx to Pluto twice. Events around now may be related to developments at the repetitions. The first instance is part of the Fingers of God 7/24-7/26 involving Jupiter (8° GE, quincunx Pluto on 7/18 – see below). The second on 8/18 duplicates this week's Finger of God with Chiron (without Venus). In each instance, the detours in which we find ourselves have the purpose of changing our thinking, revealing something or eliciting an "ah-ha" moment. When Chiron participates, a healing comes about. When Venus is in the picture, an encounter elucidates relationships or finances. Jupiter opens new vistas, bringing hope and opportunities.

★ **10** *Ceres (6°10' GE) conjunct Jupiter (6°10' GE)* The information we need is easy to find. Sweet words of encouragement and support surround us and we reap the benefits of positive conversations in the past.

★ **10** *North Node (2°49' SG) and South Node (2°49' GE) form T-square with Neptune (2°49' PI)* [This pattern is within two degrees of being exact from 5/27 to 9/17, with the Moon tangled in its web every few days.] A planet halfway between the Nodes, squaring both ends of the nodal axis, is said to be at "the bendings." It indicates a force to help turn us in a different direction. In this

Continued on next page.

case, Neptune signals the importance of our beliefs. For instance, scientists discovered their expectations of certain results in an experiment affected the outcome. This is similar to the placebo effect in clinical trials of medicines. Such an influence could cloud our view of where we need to head or conversely, may provide an inspirational vision of what we can do and what we need to leave behind to achieve it.

★ **13** *Uranus (8°32' AR) turns Retrograde* [Direct since 12/10/11; Retrograde until 12/13/12] Benefits come from re-assessing friendships and group affiliations to see whether they promote or hinder one's individuality. There is an increased need to be more authentic or to develop uniqueness. We re-examine ways to do so.

★ **14** *Mercury (12°32' LE) turns Retrograde* [Direct since 4/4; Retrograde until 8/7 (P), 8/8 (E)] This retrograde is entirely in Leo. Creative projects are subject to change or strange choices. Using the dates listed here, you can conceive and implement an undertaking in three stages. Issues of pride, ego or attention are possible. Mercury's repeating aspects include: making a Finger of God with Chiron and Pluto twice (see July 3, above); three sextiles to Jupiter (6/29, 7/24 & 8/22), stimulating mental fertility and putting you in contact with helpful people or information; and three trines to Uranus (7/4, 7/25 & 8/18), sparking ingenious thoughts or exceptional inventiveness.

★ **17** *Jupiter (7°43' GE) semisquare Eris (22°43' AR)* [again 1/17/13 & 2/14/13] A disruption breaks your train of thought or information comes to light that calls a prior assumption into question. A competitive situation could cause a problem.

★ **18** *Jupiter (7°47' GE) quincunx Pluto (7°47' CP)* [again 12/20/12 & 3/29/13] One person's insistence on the way things should be done doesn't fit with the approach others want to take. It's hard to find a happy medium between flexibility and firmness.

★ **18** *Eris (22°43' AR) turns Retrograde* [Direct since 1/8 (P), 1/9 (E); Retrograde until 1/8/13] When Eris is Retrograde, we can benefit by examining how we undermine our own efforts or bring disorder into our lives. When it's Direct, we're more likely to notice how disruption comes from sources beyond ourselves.

★ **20** *Jupiter (8°18' GE) sesquiquadrate Saturn (23°18' LI)* [again 10/15/12 & 5/19-20, 2013] Clashes between Jupiter and Saturn pose the question how much is too much or how little, too little. Adjustments must be made to rein in anything that has begun to get out of control. Conversely, what has been tightly constricted needs room to breathe. Care should be taken in communication because once something is said, it can't be retracted. Try not to overthink issues in relationships.

★ **21** *(P),* **22** *(E) Jupiter (8°30' GE) sextile Uranus (8°30' AR)* [only once, but they're within 1° of this aspect from 1/24/13 until 3/5/13] The beneficial side of Jupiter combines fortuitously with the unexpected element of Uranus to produce strokes of good luck and happy surprises. The freedom urge is strong and people break free from restrictions or express their unique nature easily.

★ **22** *Sun enters Leo* [until 8/22] Fun and innovation take center stage, whether with children or by letting our inner child out to play. Romance and risk-taking are appealing. Go after your heart's desires with unwavering determination.

★ **24** *Jupiter (8°56' GE) square Chiron (8°56' PI)* [again 1/14/13 (P), 1/15/13 (E) & 3/26/13 (P), 3/27/13 (E)] Problems stem from doing or saying too much or going too far in some way. Situations that have grown bigger than is healthy need to be brought back down to scale.

★ **24-26** *Mercury forms Fingers of God with Jupiter, Chiron and Pluto* See July 3, above.

★ **29** *Saturn (23°44' LI) sesquiquadrate Chiron (8°44' PI)* [before 10/28/10, 2/27/11, 9/17/11 & 5/11/12] We realize it takes time, commitment and effort to bring about a healing, right a wrong or improve conditions. Team up with a partner or join in a collective effort to accomplish any or all of these goals. (See May 11, above.)

AUGUST

★ **7** *Venus enters Cancer* [until 9/6] Love of home, family, tribe and nation are of utmost importance. Nesting instincts are also strong. Attention turns to decorating or increasing the value of properties. It's natural to be emotional about relationships and exhibit a caring, protective side. Be careful how feelings affect monetary matters, though.

★ **7** *(P),* **8** *(E) Mercury (1°25' LE) turns Direct* [Retrograde since 7/14; Direct until 11/6] It's as if we come out of a fog. We see things more clearly and may have to correct errors made during the Retrograde.

★ **8** *Chiron sextile Pluto* [within one degree] See April 21, above.

★ **11** *Chiron (8°12' PI) semisextile Uranus (8°12' AR)* [before 4 times 2010-11; again 11/13/12 & 17 more times 2013-2021] Letting your uniqueness shine is very healing. It should be a source of pride rather than shame. If you've felt you had to hide in the shadows because of some flaw, you will have many chances over the coming years to make improvements. Treat yourself gently regarding your imperfections rather than berating yourself. (See Long-term Influences, p. 74.)

★ **11** *(P),* **12** *(E) Vesta (12°4' GE) conjunct Jupiter (4°12' GE)* [within 1° from 8/6 to 8/17] Some people will read voraciously around now or encounter a new interest. Pursue your intellectual passions with gusto.

★ **15** *Mars (24°49' LI) conjunct Saturn (24°49' LI)* These two planets were called "malefics" (evil-doers) by ancient astrologers. Modern astrologers like to point out positive uses for them. They meet up about every two years. This time, they join in Libra, where Saturn is said to be "exalted" (well placed, behaving nicely) and Mars is in the sign opposite Aries, which it rules, and is said to be "debilitated," unable to be its usual assertive self. This time around is likely to be a milder union than it usually is. It helps us be forward about establishing or revisiting the rules of the game in a relationship, or take on responsibilities that can be handled in tandem or teams.

Together they participate in a very favorable pattern (see weekly Highlights and Aug. 19, below).

★ **15** *Venus (7°13' CN) at maximum western elongation* This is as far behind the Sun as Venus gets, rising earliest ahead of the Sun in the pre-dawn sky.

★ **19** *Saturn (25°09' LI) quintile Pluto (7°09' CP)* [before 11/11/11 & 3/28/12 but no Quintile Triangles formed then] Respect and a little work help bring about positive alterations in relationships. Those in power collaborate to shore up boundaries or rules and foster structural changes. These two planets are in a Quintile Triangle with the indicator of the path of least resistance, the South Node (around 1° GE), which was biquintile Pluto 8/7 and is biquintile Saturn 8/16. The formation is close enough to exact throughout most of August to create additional Quintile Triangles. Mars passes Saturn 8/15, joining in the pattern. The Moon (around 13° LE) makes quintiles and biquintiles to them on 8/16, expanding this triangle to one point short of a 5-pointed star. If you have anything near 19° Pisces in your natal chart, it creates a perfect pentagram midday 8/16 and all day on 8/22, when Mercury moves through 13° LE. Such a formation can be used to great advantage to set intentions in motion.

★ **22** *Sun enters Virgo* [until 9/22] We're patient, polite and humble – except when taking pride in a job well done. Being of help comes naturally and great care can be given to all the little things. Most of us shy away from big risks. Watch out for Virgo's down side: "analysis leads to paralysis."

★ **23** *Mars enters Scorpio* [until 10/6] This is a time to make changes and purge what isn't working in our lives. With Mars' anger tendency added to Scorpio's explosive side, sensitivities easily escalate into arguments. We're more intense in our physical activities (workouts, sex, etc.).

★ **24** *Chiron (7°36' PI) semisquare Eris (22°36' AR)* [before 3/20/12; again 1/12/13 (P), 1/13/13 (E)] See March 20, above.

★ **29** *True North Node enters Scorpio, True South Node enters Taurus* [until 2/18/14] See Sept. 1, below.

★ **31** *Mercury enters Virgo* [until 9/16] As you pay close attention to your work, don't get lost in details. Those who tend to be conscientious about helping others might put themselves on the back burner. Health is on our minds.

★ **31** *Blue Moon?* Depends on your definition. As originally used, if there were four full moons in a season of three months, the third was designated as blue. The Full Moon on 8/20/13 will qualify in that strict sense. Common usage today considers a second full moon in a calendar month as blue, like this one.

SEPTEMBER

★ **1** *North Node enters Scorpio, South Node enters Taurus* [until 3/22/14] You might see a different date (Aug. 29) elsewhere for the Nodes changing signs. There are two ways of calculating the Nodes' positions. This calendar uses the average motion, called the Mean Node, which continually marches backward through the zodiac at a fairly consistent pace. The other method, called the True Node, has a more variable speed and vacillates between forward and backward motion (see the ephemeris, p. 63). The North Node's sign shows experiences we need to assimilate or traits we should incorporate for our growth, while the South Node's sign points to what we need to release or it will hold us back. Now that the Nodes have left Sagittarius and Gemini, everything must be pursued to a greater depth; superficial treatment of any subject will no longer suffice. Willingness to go to extremes comes with the Scorpio territory. The Taurus South Node requires us to step out of our comfort zone and let go of a need for stability. Both are persistent signs, thus our level of tenacity increases. Both can be jealous or resentful; beware these deterrents to clean karma in relationships. The Nodes are the intersections of two orbits: earth around the Sun and the Moon around earth. Eclipses occur when New or Full Moons are in the vicinity of the Nodes and the earth, Sun and Moon align perfectly. With the changing of the Nodes' signs, the signs for eclipses also shift.

★ **6** *Chiron (6°59' PI) sextile Pluto (6°59' CP)* See April 21 and May 12, above.

★ **6** *Venus enters Leo* [until 10/3] We're generous and dramatic in our affections, as well as loyal and steadfast. All forms of entertainment delight us and some people will yearn for the spotlight.

★ **12** *Finger of God: Venus (6°41'-57' LE) quincunx Chiron (6°41' PI) & Pluto (6°57' CP), which are sextile (exact 9/6)* Venus helps accomplish the transformative healing that the Chiron-Pluto sextile offers through love, contribution of funds or putting a good mix of people together as a team.

★ **16** *Mercury enters Libra* [until 10/5] Fairness is on our minds. Social conversation is easy, aimed at keeping the peace by using negotiating skills. We're easily able to conceptualize and understand abstractions and we enjoy a good debate.

★ **17** *(P),* **18** *(E) Pluto (6°57' CP) turns Direct* [Retrograde since 4/10; Direct until 4/12/13] Financial matters involving more than one person's money (banking, investments, insurance, inheritance, grants, etc.) function more smoothly when Pluto is Direct. Examining the foundation of situations and people's motives helps us understand them better. It's time to make progress in letting go of what's outworn in our lives.

★ **18** *(P),* **19** *(E) Uranus (6°57' AR) square Pluto (6°57' CP)* [before 6/24; again 5/20/13, 11/1/13 & 4/21/14] See June 24, above.

★ **22** *Autumn Equinox* See Seasonal Synopses, p. 75.

★ **22** *Sun enters Libra* [until 10/22] Relationships are foremost on our radar screen. Social obligations keep us busy, to the detriment of personal objectives. Seek balance in your life and harmony in your soul. [See Mutual Receptions near the beginning of the Star Pages.]

★ **26** *Ceres enters Cancer* [until 12/3; again 4/4-6/22/13 because it goes Retrograde here] We realize the emotions we ingest and feed to others have a strong

Continued on next page.

impact, thus we become more careful and caring. Greater attention is paid to family matters, the housing market, eating and nutrition, the food supply and the problems of starvation and obesity.

OCTOBER

★ **3** *Venus enters Virgo* [until 10/28] Social niceties and etiquette are important. Appreciate refinement and when care is given to details. Try to avoid being critical in relationships. Be selective in accepting social invitations, choosy about partners or friends, and careful in finances.

★ **4** *Jupiter (16°23' GE) turns Retrograde* [Direct since 12/25/11; Retrograde until 1/30/13] For the next four months, we may feel less optimistic and expansive, needing to rein ourselves in and stay grounded. Some will experience backsliding or challenges in the areas of higher education, travel, media, promotion and legal affairs. Re-examine your philosophies. Try to create your own luck rather than wait for breaks from other people.

★ **5** *Mercury enters Scorpio* [until 10/28 (P), 10/29 (E); again 11/13 (P), 11/14 (E) - 12/10 because it Retrogrades back into Scorpio from Sagittarius] Our minds may be on survival matters, finances, sex or reproduction, and our thinking is impacted by deep feelings. We have a sharp understanding of motives (including our own) and what makes people tick.

★ **5** *Saturn enters Scorpio* [until 12/23/14; again 6/14/15-9/17/15] Hard work and discipline are brought to bear in areas needing major transformation. Perseverance and a "do or die" attitude ensure seeing things through to conclusion, no matter how long it takes – and it could be quite some time! (The down side is "beating a dead horse.") This is a good period for undertaking monumental projects, especially if these require the efforts and resources of many people. Saturn generally has a contracting effect and Scorpio and its ruler Pluto are related to the economy, pointing to the potential for a protracted period of slow or no growth. However, in recent history, the opposite has been the case when Saturn was in Scorpio: the Roaring 20s, mid-50s and mid-80s were all boom times. Perhaps the regulatory climate (under Saturn's bailiwick as ruler of laws) is an important factor. (See Mutual Receptions, p. 74.)

★ **6** *Mars enters Sagittarius* [until 11/16] We reach far and wide, wanting the world, but we may try for too much and miss the mark. Though we're confident we can juggle multiple tasks at once, they will each turn out better if we slow down and concentrate on one thing at a time.

★ **10** *Saturn (0°37' SC) trine Neptune (0°37' PI)* [again 6/11/13 & 7/19/13] These two planets don't have much in common. Saturn is concerned with reality while Neptune dwells in the depths of imagination. When they cooperate like this, we are inspired to give form to ideas and find outlets for creativity. A potential downside is a tendency to trust that everything will just gel without any effort, which could dilute ambition. Saturn in Scorpio provides the desire to make a difference while Neptune in Pisces adds the compassion to help those at

a disadvantage. From the beginning of October until Thanksgiving weekend, Ceres in Cancer forms a water-sign Grand Trine with Saturn and Neptune, enhancing charitable efforts and bolstering the support we give to family members who may be in need. (The Sun and Moon at the Oct. 29 Full Moon join in, expanding the formation into a Kite.) Religious and non-profit organizations try to make up for the slack from slim government funds. This autumn should be a very fruitful period for artistic projects and is a great time for home decorating. (See Long-term Influences, p. 74.)

★ **15** *Jupiter (16°10' GE) sesquiquadrate Saturn (1°10' SC)* [before 7/20/12; again 5/19/13 (P), 5/20/13 (E)] See July 20, above. A nuance of difference in the expression of these planets in this instance and the last is that Saturn has moved into Scorpio. There's not so much of an emphasis on relationships any longer. Instead, the focus is on finances and power, with the likelihood that something under wraps is exposed. Expect excessive discussions about how to control spending or the manner of allocating funds.

★ **15-16** *Quintile Triangle: Venus (15° VI) quintile Ceres (3° CA) and quintile North Node (27° SC)* (North Node biquintile Ceres is exact on 10/21) Being careful and protective about money matters leads to positive results. Assess what expenditures are worth the cost and which investments will yield a good return.

★ **22** *Sun enters Scorpio* [until 11/21] For the next four weeks, try to change your life in some way, applying will power and intention to move past blocks and obstacles. Begin a new chapter with a greater sense of control. Tenacity won't let anything get the better of you.

★ **25** *(P),* **26** *(E) Mercury begins repeated aspects of Retrograde cycle)* See Nov. 6, below.

★ **28** *Venus enters Libra* [until 11/21] Fairness and equality are top values now, and we want relationships to be balanced and healthy. People act with more gentility and diplomacy. Romance flourishes.

★ **28** *(P),* **29** *(E) Mercury enters Sagittarius* [until 11/13 (P), 11/14 (E); again 12/10 - 12/31] Minds are quick and intuition is strong, though our attention span may be shorter than usual. Reading and learning (perhaps a new language) are appealing. This doesn't have to mean books and the library; the internet is a rich source of information. After backtracking into Scorpio, when something hidden comes to light, we re-approach matters with a wider perspective and more wisdom.

★ **31** *Ceres (3°43' CN) turns Retrograde* [Direct since 11/6/11; Retrograde until 2/4/13, backtracking into Gemini – see June 23] Nurture yourself instead of looking to others for your care and emotional support. This is a good period to make improvements in your home environment so you're more comfortable there.

Want to learn more about astrology?
Visit the Study Booth at
JanetsPlan-its.com

NOVEMBER

★ **1-7** *Quintile Triangles: Venus and Mars with Neptune, then Chiron. Mars (18°23 SG) quintile Neptune (0°23' PI) on 11/1; Venus (6°22' LI) biquintile Neptune (0°22' PI) on 11/2; Venus (8°44' LI) quintile Mars (20°44' SG) on 11/4; Venus (11°0' LI) biquintile Chiron (5°0' PI) on 11/6; Mars (23°0' SG) quintile Chiron (5°0' PI) on 11/7.* Time for guys and gals to make magic! This is the week for love to help you get over hurts, whether those stemmed from romance or not. Just knowing someone understands and cares can make a difference. It's also a good time to bring people together for creative projects, travel or education.

★ **6** *Mercury (4°18' SG) turns Retrograde* [Direct since 8/7 (P), 8/8 (E); Retrograde until 11/26] Backtracking from Sagittarius into Scorpio, issues now involve transparency versus what's hidden or kept private. Prepare to encounter new vistas by first clearing the cobwebs of obsessive thoughts from your mind. With Mercury turning tail on Election Day, observe the influence and behavior of the media. Lessons of this cycle include: mouthing off can create enemies; respect confidentiality; be true to your core values; and maintain hope in the midst of dire straits or big changes. Mercury repeats two key aspects in this cycle. It's conjunct the North Node in Scorpio (10/26, 11/17 and 12/6), forcing us to look into dark corners or address taboo subjects. Its square to Neptune (10/29, 11/13 and 12/11) brings belief and trust into question. Some will fall prey to projecting their own issues onto others.

★ **10** *(P),* **11** *(E) Neptune (0°21' PI) turns Direct* [Retrograde since 6/4; Direct until 6/7/13] After months of turning to ourselves for spiritual guidance, now we incorporate input from others in matters of faith. We find it easier to trust people.

★ **13** *Chiron (4°59' PI) semisextile Uranus (4°59' AR)* [before 4 times 2010-11 & 8/11/12; again 17 more times 2013-2021; next 8/21/13] (See Aug. 11, above.) Both these planets currently make aspects to Saturn, a quincunx from Uranus (see Nov. 15) and a trine from Chiron (see Nov. 16). Since this instance occurs on the same day as a Solar Eclipse (see below), its influence is carried forward for at least the next six months.

★ **13** *Solar Eclipse New Moon (21°57' SC)* a total eclipse visible in extremely northern Australia and the Pacific east of there. Dramatic changes which could happen quite suddenly are becoming the norm nowadays and this eclipse promises more of the same. The Moon and Sun are semisquare Pluto and sesquiquadrate Uranus, pointing to the need to shed outworn feelings and notions of our purpose or identity. The eclipse occurs close to the North Node, showing that transitions are not second nature but necessary and take effort. Mercury is about to pass the North Node, putting conscious attention on the process of change. Nurturing support should be part of the formula, as indicated by Ceres in Cancer in three key patterns. It continues in a long-lasting Grand Trine (see Oct. 10, above), comes close to forming a T-square with Uranus and Pluto (discussed in the Nov. 5-11 Highlights), and is part of a Quintile Triangle with Eris and the North Node. This last formation creates a safe atmosphere in which confidence and persistence assist

in getting rid of what's no longer needed or holding us back. Diplomacy between countries may be dicey due to two wild cards: an out of bounds Mars in Sagittarius and Jupiter in a condition called "unaspected" (without any connections to other planets to help express its influence).

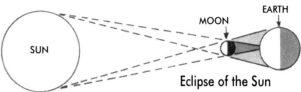

Eclipse of the Sun

★ **13** *(P),* **14** *(E) Mercury re-enters Scorpio* [before 10/5-10/28 (P), 10/29(E); until 12/10] See Oct. 5, above.

★ **14** *Chiron (4°59' PI) turns Direct* [Retrograde since 6/12; Direct until 6/16/13] The past five months were a time to address our internal wounds and be our own inspiration for improvement. Going forward, we can seek such support externally and more easily provide it to others, as well. As both Neptune and Chiron advance rather than retreat, health matters are more likely to improve.

★ **15** *Saturn (4°56' SC) quincunx Uranus (4°56' AR)* [again 4/12/13 & 10/4/13 (P), 10/5/13 (E)] Discomfort arises when you want to be on top of things but can hardly keep up with the pace of change. Something seems to be in the way of making a fresh start. There's a mismatch between impatience and a desire to take a slow, thorough approach.

★ **16** *Saturn (4°58' SC) trine Chiron (4°58' PI)* [again 3/21/13 & 10/2/13] We have the strength to address pain and problems, whether they're others' or our own. We're willing to invest time and resources to find solutions and make improvements. People may not show the depth of their feelings but their actions demonstrate it.

★ **16** *Mars enters Capricorn* [until 12/25] It's time to get organized and focus on achievement. Ambitions and concentration help us reach our objectives. It's easy to be pragmatic and practice patience.

★ **21** *Sun enters Sagittarius* [until 12/21] The sky's the limit! Stretch yourself upward and onward. It's a good time for travel, study, law, journalism, and contact with those at a distance – anything that increases our knowledge and understanding.

★ **21** *Venus enters Scorpio* [until 12/15] Your level of passion increases for people and things to which you're attracted. Any insecurity you might have about love or money is more likely to surface now. Extremes are possible in fashion or spending; this is not when you stick to the middle road.

★ **26** *Mercury (18°10' SC) turns Direct* [Retrograde since 11/6 (E); Direct until 2/23/13] Wrap up anything you've been researching; it's time to draw conclusions. You can now put to use what you have uncovered. You'll feel like you're making good progress by Dec. 14, when Mercury moves past the point where it turned Retrograde, possibly as soon as when it re-enters Sagittarius on Dec. 10.

★ **28** *Lunar Eclipse Full Moon (6°47' GE)* Three slower moving planets are creeping into position for a potent Finger of God triangle, exact next month (see Dec. 20, below). They are joined now by a flurry of quick planets that form the Finger temporarily like a preview of coming attractions. The base of the triangle is the long-term Saturn-Pluto sextile (see Dec. 26, below). Jupiter will soon be quincunx to each (Dec. 20 and 22). Venus is just past Saturn while Mars pairs with Pluto. The Moon nears Jupiter and the Moon-Sun opposition of the Full Moon splits the triangle down the middle at this eclipse. It's a powerful set-up for one strange event leading to another to bring movement in a situation where needed changes have been slow in coming. Likely realms affected are finances, relationships, education, transportation and communication. The Moon and Sun are also in a T-square with Chiron so it may be a time when fresh wounds are suffered or a healing from prior hurts takes place, maybe even some of both. Problems are more likely in situations that involve rivalry or competition, since Eris is halfway between Chiron and the Moon, sesquiquadrate the Sun. The more you can view circumstances in light of spiritual growth and acceptance, the easier you can flow with the adjustments in store.

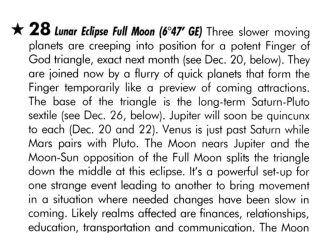

Eclipse of the Moon

★ **29** *Ceres at zero degrees of Cancer* [until it retreats into Gemini 12/4; again 4/4/13 - 4/8/13] Any planet at the degree where the Sun is at a solstice (such as this degree) or an equinox is at a power point of the zodiac and can signal important events that impact many people. Ceres is often related to harvests and the food supply, while Cancer is a sign of nutrition. Famine or food contamination may be in the news.

DECEMBER

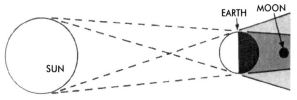

★ **4** *Ceres re-enters Gemini* [before 6/23-9/26; until 4/4/13] See June 23, above.

★ **10** *Mercury re-enters Sagittarius* [before 10/28 (P), 10/29 (E)-11/13 (P), 11/14 (E); until 12/31] See Oct. 28-29, above.

★ **13** *Uranus (4°36' AR) turns Direct* [Retrograde since 7/13; Direct until 7/17/13] The past five months, we've turned inward to seek a spark for self-development. While Uranus is Direct, our individuality is recognized and promoted by others. When Uranus is Retrograde, we sometimes rebel against our own advice to ourselves. When it's in forward motion, we're more likely to revolt against other people's orders.

★ **15** *Venus enters Sagittarius* [until 1/8/13] Optimism in romance is much easier than earlier this month. Significant others are supportive and beneficial. Better possibilities are ours for the taking in social and/or financial matters.

Connect with people far and wide, whether in person or via mail/phone/internet.

★ **20** *Jupiter (8°56' GE) quincunx Pluto (8°56' CP)* [before 7/18; again 3/29/13] See July 18, above.

★ **20-26** *Finger of God: Jupiter quincunx Pluto and Saturn, which are sextile* [12/20 (see above) Jupiter quincunx Pluto; 12/22 (see below) Jupiter quincunx Saturn; 12/26 (see below) Saturn sextile Pluto] The goal is to bring about progress through good organization and careful planning. Avoid the impulse to speed up the process; shooting from the hip could undermine all your hard work.

★ **21** *Winter Solstice* See Seasonal Synopses, p. 75.

★ **21** *Sun enters Capricorn* [until 1/18/13 (P), 1/19/13 (P)] A focus on work and career, coupled with conscientious effort, helps us achieve goals and win appreciation on the job. We care what people think about us and strive to maintain a good reputation.

★ **22** *Jupiter (8°45' GE) quincunx Saturn (8°45' SC)* [before 5/16; again 3/23/13] See May 16, above.

★ **22** *Venus (8°42' SG) at "release point" of Finger of God, opposite Jupiter (8°42' GE); Venus semisextile Saturn (8°49' SC) & Pluto (9°1' CP) on 12/23* Being open-hearted and generous allows you to connect with people who are cautious or private. This is a very positive indicator for business dealings, especially if they involve the media or the internet.

★ **25** *Mars enters Aquarius* [until 2/1/13] You're likely to act on what you "know" to be true (even if it's just your own opinion). Take a stand for a friend or for humanity's sake, or serve in a leadership position in a group to which you belong.

★ **26** *Saturn (9°8' SC) sextile Pluto (9°8' CP)* [again 3/7/13 (P), 3/8/13 (E) & 9/20/13 (P), 9/21/13 (E)] If you steel yourself against any hurdles, there's not much that can stop you from attaining your goals, even though the process may be lengthy. You have patience. Determination is strong as is the ability to bounce back from adversity. You're good at organizing and ensuring needed resources are at hand. (See Finger of God comments on Dec. 20, above.)

★ **29-30** *Sun (8° - 9° CP) quincunx Jupiter (8° GE) 12/29, conjunct Pluto (9° CP) & sextile Saturn (9° SC) on 12/30, joining their Finger of God* (see Dec. 20-26), extending its influence. Leadership or creativity helps bring about change to form a stronger foundation for the future. By expanding discussions, more wisdom and resources become involved.

★ **31** *Mercury enters Capricorn* [until 1/18/13 (P), 1/19/13 (E)] Mercury, the messenger planet, is associated with announcements or headlines. When it enters a season-changing sign like this, there's potential for a wide impact. While in Capricorn, Mercury moves us to streamline information systems and get down to brass tacks. This is a good time to arrange files, set up schedules and make checklists. Our minds operate like efficient machines, with little room for emotions.

LOOKING AHEAD TO JANUARY 2013

See 2013 On a Page (p. 88).

★ **5** *(P),* **6** *(E) Mercury (7° - 9° CP) quincunx Jupiter (7° GE) 1/5, conjunct Pluto (9° CP) & sextile Saturn (9° SC) 1/6, joining their Finger of God (see Dec. 20-26),* for the finale of its influence. Even though some people employ humor to make light of a heavy situation, thoughts and words are powerful now, able to turn things in a better direction. One thing leads to another and we find out what we need to know and say what we need to convey.

★ **8** *Eris (21°37' AR) turns Direct* [Retrograde since 7/18; Direct until 7/19/13] There's likely to be more disorder and disruption when Eris is at a standstill for a couple weeks on either side of its change of direction. Once it's moving forward again, we're better able to assert our independence, handle disruptions and deal with competition.

★ **8** *Venus enters Capricorn* [until 2/1/13] We're more serious about relationships and seek assurances or commitment from a significant other. The importance of interpersonal boundaries may be demonstrated by people crossing the line. We tend to be frugal or at least aim for a deal on purchases. This is a good time for budgeting and long-term financial planning.

Do you have your 2013 Janet's Plan-its Celestial Planner?

Global Pledge of Allegiance

I pledge allegiance to the earth and to the universal spirit which gives us life; one planet, indivisible, with peace and justice for all.

I pledge to do my best to uphold the trust bestowed in the gift of my life, to care for our planet and our atmosphere, to respect and honor all her inhabitants, all people, animals, plants and resources, to create a legacy for our children and our children's children in a world of harmony and love.

I pledge allegiance to the universal spirit, by whatever name it may be called.

I align my life with the on-going process of creation; to grow myself with care, to act from my own integrity, to be for others how I would want them to be for me.

Together, may we carry this vision in our hearts, into our daily choices, and through our expanding consciousness within and beyond our planet.

Edna Reitz, Copyright 1988

Janet Booth is available for readings by phone and Skype.
Readings are recorded for your convenience.
Visit JanetsPlan-its.com for details.

2013 Janet's Plan-its™ On a Page

	MERCURY	VENUS	MARS	CERES	JUPITER	SATURN	CHIRON	URANUS	NEPTUNE	PLUTO	MOON PHASES
(top)				R 10/31/12, 3°43' CN	R 10/4/12, 16°23' GE	B 11/14/12, 4°49' SC	D 11/14/12, 4°59' PI	D 12/13/12, 4°36' AR	D 11/11/12, 0°21' PI	B 12/22/12, 8°59' CP	(E) = ECLIPSE
JANUARY					D 1/30, 6°20' GE					(next R shadow) E 1/7, 9°34' CP (prior R shadow)	New 1/11, 21°46' CP Full 1/26, 7°24' LE
FEBRUARY	B 2/8, 5°38' PI R 2/23, 19°52' PI			D 2/4, 19°45' GE		R 2/18, 11°32' SC	B 2/23, 9°7' PI (next R shadow)		B 2/14, 2°35' PI (next R shadow)		New 2/10, 21°43' AQ Full 2/25, 7°24' VI
MARCH	D 3/17, 5°38' PI						E 3/5, 9°45' PI (prior R shadow)	E 3/29, 8°32' AR B 3/30, 8°35' AR	E 3/1, 3°9' PI (prior R shadow)		New 3/11, 21°24' PI Full 3/27, 6°52' LI
APRIL	E 4/6, 19°52' AR			E 4/16, 3°43' CN	E 4/25, 16°23' GE					R 4/12, 11°35' CP	New 4/10, 20°41' AR Full 4/25, 5°46' SC (E)
MAY											New 5/9, 19°31' TA (E) Full 5/25, 4°8' SG (E)
JUNE	B 6/9, 13°22' CN R 6/26, 23°6' CN					R 6/16, 13°50' PI			R 6/7, 5°22' PI		New 6/8, 18°1' GE Full 6/23, 2°10' CP
JULY	D 7/20, 13°22' CN					D 7/8, 4°49' SC		R 7/17, 12°31' AR			New 7/8, 16°18' CN Full 7/22, 0°6' AQ
AUGUST	E 8/3, 23°6' CN				B 8/12, 10°27' CN						New 8/6, 14°35' LE Full 8/20, 28°11' AQ
SEPTEMBER										D 9/20, 8°59' CP	New 9/15, 13°4' VI Full 9/19, 26°41' PI
OCTOBER	B 10/1, 2°30' SC R 10/21, 18°23' SC					E 10/14, 11°32' SC					New 10/4, 11°56' LI Full 10/18, 25°45' AR (E)
NOVEMBER	D 11/10, 2°30' SC E 11/27, 18°23' SC	B 11/20, 13°33' CP			R 11/7, 20°31' CN	B 11/26, 16°39' SC	D 11/19, 9°7' PI		D 11/13, 2°35' PI	B 12/24, 11°0' CP	New 11/3, 11°16' SC (E) Full 11/17, 25°26' TA
DECEMBER	R 12/21, 28°59' CP D 1/31/14, 13°33' CP	R 12/21, 28°59' CP D 1/31/14, 13°33' CP	B 12/26, 9°2' LI R 3/1/14, 27°32' LI	B 12/21, 18°32' LI R 2/27/14, 1°53' SC	D 3/6/14, 10°27' CN	R 3/2/14, 23°19' SC	E 3/10/14, 13°50' PI	D 12/17, 8°35' AR E 4/2/14, 12°31' AR	E 3/3/14, 5°22' PI	(next R shadow) E 1/10/14, 11°35' CP (prior R shadow)	New 12/2, 10°59' SG Full 12/17, 25°36' GE

NOTE: The shadows of Chiron, Neptune and Pluto can overlap, creating a brief double shadow [darker shading]. Eris begins 2013 Retrograde, turning Direct 1/8 at 21°37' AR. It has overlapping shadows from 3/1 to 5/26, turning Retrograde 7/19 at 22°57' AR. It next turns Direct 1/9/14 at 21°51' AR. It doesn't make much forward progress in a year!

2013 Calendar

JANUARY
SU	M	TU	W	T	F	S
		1	2	3	4	5
6	7	8	9	10	11	12
13	14	15	16	17	18	19
20	21	22	23	24	25	26
27	28	29	30	31		

FEBRUARY
SU	M	TU	W	T	F	S
					1	2
3	4	5	6	7	8	9
10	11	12	13	14	15	16
17	18	19	20	21	22	23
24	25	26	27	28		

MARCH
SU	M	TU	W	T	F	S
					1	2
3	4	5	6	7	8	9
10	11	12	13	14	15	16
17	18	19	20	21	22	23
24	25	26	27	28	29	30
31						

APRIL
SU	M	TU	W	T	F	S
	1	2	3	4	5	6
7	8	9	10	11	12	13
14	15	16	17	18	19	20
21	22	23	24	25	26	27
28	29	30				

MAY
SU	M	TU	W	T	F	S
			1	2	3	4
5	6	7	8	9	10	11
12	13	14	15	16	17	18
19	20	21	22	23	24	25
26	27	28	29	30	31	

JUNE
SU	M	TU	W	T	F	S
						1
2	3	4	5	6	7	8
9	10	11	12	13	14	15
16	17	18	19	20	21	22
23	24	25	26	27	28	29
30						

JULY
SU	M	TU	W	T	F	S
	1	2	3	4	5	6
7	8	9	10	11	12	13
14	15	16	17	18	19	20
21	22	23	24	25	26	27
28	29	30	31			

AUGUST
SU	M	TU	W	T	F	S
				1	2	3
4	5	6	7	8	9	10
11	12	13	14	15	16	17
18	19	20	21	22	23	24
25	26	27	28	29	30	31

SEPTEMBER
SU	M	TU	W	T	F	S
1	2	3	4	5	6	7
8	9	10	11	12	13	14
15	16	17	18	19	20	21
22	23	24	25	26	27	28
29	30					

OCTOBER
SU	M	TU	W	T	F	S
		1	2	3	4	5
6	7	8	9	10	11	12
13	14	15	16	17	18	19
20	21	22	23	24	25	26
27	28	29	30	31		

NOVEMBER
SU	M	TU	W	T	F	S
					1	2
3	4	5	6	7	8	9
10	11	12	13	14	15	16
17	18	19	20	21	22	23
24	25	26	27	28	29	30

DECEMBER
SU	M	TU	W	T	F	S
1	2	3	4	5	6	7
8	9	10	11	12	13	14
15	16	17	18	19	20	21
22	23	24	25	26	27	28
29	30	31				

2013 Moon Phases

NEW

1/11 • 2/10 • 3/11 • 4/10 • 5/9 • 6/8 • 7/8 • 8/6 • 9/5 • 10/4 • 11/3 • 12/2

FIRST QUARTER

1/18 • 2/17 • 3/19 • 4/18 • 5/18 • 6/16 • 7/15 • 8/14 • 9/12 • 10/11 • 11/10 • 12/9

FULL

1/26 • 2/25 • 3/27 • 4/25 • 5/25 • 6/23 • 7/22 • 8/20 • 9/19 • 10/18 • 11/17 • 12/17

THIRD QUARTER

1/4 • 2/3 • 3/4 • 4/3 • 5/2 • 5/31 • 6/30 • 7/29 • 8/28 • 9/26 • 10/26 • 11/25 • 12/25

Dates based on Eastern time zone.

Cycles of Eight, of Transformation, on Earth and Within Your Life!

Eight Phases of the Sun, defining the seasons of each Solar Year and the stages of plant life.
Eight Phases of the Moon, by month, and by your own lifetime progressed Lunar Phase Cycle.

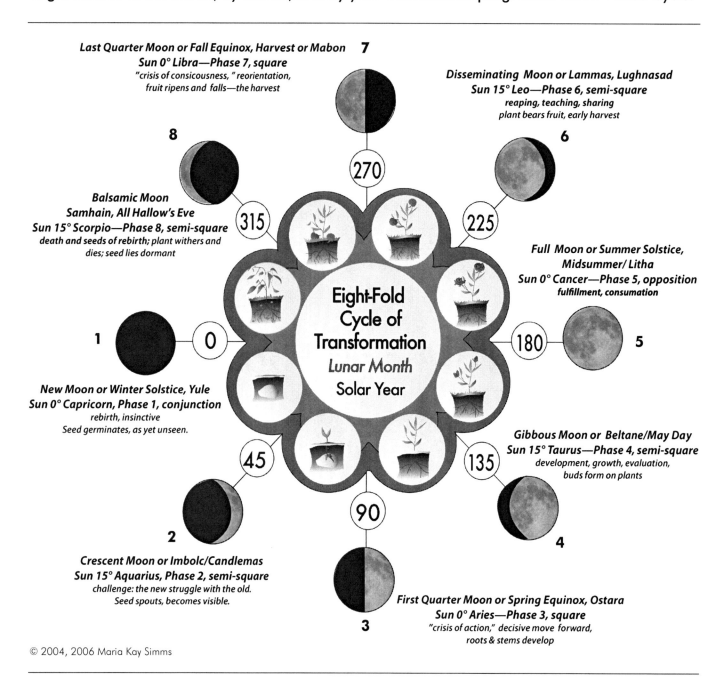

Last Quarter Moon or Fall Equinox, Harvest or Mabon 7
Sun 0° Libra—Phase 7, square
"crisis of consicousness," reorientation,
fruit ripens and falls—the harvest

Disseminating Moon or Lammas, Lughnasad
Sun 15° Leo—Phase 6, semi-square
reaping, teaching, sharing
plant bears fruit, early harvest

Balsamic Moon
Samhain, All Hallow's Eve
Sun 15° Scorpio—Phase 8, semi-square
death and seeds of rebirth; plant withers and
dies; seed lies dormant

Full Moon or Summer Solstice,
Midsummer/ Litha
Sun 0° Cancer—Phase 5, opposition
fulfillment, consumation

New Moon or Winter Solstice, Yule
Sun 0° Capricorn, Phase 1, conjunction
rebirth, insinctive
Seed germinates, as yet unseen.

Eight-Fold Cycle of Transformation
Lunar Month
Solar Year

Gibbous Moon or Beltane/May Day
Sun 15° Taurus—Phase 4, semi-square
development, growth, evaluation,
buds form on plants

Crescent Moon or Imbolc/Candlemas
Sun 15° Aquarius, Phase 2, semi-square
challenge: the new struggle with the old.
Seed spouts, becomes visible.

First Quarter Moon or Spring Equinox, Ostara
Sun 0° Aries—Phase 3, square
"crisis of action," decisive move forward,
roots & stems develop

This graphic from my book, **Moon tides, Soul Passages**, summarizes the Eight-fold Cycle of Transformation, each lunar phase with its corresponding phase in the solar seasonal cycle. Just as Moon passes through 8 phases each month of about 30 days, the secondary progressed cycle of our natal Moon defines the 8 phases in each 30 years of life. Our life begins with the phase we are born within, and progresses from there. Our birth phase defines an important aspect of who we are, and our progression into each successive phase becomes a powerful method to understand the inner and outer changes we are experiencing, as well as to anticipate what may lie ahead.

– Maria Kay Simms

Moon Tides, Soul Passages
Lunar Phases and the Seasons of Life

Moon, Sun and Earth show us the seasons of life, and the archetypical spirit, soul and body of all three live within. The Moon has 8 distinct phases, as first defined by Dane Rudhyar. By secondary progression, the 8 lunar phases can be defined as a 29-1/2 – 30 year cycle of life experience.

I've been long fascinated with this powerful cycle of 8–especially its progressed phases that I've found to "work" well in my life, as well as in anyone else's I've studied. I'm also intrigued with the correlation of the 8 phases with the themes of the solar-seasonal cycle of 8, basic to ancient pagan sabbats. The core significance of the sabbats (though many are unaware of the origin) lives on in major holidays that fall on or very near the onset of each seasonal phase.

New Moon
New Moon, like the Maiden Goddess dances out of chaos, independent and free. As New Moon born, you project yourself onto your world, acting on instinct. At progressed New Moon, we enter a new major phase of life. Something significant to our past is ending, but we don't analyze; we just act. We make changes, driven by instinct.

Ritual/Action: New Moon is good for brainstorming. Get a pad & pen, dance to drumming or recorded music to raise energy, then chant this rhyme 9 times: *By magic charm, by 3 times 3, new ideas come to me! Jot them down!*

Crescent Moon
The dark is over and there's a sense of anticipation. Born at Crescent phase, you try to pull away from the past to forge something new. You have a vision, but must overcome something from the past to move forward. In progressed Crescent phase, it may feel as though each time you take two steps forward, there's a step back. You may know what you want, but there's resistance. that you must overcome.

Ritual/Action: When you see the waxing Crescent above, lift and cup your hands around her. Draw down her light and say: *Maiden Moon, come to me, Flow of bright new energy. My spirit lifts, my path is clear, my will is charged, my goal is near. Praise to thee and blessed be!*

First Quarter Moon
Now half light, half dark, the challenge is to move forward—act NOW! This is the "crisis of action!" If your birth phase, you like things that way! During progressed First Quarter, you've become very aware of the new direction that has been brewing. Now you make a clean break with what's past and move forward without looking back. Instinct still drives you, but now with a greater sense of direction.

Ritual/Action: Turn to each of the four directions, now with respect, say the appropriate phrase and listen to Spirit: *To the East I turn for clarity. To the South I turn for energy. To the West for intuition true. To the North for strength to see it through.* Then give thanks for insight received.

Gibbous Moon
Almost Full...but not quite...born at Gibbous phase, you constantly strive for an ideal, and your drive to reach it is strong. In progressed Gibbous, your goal is clear, but you're not quite there yet. There are still things to do. Persist — perfect your method.

Ritual/Action: Plant flowers with your pledge to bring your goal to full flower. As you plant say: *Lovely flowers, as you grow, strength and beauty I will see, Inspiring me to grow as well, In Her service, blessed be!*

Full Moon
Born at Full Moon, you have a deep sense of inner purpose, and must weigh opposing forces to balance and fulfill your intent. At progressed Full Moon, you reach a culmination that can be seen. If you remain vested in your purpose, you'll continue. If not, you may move on to create something else.

Ritual/Action: Draw down the Full Moon, a powerful experience. Cup her within your hands and draw her energy down through you, then send energy back to Her. Speak words of thanksgiving for what has been achieved.

Disseminating Moon
This is a phase of sharing, of giving back from what has been learned, achieved. If your natal phase, you are to demonstrate, teach and be a good example. The same theme holds for the 3-1/2 year progressed phase. Show what you can do!

Ritual/Action: Donate your time to a worthy charity to do a talk or demonstrate what you can do well.

Third Quarter Moon
Key phrase for this phase is "crisis of consciousness." If your natal phase, you are an iconoclast that doesn't fit into the mainstream. In the progressed phase, you experience an inner reorientation. Tired of what you've been doing, you begin a process of inner change.

Ritual/Action: Take a symbol of what you feel ready to let go of, and let it go with thanks, into an element of your choice: fire, air, earth or water.

Balsamic Moon
The waning crescent appears, and the lunar cycle draws to a close. The balsamic born are often visionary, and somehow feel different. At the progressed phase, we feel a sense of ending, perhaps a sense of isolation, a need to "be" rather than "do." But seeds of the new are stirring within.

Ritual/Action: Light a candle for guidance. Say: *Lady, guide me through the night, until new light I see. Inspire me toward my highest good. In love and trust, so mote it be!*

Anatomical Man

This famous illustration was painted by the Limbourg brothers for their patron, the Duc de Berry (brother of Charles V of France).
It shows the signs associated with various parts of the body, from the ram on the woman's head to the fish at her feet.
At her back, a man faces the opposite direction. Together they represent the feminine and masculine polarities.
The zodiac signs surround them in typical order from Aries at the top left, circling counterclockwise to Pisces at the top right.

"Anatomical Man" Annotated

by Diane L. Cramer, M.S., NCGR IV

The signs of the zodiac seen on the Anatomical Man are associated with different parts of the body. Each sign also has attributes describing their action and reaction in the body. Various health issues are common to each sign, as well. Due to polarity (see Keywords, p. 98), the signs are subject to ailments affiliated with the opposite sign. A pair of opposite signs may share a connection to a particular function or to related bodily systems. For example, Gemini and Sagittarius might indicate locomotive disorders; Leo and Aquarius can affect the heart and circulation. The following descriptions are applicable to one's Sun sign, rising sign, and in some instances, to the sign of the Moon.

ARIES
The ram on the top of the head represents Aries, a fire sign, which rules the brain, skull, outer ears, eyeball, upper jaw, adrenal medulla and pituitary gland. The head, face and teeth can be areas of distress. Aries shuns limits and needs to conserve energy or have a sound exercise program as an outlet for excess energy. Aries needs iron and may require meat more than other signs. Problems: fever, inflammation. Aries is also linked with renal function due to polarity with its opposite sign, Libra. Helpful herbs: ginseng or bergamot for mental exhaustion, lavender for headaches and borage for depletion of energy.

TAURUS
Taurus, the first of the earth signs, is represented by the bull at the back of the neck. Taurus rules the neck, throat, inner ears, gums, vocal chords and thyroid. Taurus tends to have endurance and a strong constitution but can be inflexible, which leads to a tense or stiff body. Body massages are useful for Taurus. Ruled by Venus, Taurus tends to overindulge in rich food and needs roughage and variety in the diet. Problems: sensitive vocal cords subject to infections, sore throats and hearing disorders. Helpful foods and herbs: black currants, coltsfoot and fenugreek to control sore throats; parsley and oregano to liven up the system; and root vegetables to help clean the digestive tract.

GEMINI
Gemini, the first of the air signs, is represented by the twins peeking around the shoulders. Gemini rules the arms, shoulders, hands, tongue, trachea and bronchi. Gemini rules all tubes in the body. Worry is a negative attribute which Gemini needs to overcome by positive thinking. Problems: nervous or respiratory disorders, allergies and weak lungs. Helpful: deep breathing exercises and aerobics as an outlet for Gemini's nervous energy; vitamins A, B, C and D to aid the lungs; herbs like skullcap for nervous excitability, flaxseed for coughs and bronchial complaints and bergamot for relaxation and sleep.

CANCER
The first of the water signs, Cancer is represented by the crab on the breastbone. Cancer rules all containers and coverings in the body. This includes the breasts, rib cage, sinus cavity, stomach, womb and the pleura of the lungs. Problems: a tendency toward water retention and disorders of the stomach. Helpful: raw enzymes to aid digestion from foods such as pineapple or papaya, and herbs such as bilberry for water retention, cloves for stomach gas, and honeysuckle and arrowroot to calm the stomach. Cancer needs to include fiber like bran and whole fruits in the diet. Lettuce, a Cancer plant, soothes the stomach.

LEO
Leo, the second of the fire signs, represented by the lion at the heart, is a sign of energy and vitality. The constitution is strong and when ill, Leo recovers quickly. Leo rules the heart muscle, spine and middle back. Rich foods tend to increase cholesterol levels so Leo would do well to avoid fatty foods. Problems: heart and muscle strain, backache, sunstroke and high fevers or inflammatory disorders. Helpful: herbs such as angelica for heartburn, dandelion as a tonic and blood purifier, rosemary as a heart tonic and mustard to alleviate back pains. Also beneficial: Vitamin E, magnesium and activities such as yoga that encourage flexibility in the torso and back.

VIRGO
Virgo, the second earth sign, represented by the virgin on the stomach, is a sign of assimilation and utilization. Virgo has a sensitive constitution and needs to keep the bowels and nervous system functioning in good order. Virgo rules the small intestines, pancreas, duodenum, the enzyme action of the liver and peristalsis of the bowels. Virgo has strong preferences and dislikes, and does well on a diet of natural foods, including plenty of fiber and whole grains. Problems: digestive disturbances, weak intestines, nervous complaints and illness due to poor nutrition. Helpful herbs: balm and borage for nervous troubles, angelica to stimulate the digestive tract, fenugreek for inflammation of the intestines, fennel seeds for gas and skullcap to tone the nervous system.

Continued on page 94

Disclaimer: This material is for informational and entertainment purposes only and does not replace nor is it to be used for the purpose of medical diagnosis or treatment. For medical attention, see a licensed medical professional.

LIBRA

Libra, the second of the three air signs, represented by the scales at the midsection, is a sign of balance and harmony. Libra needs to live a balanced and harmonious life and benefits from a balanced diet. Libra rules the kidneys, the lower back and the skin, from a cosmetic standpoint. Libra can be weak in the kidney area and would benefit from drinking lots of water every day to keep the kidneys flushed. Problems: headaches, lower back pains, skin complaints and health disorders due to Libra's love of sweets. Helpful herbs: bilberry and borage to promote kidney action, burdock for kidney weakness, feverfew to strengthen and cleanse the kidneys, and thyme for headaches.

SCORPIO

Scorpio, the second of the water signs, represented by the scorpion at the loins, is a sign of transformation, elimination and regeneration. Scorpio has a strong constitution with much vital force. Scorpio rules the eliminative and procreative organs in the body. As a fixed sign, Scorpio can be tense at times so would benefit from walking to increase flexibility. Scorpio may also be attracted to alternative healing methods, such as acupressure and biofeedback. Problems: bladder or bowel disorders; female complaints; a weak prostate in men; and predisposition to hemorrhoids, constipation and hernia in both genders. Helpful: daily roughage; fruits and vegetables; herbs such as chicory as a laxative, witch hazel for hemorrhoids, lavage as a general tonic and blessed thistle to force out impurities in the body; and a diet containing leeks, prunes, onions, beans and barley for energy.

SAGITTARIUS

Sagittarius, the last of the three fire signs, is represented by the archer at the thighs. Sagittarius can be expansive, optimistic and generous. However Sagittarius tends to excess and may overindulge in sweets, alcoholic beverages and meat. Sagittarius rules the hips, thighs and liver. Problems: gout, sciatica, hip injuries, obesity, rheumatism and diabetes or hypoglycemia. Helpful: discipline in dietary habits; foods such as cucumber to soothe the system, asparagus as a cleanser and spices such as sage, cloves and nutmeg. Herbs such as chicory address liver impurities; dandelion is an aid to the liver and a general tonic; red clover is a good blood purifier; and thyme and rosemary are tonic for the liver.

CAPRICORN

The last of the three earth signs, Capricorn, is represented by the goat at the knees. This is a sign that strengthens as it ages. Capricorn rules the skin, knees, joints, hair, teeth and nails. Capricorn does best in a warm environment as getting chilled can lead to illness. Capricorn needs sufficient calcium to maintain bones and teeth. Problems: falls, bruises, colds and chills, weak knees, skin disorders, dental problems and stiff joints. Helpful Herbs: bay for skin trouble, camphor rub for chills, chamomile and cloves for toothache, rose hips to retain flexibility of cartilage and slippery elm to strengthen the skeletal system. A dogmatic sign, Capricorn needs to loosen up by swimming, stretching, deep breathing exercises or massage.

AQUARIUS

The last of the air signs, Aquarius, a sign of oxygenation, is represented by the water bearer at the shins. Aquarius can become high strung and restless due to an abundance of nervous energy. Aquarius rules the electrolytes of the body, the lower legs and ankles, the valves of the heart and the retina of the eyes. Problems: circulatory complaints, leg complaints, varicose veins, nervous disorders, hormonal imbalance, sprained or broken ankle and impurities of the bloodstream. Helpful: exercises such as bicycling, yoga and deep breathing, and a good night's sleep to recharge the nervous system. Herbs such as bergamot aid relaxation, borage cleanses the bloodstream and is helpful for sprains, rosemary stimulates circulation and valerian quiets the nerves. Aquarius would do well to avoid chemicals and processed foods.

PISCES

Pisces, the last of the water signs, is represented by the fish at the feet. Pisces can experience low energy and needs plenty of vitamins and minerals to build up the vital powers in the body. The ability to imagine and help others is an aid to good health in Pisces. This sign rules the lymphatic system of the body, the feet and the toes. Problems: a tendency toward bunions, gout, swelling of the feet, colds and infections, weak lungs, psychosomatic illnesses and alcoholism. Helpful: living near water, swimming, walking and meditation. Pisces may benefit from ginseng as a tonic, chicory to eliminate mucous and kelp as a source of iron. Foods high in iron such as liver, raisins or dried apricots, are beneficial to Pisces.

Disclaimer: This material is for informational and entertainment purposes only and does not replace nor is it to be used for the purpose of medical diagnosis or treatment. For medical attention, see a licensed medical professional.

BEST AND WORST DAYS
FOR VARIOUS ACTIVITIES

"Best" and "worst" are relative terms. You might think of these dates as "better" or "worse" than the other days of the year specifically for the activities listed. Sometimes "best" is "as good as it gets" in light of other factors in place, and certainly not perfect. Every attempt was made to find at least one "best" and one "worst" for each month in each category.

To put a date into context or to select a particular part of a day, see the weekly Highlights, daily messages, 2012 On a Page and the Star Pages (including the sections on Mutual Receptions and planets Out of Bounds). As usual, take precautions when Mercury or Venus is Retrograde, especially for activities related to these planets. And of course you wouldn't undertake important action when the Moon is Void. See Using This Planner (p. 2) to check if your birthday is on the list.

In many cases, only part of a day is better or worse for a type of activity. The parentheses after the date point you to morning (morn), afternoon (aft) or evening (eve). Sometimes "best" or "worst" applies to all but a portion of the day and the parentheses might say (not morn), meaning just the afternoon and evening apply. "Worst" days are warnings that these activities are likely to run into problems if undertaken then. These time frames apply to time zones in North America, from Atlantic (one hour earlier than Eastern) to Pacific, and they take Daylight Saving Time into account.

After the type of activity, the planets and signs associated with the arena are listed in brackets. If you know additional activities associated with these factors, they are also impacted. See the Keywords (p. 98) and at Janet's Plan-its.com.

♈ ♂
PHYSICAL ACTIVITIES, SPORTS, COMPETITION, RISK-TAKING
[Aries, Mars]

BEST: 1/13, 1/27, 2/27 (not eve), 3/14 (morn), 3/15 (eve), 4/21, 5/13, 6/2 (morn), 7/4 (eve), 7/8, 8/26 (not eve), 9/3 (morn), 10/22 (eve), 11/25, 12/6 (not eve).

WORST: 1/30, 2/1, 2/22, 3/10, 3/18, 3/22, 3/27, 4/6, 5/3, 5/5, 5/10, 5/17, 5/28 (eve), 6/4, 6/7, 7/17, 7/18, 8/11, 9/25, 9/29, 10/7, 10/14, 11/9, 12/7, 12/8.

♉ ♀ ♏ ♆
FINANCES, PURCHASES, INVESTMENTS
[Taurus, Venus, Scorpio, Pluto]

BEST: 1/13, (not morn), 2/20 (morn), 3/14 (morn), 3/25 (not eve), 4/14 (morn), 4/21, 5/19, 5/22, 6/15, 6/22 (morn), 7/5, 7/20 (morn), 8/8, 9/21 (not morn), 10/2, 10/26 (morn), 11/25, 12/6 (aft), 12/11 (not eve).

WORST: 1/19, 1/30, 2/14 (morn), 2/17 (not morn), 2/21 (not eve), 2/25, 2/29, 3/4, 3/7 (eve), 3/14 (eve), 3/18 (not eve), 3/22, 3/26, 4/3, 4/16, 5/2, 5/15, 6/4, 6/16, 7/7, 8/24, 8/30, 8/31, 9/25, 10/3, 10/4 (morn), 10/30, 11/3, 11/11, 11/13, 11/15, 12/7, 12/21

♊ ☿
COMMUNICATION, LOCAL TRAVEL OR TRANSPORTATION, NEIGHBORS, SIBLINGS
[Gemini, Mercury]

BEST: 1/1 (eve), 1/7 (not eve), 2/2 (not eve), 2/13 (morn), 2/16, 3/17 (not morn), 4/29, 5/19 (eve), 5/22, 6/26, 7/5 (morn), 8/22, 9/10 (morn), 10/26 (morn), 11/28 (eve), 12/6 (aft). (*Best days to mail holiday packages: 11/28 (aft), 12/6.*)

WORST: 1/22 (morn), 1/30, 2/1, 2/14, 2/22, 2/25, 3/9 (not eve), 3/15 (not eve), 3/27, 4/22 (eve), 4/25, 4/26 (eve), 5/4, 5/20, 5/24, 5/28, 6/11, 6/17, 6/20, 7/12 (eve), 7/29 (morn), 8/19, 9/20, 9/26, 10/20, 10/31, 11/4, 11/11, 11/13, 11/19, 12/11, 12/14-12/17, 12/27.

BEST AND WORST DAYS FOR VARIOUS ACTIVITIES

♋ ☽ ⚳

REAL ESTATE, DOMESTIC/ FAMILY MATTERS

[Cancer, Moon, Ceres]

BEST: 1/13 (not morn), 1/21 (morn), 2/16, 3/15 (eve), 3/25 (not eve), 4/21, 5/14, 5/19, 6/19, 6/22 (morn), 7/5 (morn), 8/8, 9/21 (eve), 10/11 (aft), 10/19, 11/12, 11/25, 12/1 (morn).

WORST: 1/30, 2/7, 2/25, 3/4, 3/9 (not eve), 3/30 (not eve), 3/31 (eve), 4/3, 4/6, 4/23 (eve), 5/2, 5/10, 5/23 (eve), 5/24, 5/28, 6/9, 6/12, 7/17, 7/27, 8/13 (not morn), 8/24, 8/27, 8/31, 9/19, 9/29, 10/3, 10/7, 10/8, 10/30, 11/3, 11/4, 11/10, 12/21.

♌ ☉ ♀ ♆

ART, CREATIVITY, ACTIVITIES FOR CHILDREN

(or your inner child)

[Leo, Sun, Venus, Neptune]

BEST: 1/13, 2/16, 3/11 (morn), 4/1 (not eve), 4/21, 4/29, 5/25 (eve), 6/22 (morn), 7/23 (not morn), 8/6, 8/8, 8/17, 9/10 (morn), 10/19, 11/17 (not eve), 12/22 (aft).

WORST: 1/19, 2/7, 2/21 (not eve), 2/25, 3/4, 3/7 (eve), 3/14 (eve), 3/18 (not eve), 3/30 (not eve), 4/6, 4/12, 5/24, 5/28, 6/7, 6/29, 7/9, 7/14, 8/13 (not morn), 8/24, 8/30, 8/31, 9/8, 9/29, 10/11 (eve), 10/14, 11/10, 12/2.

♎ ♀

RELATIONSHIPS, PARTNERSHIP

[Libra, Venus]

BEST: 1/6 (eve), 1/20 (morn), 2/20 (morn), 3/11 (morn), 3/14 (morn), 4/14 (morn), 5/22, 6/22 (morn), 7/5 (morn), 8/8, 9/21 (not morn), 10/2, 10/9, 10/26 (morn), 11/25, 12/11 (not eve).

WORST: 1/30, 2/1, 2/10, 2/21 (not eve), 2/25, 2/29, 3/4, 3/7 (eve), 3/14 (eve), 3/18 (not eve), 4/6, 4/12, 4/16, 5/2, 5/11 (not morn), 5/15, 6/20, 7/7, 8/24, 8/30, 8/31, 9/25, 10/3, 10/4 (morn), 10/30, 11/3, 11/11, 11/13, 11/15, 12/7, 12/21.

♎ ♀

MARRIAGE

[Libra, Venus]

It's advisable to get both partners' birth time and work with an astrologer to find a suitable date. Sometimes a day that's not great on its own can bring out the best in a couple's charts. Even on recommended days, certain hours are better than others. Get legally married at a good time; then re-enact vows and have your reception when you want.

BEST: 1/6, 1/7, 10/19 (before the Void period is better than after).

WORST: When Venus is out of bounds (4/2-6/3) or Retrograde (5/15-6/27), and on Worst Days for Relationships.

Acceptable at times*: 4/28, 7/3, 8/21 (late aft/eve), 9/22, 12/22 (after Moon enters Taurus).

** depends on location; consult an astrologer for exact times.*

HEALTH

[Virgo, Pisces, Neptune, Chiron] ♍ ♓ ♆ ⚷

BEST: 1/16, 2/16, 2/21 (eve), 3/11 (morn), 4/21, 5/18 (not eve), 6/14 (aft), 7/30 (morn), 8/8, 9/10 (morn), 9/28 (not morn), 10/24 (not eve), 10/26 (morn), 11/8 (aft), 12/9 (eve).

WORST: 1/18, 2/25, 3/10 (morn), 3/13, 3/16, 3/27, 4/3, 4/12, 5/4, 5/24, 5/28, 6/17 (morn), 7/7, 7/18, 8/19, 9/20, 9/26, 10/31, 11/4, 11/13, 11/19, 12/2, 12/11, 12/14, 12/16.

BEST AND WORST DAYS FOR VARIOUS ACTIVITIES

♏ ♆ ♑ ♄

BUSINESS
(also see FINANCE and if applicable, PARTNERSHIP)

[Scorpio, Pluto, Capricorn, Saturn]

BEST: 1/21 (morn), 2/13 (morn), 3/14 (morn), 3/15 (eve), 3/25 (not eve), 4/21, 5/1, 5/9 (aft), 6/1 (eve), 7/12 (not eve), 8/8, 8/16, 9/14 (aft), 10/2 (morn), 11/12, 12/28 (morn).

WORST: 1/7 (eve), 2/14 (morn), 3/9 (not eve), 3/30 (not eve), 4/8, 5/6, 5/30, 6/16, 7/17, 8/13 (not morn), 9/16 (not morn), 9/19, 9/29, 10/3, 11/3, 11/10, 11/13, 11/19, 12/4.

♑ ♄ ♍

CAREER MATTERS, ORGANIZING, PLANNING

[Capricorn, Saturn, Virgo]

BEST: 1/7 (not eve), 1/13, 2/12 (not eve), 3/19 (aft), 4/15 (eve), 4/25 (aft), 5/22, 6/8 (eve), 7/30 (morn), 8/16, 9/15 (not morn), 10/2, 10/11 (aft), 10/19 (eve), 11/12, 12/26 (not morn).

WORST: 1/19, 1/22, 2/22, 3/4, 3/31 (eve), 4/16, 4/20, 5/6, 5/10, 5/28, 6/6, 6/20, 7/14, 7/15, 8/31, 9/24, 10/18 (eve), 11/9 (not eve), 12/14, 12/27.

♐ ♃

EDUCATION, PROMOTION, LONG DISTANCE TRAVEL, CONTACT AT A DISTANCE
(includes online), LEGAL MATTERS

[Sagittarius, Jupiter]

BEST: 1/2 (eve), 2/16 (not morn), 2/26 (eve), 3/14 (morn), 4/22 (not eve), 5/22, 6/26, 7/5 (morn), 7/19 (eve), 8/6, 9/21 (not morn), 10/18 (eve), 11/28 (not morn), 12/30 (aft).

WORST: 1/19, 2/19 (not eve), 3/8, 4/8, 4/9, 5/6, 5/7, 6/27, 7/25, 8/24, 9/8, 10/15, 11/21 (not eve), 12/2, 12/12 (morn), 12/18.

♒ ♅ ♀

SOCIALIZING, MEETINGS, COOPERATION, FRIENDS

[Aquarius, Uranus, Venus]

BEST: 1/13, 1/27 (aft), 2/16 (eve), 3/4 (eve), 4/1 (not eve), 4/14 (morn), 5/26, 6/22 (morn), 7/4, 7/5 (morn), 8/1 (aft), 9/12 (morn), 10/22 (morn), 11/18 (morn), 12/11 (eve).

WORST: 1/30, 2/6, 2/7, 3/9 (not eve), 3/18, 4/22 (eve), 5/6, 5/30, 6/5, 7/13, 7/17, 8/13 (not morn), 9/16 (not morn), 9/19, 9/29, 10/20, 11/10, 12/4.

♓ ♆

CHARITABLE, SPIRITUAL

[Pisces, Neptune]

BEST: 1/16, 1/20 (aft), 2/21 (eve), 3/11 (morn), 3/24 (eve), 4/21, 5/18 (not eve), 6/19, 7/30 (morn), 8/8, 9/28 (not morn), 10/11 (aft), 10/24, 11/12 (not eve), 11/20 (not morn), 12/9 (eve).

WORST: 1/8 (eve), 2/8, 2/25, 3/6 (eve), 4/3, 4/6, 4/23 (eve), 5/24, 6/3, 6/9 (not morn), 6/30 (eve), 7/10, 8/3, 8/24, 9/14 (not eve), 10/3, 10/4, 10/7, 11/4, 12/7, 12/8, 12/11.

JANET'S PLAN-ITS KEYWORDS FOR ASTROLOGICAL TERMS

HEAVENLY BODIES/PLANETS

☉ **SUN** leadership, ego, will power, creativity, vitality, spirit, purpose, identity

☽ **MOON** responses, habit patterns, feelings, receptivity, sensitivity, nurturing

☿ **MERCURY** rational mind, thinking processes, all forms of communications, local travel/transportation matters

♀ **VENUS** affections, attraction, aesthetics, desire for beauty, balance, values, harmony

♂ **MARS** aggressiveness, assertiveness, initiative, independence, pioneering, competition

⚳ **CERES** harvest, fertility, abundance, nurturing

♃ **JUPITER** growth, philosophy, higher education, long distance travel or communication

♄ **SATURN** structure, definition, limits, restriction, responsibility, organization, authority, maturity

⚷ **CHIRON** (asteroid) "Wounded Healer," hurts, healing, innovation, teaching

♅ **URANUS** the unusual or unexpected, uniqueness, individuality, revolution, reform

♆ **NEPTUNE** imagination, psychic sensitivity, confusion, fears, spirituality, the arts

♇ **PLUTO** (plutoid) finances, shared resources, transformation, death, re-birth, afterlife, sex

⚸ **ERIS** (plutoid) chaos, discord, strife, rivalry

SIGNS [followed by their ruling planets]

♈ **ARIES** [ruler: Mars] enthusiastic, outgoing, self-centered, energetic, pioneering, assertive

♉ **TAURUS** [ruler: Venus] stable, steadfast, patient, practical, stubborn, jealous, artsy

♊ **GEMINI** [ruler: Mercury] communicative, inquisitive, adaptable, versatile

♋ **CANCER** [ruler: Moon] sensitive, nurturing, receptive, home/family-oriented, emotional

♌ **LEO** [ruler: Sun] generous, showy, dramatic, creative, a leader, egotistical, fun-loving

♍ **VIRGO** [ruler: Mercury] analytical, discriminating, critical, detail-oriented, service-minded, useful

♎ **LIBRA** [ruler: Venus] diplomatic, other-oriented, peace-loving, refined, flirty, indecisive

♏ **SCORPIO** [ruler: Pluto] magnetic, powerful, intense, persevering, passionate, extreme

♐ **SAGITTARIUS** [ruler: Jupiter] idealistic, optimistic, scattered, honest, exaggerative, restless

♑ **CAPRICORN** [ruler: Saturn] ambitious, responsible, economical, efficient, disciplined, insensitive

♒ **AQUARIUS** [ruler: Uranus] impersonal, detached, original, humanitarian, independent, rebellious

♓ **PISCES** [ruler: Neptune] sympathetic, sentimental, caring, responsive, psychic, spiritual, escapist

Please note: Planets and signs are related to many more matters than the most common associations listed here.

ASPECTS (Angular distance between planets, linking their influences; multiple aspects can form patterns)

☌ **CONJUNCTION (0°)** [Planet joins/passes another] powerful emphasis, strength in the sign

⚺ **SEMISEXTILE (30°)** [one-twelfth of the sky apart] like sextile but weaker, favorable combo

∠ **SEMISQUARE (45°)** [one-eighth of the sky apart] similar to Square, grating

✻ **SEXTILE (60°)** [one-sixth of the sky apart] ease, put in effort for best results

□ **SQUARE (90°)** [a quarter of the sky apart] conflicting desires, inner struggles lead to action

△ **TRINE (120°)** [a third of the sky apart] automatic benefits, harmony, ease

⚼ **SESQUIQUADRATE (135°)** [three-eighths of the sky apart] similar to Square, friction, tension

Q **QUINTILE (72°)** and **Q²** **BIQUINTILE (144°)** [one-fifth and two-fifths of the sky apart] a talent or a choice to make between planets' influences

⚻ **QUINCUNX (150°)** [five-twelfths of the sky apart] a disconnect, need adjustment or compromise

☍ **OPPOSITION (180°)** [half of the sky apart] conflict, difficulties from outside oneself or differences requiring resolution, brings awareness

Learn about HOUSES on page 5.

Signs are grouped according to three characteristics – **Modes**, **Elements** and **Polarity** – indicating shared traits.

Modes *(also called Qualities)*

CARDINAL *(beginning of each season)* [Aries, Cancer, Libra, Capricorn]
active, energetic, dynamic, initiating, thrives on crisis

FIXED *(middle of each season)* [Taurus, Leo, Scorpio, Aquarius]
stable, persistent, willful, stubborn, resistant to change

MUTABLE *(end of each season)* [Gemini, Virgo, Sagittarius, Pisces]
adaptable, variable, restless, easy-going, scattered

Elements

FIRE *[Aries, Leo, Sagittarius]* impulsive, inspirational, enthusiastic, intuitive, energetic

EARTH *[Taurus, Virgo, Capricorn]* practical, materialistic, dependable, utilitarian, conservative

AIR *[Gemini, Libra, Aquarius]* intellectual, communicative, abstract, idealistic, cooperative

WATER *[Cancer, Scorpio, Pisces]* emotional, sensitive, protective, responsive, nurturing, psychic

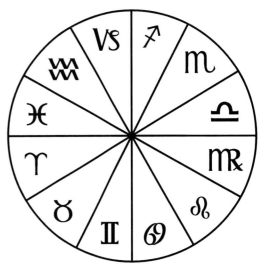

Look for squares and oppositions in the
same mode, trines in a shared element,
or sextiles and oppositions in a polarity.

Polarity

YANG *[Fire and Air signs]* extroverted, out-going, assertive   **YIN** *[Earth and Water signs]* introverted, passive, receptive
Opposite signs share the same polarity. They often relate to a common theme, reflecting both ends of a spectrum.

Retrograde Motion   ℞

A planet's apparent backward motion. Shows a need to re-experience, review, or re-do according to sign and aspects.

Lunar Phases

● New Moon

◐ First Quarter Moon

○ Full Moon

◑ Third Quarter Moon

Void of Course Moon

A period of time when the Moon has finished
its aspects in its current sign. Until entering the
next sign, motivation is low and actions "run
out of steam." It's not a good time to make
major purchases or begin important activities.

Eclipses

🖉 Solar Eclipse

🖉 Lunar Eclipse

Read about lunar cycles
on page 90.

Moon's Nodes *(intersection of the Moon's orbit around the earth with the earth's orbit of the Sun)*

☊ **NORTH NODE** direction for progress, what is difficult to do but growth-producing, what one needs to develop
☋ **SOUTH NODE** path of least resistance, not growth-producing, traps from old habits

Aspect Patterns

FINGER OF GOD (YOD): 2 planets sextile, both quincunx a third – strange twists of fate with a positive outcome

GRAND TRINE: 3 planets in an equilateral triangle, all trine one another *(usually with components in the same Element)*
        – an easy flow of energy between planets, may yield luck in circumstances related to planets & signs involved

GRAND CROSS (GRAND SQUARE): a cross or square box formed by 2 perpendicular oppositions, contains 4 squares
        (usually has components in same Mode) – big difficulties for planets & signs involved

KITE: Grand Trine with a planet opposite 1 point, sextile the other 2 – a challenge maximizes the Grand Trine

MYSTIC RECTANGLE: sextiles and trines on the sides, diagonal oppositions – cooperative and complementary energies mix

QUINTILE TRIANGLE ("QT"): a triangle comprised of quintiles and biquintiles – multiple talents or fortunate circumstances

STAR OF DAVID (Grand Sextile): 2 overlapping Grand Trines, with 6 sextiles *and* 3 oppositions (= 3 connected Kites)

T-SQUARE: 2 planets in opposition, both square a third – problems and dilemmas that force decisions or action

Resources

Contributors to Janet's Plan-its 2012 Celestial Planner

Bryan R. Bonina

Bryan R. Bonina, a visual artist and graphic designer for 25 years, has managed layout and design of the Celestial Planner since 2001. In addition to the calendar, he also produces Janet's collateral print material while providing her with marketing consulting services. Bryan's freelance business, Always Amazing Results ~ A Marketing & Communications LLC, is based in Farmington, CT. Contact: bryan_r_bonina@sbcglobal.net.

Diane Cramer

Diane Cramer, MS, NCGR IV, wrote the companion article to the medieval illustration, Anatomical Man (p. 92), discussing astrological associations with the human body and health indications for the signs. A Consulting Astrologer certified by the National Council for Geocosmic Research (NCGR), she is a lecturer and teacher in all aspects of astrology, specializing in medical astrology and nutrition. Her four books – *Managing Your Health & Wellness, How to Give an Astrological Health Reading, Dictionary of Medical Astrology* and *Medical Astrology Let The Stars Guide You to Good Health* – are available at dianecramer.com. Her email is astroldiane@yahoo.com.

Sally Faubion

Sally Faubion, a professional numerologist from San Francisco, CA, offered insights into the year 2012 from a numerological standpoint for the Overview (p. 1). Her book, *Motivational Numerology And How Numbers Affect Your Life* is great! On her website, sfnumber.com, you can enter your birth data and read her Wizard Star interpretation, order her book or buy her new iApp, "CosmicMates." Input birth dates of two people and see a rating of how they get along and their relationship potentials.

Dietrech Pessin

Dietrech Pessin, a professional astrologer noted for her discovery of "moon families." *Lunar Shadows III The Predictive Power of Moon Phases and Eclipses* is a comprehensive study of this ingenious predictive tool, with tables covering 1927-2034. (See the excerpt for 2012 on p. 69.) At lunar-shadows.com, you can read and listen to her weekly astrology report, broadcast Saturday at 9:30 am Eastern on 90.3 FM WZBC in Newton, MA. Her book is available from her website or Amazon.com. Her email is dietrechpessin@lunar-shadows.com.

Ray Pioggia

Janet's portrait photos on the calendar back cover and on her website are by photographer **Ray Pioggia**. The Blazing Sun art on her homepage is by his wife, artist Laurie Tavino. The creative couple owns and operates Lauray Studio & Gallery in Suffield, CT (lauraystudio@yahoo.com).

Maria Kay Simms

Maria Kay Simms (maria@astrocom.com), a professional astrologer and Wiccan High Priestess, contributed the article about the 8 phases of the Moon (p. 90), drawing from her book *Moon Tides, Soul Passages Your Astrological Cycles for Personal and Spiritual Development*. The book comes with software to calculate and print your astrological information to apply the book's interpretations. Maria was the first woman elected Chair of the National Council for Geocosmic Research (NCGR), serving from 1999 to 2004. She holds two professional certifications as an astrologer, NCGR Level IV and PMAFA from the American Federation of Astrologers. Her companies, ACS Publications and Starcrafts, LLC, generously granted permission to reprint the 2012 ephemeris in Janet's Plan-its, excerpted from *The American Ephemeris for the 21st Century at Midnight*, by Neil F. Michelsen and Rique Pottenger, published by ACS Publications, an imprint of Starcrafts LLC (astrocom.com), also available in a noon version.

Ilene J. Wolf

Ilene J. Wolf, MS, is a nationally recognized specialist in emotional wellness and issues around recovery. She founded the nonprofit Healing Emotionally Abused Lives (HEAL), emotionalheal.org. She also has a coaching practice, Healing Wolf Tracks at healingwolf.net. Ilene runs workshops, i-publishes "Wolf's Daily Howl" and serves as the editor for Janet's Plan-its.

Janet's Picks

These picks are among many listed in the
Links section of the Information Booth at
AstrologyBooth.com
home of
JanetsPlan-its.com

Looking for top-of-the-line monthly forecasts for the Sun signs?
I highly recommend Susan Miller's
astrologyzone.com

Find cool celestial stuff, from A to Z at:
ArttoZen.com and Zodiacts.com

An excellent resource to learn about the Mayan calendar and daycount is
Jaguar Nights
by Gevera Bert Piedmont (ObsidianButterfly.com)

This is the name of both her annual calendar and a new companion book
covering the existing base of knowledge thoroughly and adding significantly
to it with her own insights and the unique techniques she's developed.

For more information about the Passage of Venus (June 5, 2012), check out
Venus Star Rising: A New Cosmology for the 21st Century
by Arielle Guttman (sophiavenus.com),
Sophia Venus Productions, Santa Fe, NM.

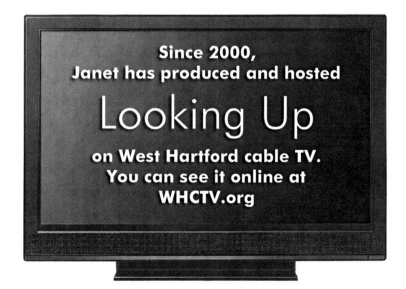

CPSIA information can be obtained at www.ICGtesting.com
Printed in the USA
BVOW052308081211

277931BV00003B/7/P